Comparative narrative poetry

Edited by Olivia M. Cooke

NOBLE AND NOBLE, PUBLISHERS, INC.
750 Third Avenue, New York City 10017

COMPARATIVE NARRATIVE POETRY

Present and Past

■ ACKNOWLEDGMENTS

We offer grateful acknowledgment to the following publishers and authors for their permission to use copyrighted material:

THE ATLANTIC MONTHLY PRESS and MAXINE W. KUMIN: for "The Microscope," by Maxine W. Kumin. Reprinted from *The Atlantic*, March, 1963.

BODLEY HEAD, LTD.: for "A Ballad of Marjorie," by Dora Sigerson. Reprinted by permission of The Bodley Head, Ltd.

COWARD-MC CANN, INC.: for "Daniel Webster's Horses," from *Compass Rose*, by Elizabeth Coatsworth, copyright 1929, renewed 1957, by Coward-McCann, Inc. Reprinted by permission of Coward-McCann, Inc.

CURTIS BROWN, LTD.: for "Dunkirk," by Robert Nathan. Reprinted by permission of Curtis Brown, Ltd.

DODD, MEAD & COMPANY: for "The Cremation of Sam McGee" and "Fleurette," from *The Collected Poems* of Robert W. Service; "Cerelle," from *Lanterns in the Dusk*, by Margaret Bell Houston; "Jesse James" and "The Skater of Ghost Lake," from *Golden Fleece*, by William Rose Benét. "Vitaï Lampada," by Henry Newbolt; "Kitty-hawk," from *With Wings as Eagles*, by William Rose Benét, copyright 1940 by Dodd, Mead & Company. All reprinted by permission of Dodd, Mead and Company, Inc.

E. P. DUTTON AND COMPANY, INC.: for "The Sands of Dee," by Charles Kingsley, from *Poems* by Charles Kingsley. Reprinted by permission of E. P. Dutton, Inc., and Everyman's Library.

MRS. NORMA MILLAY ELLIS: for "The Ballad of the Harp-Weaver," from *Collected Poems*, by Edna St. Vincent Millay, published by Harper and Row, Inc., copyright 1922, 1950 by Edna St. Vincent Millay. Reprinted by permission of Mrs. Norma Millay Ellis.

MRS. ARTHUR GUITERMAN: for "The Legend of the Bronx," by

◼ THE COMPARATIVE CLASSICS

In recognition of the demand for a broader choice of literature, and in the belief that a study of the Classics is greatly
enhanced by comparison, the publishers have launched a new
series, *The Comparative Classics*, based upon a new idea:
that of presenting older classics in the same volume with
modern ones of the same type. This plan has several advantages. There has been a strong demand for more modern literature in secondary courses; there is at the same time a feeling that no English education is complete without some
knowledge of the great classics. The present plan meets both
demands. Furthermore, it is generally recognized that one of
the most fruitful ways of studying literature is by the comparative method. To place side by side two plays or a series
of poems or essays in which the same theme is treated by
different authors makes clear at once the various characteristics of the writers. It also affords a means of studying the
larger aspects of the works involved, of comparing them in
theme and treatment, rather than concentrating upon the
text of one. It is the practice of many teachers, after studying
a classic, to assign as supplementary reading modern works of
the same type. Here both types of material are conveniently
placed within a single cover.

■ NOBLE'S COMPARATIVE CLASSICS

COMPARATIVE NARRATIVE POETRY—PRESENT AND PAST

MACBETH—THE EMPEROR JONES

ROBINSON CRUSOE—THE RAFT—THE ANCIENT MARINER

SILAS MARNER—THE PEARL

JULIUS CAESAR—ELIZABETH THE QUEEN

ROMEO AND JULIET—CYRANO DE BERGERAC

IDYLLS OF THE KING—THE KING'S HENCHMAN

HAMLET—ELECTRA—BEYOND THE HORIZON

COMPARATIVE ESSAYS—PRESENT AND PAST

A TALE OF TWO CITIES—THE MOON IS DOWN

A MIDSUMMER NIGHT'S DREAM—BERKELEY SQUARE

COMPARATIVE COMEDIES—PRESENT AND PAST

(*She Stoops To Conquer, The Rivals, Holiday, Goose Hangs High*)

◼ CONTENTS

■ FOREWORD

Comparative Narrative Poetry is a textbook for students in the early years of high school. The titles include a wide variety of American and British narrative poems—old and new —from which teachers can make selections geared to the varying interests and abilities of their students.

The major objective of the book is to develop the student's capacity to read and enjoy narrative poetry. The pleasurable aspects of poetry are emphasized; for example, the present interest in folk singing is coordinated with an extensive study of the ballad—old folk songs and imitation ballads.

The poems have been grouped in ten sections, titled as follows: "The Story in a Narrative Poem," "Sound in Poetry," "Imagery," "Setting and Mood," "The Ballad," "Character Portraits," "Humor and Pathos," "Courage and Conflict in War," "The Quest for the Good," "More Poems for Enrichment." (The last section is adapted particularly for the advanced student who reads independently.) These classifications serve two purposes: to provide many opportunities for comparison and contrast of the poems in each category;

and to introduce students informally and pleasantly to the elements, themes, and language of poetry.

Each of the sections begins with a brief introduction to the topic around which the poems are grouped and follows with questions and activities on each poem aimed to develop understanding and appreciation. Comparative study questions in each section alert the students to compare, contrast, and discuss the stories, characters, and other elements common to the poems.

An introduction to poetry and a list of memorable quotations are included for use as class needs and interests indicate. To facilitate teacher and student use of the book, other editorial material has been provided: author, title, and first line indexes, and biographical notes about the authors. Side-notes and introductory explanations about the poems are given only if they are necessary to clarify the meaning. Further explanation is available in the study questions and in the footnotes.

For many of the students this book will be the first collection of poetry since their nursery-rhyme days; and this reading experience must be a pleasant and challenging one if it is to lead to an appreciation of the poetry they will be reading in later years of school and (we hope) in adult life. To foster students' interest, much of the poetry should be *heard* during class through individual and group reading, recordings, and perhaps an occasional "sing-along" in the spirit of the folk singers.

The major objective aimed at in the preparation of this book is to develop the student's ability to understand and enjoy these narrative poems. The textbook is only a tool; the teacher must supply the magic which can make poetry a lifetime enrichment for the student.

■ TO THE STUDENTS

This collection of story poems of the past and present has been compiled specifically for you. Are any of you asking, "Why a book of *poetry*?" The emphatic reply to your question is, "For your enjoyment!"

A narrative poem is not merely a collection of printed words on white paper; it is an experience, a story, a song. Throughout the ages people have sung, recited, read, listened to, and composed poetry just because they enjoyed it. For a moment imagine yourself back in the Middle Ages sharing the experiences of a group of people around a campfire listening to a minstrel sing a narrative poem. That poem is a surge of excitement—the deeds of heroes recited to the strumming of a lute to stir men's hearts on the eve of battle or to celebrate a victory. Now come to a "television program" with villagers gathered in a cottage around a fireside to hear a folk song about a local happening—a shipwreck, an elopement, a tragic love story, a family quarrel, a chivalrous deed.

Today the widespread popularity of hootenanny demonstrates that stories set to music are as enjoyable as they were in the past. The poems in this book can give you similar pleasure. In reading these narrative poems, old and new, American and British, you will span time and distance and share in the varied experiences of many kinds of people. You will find that, as you compare the stories, music, and characters in these poems, you will develop an increasing ability to understand and appreciate narrative poetry. You will increase your enjoyment of poetry by oral reading at home and in class, by listening to recordings of some of the poems, and by singing the songs. Sound and meaning are blended in poetry, and the effect of the sense of poetry is enhanced by the music of its words.

As you read and discuss the poems, think of them as stories of life experiences; compare and contrast the outlook on life, the problems, and achievements of their characters. Enjoy the sounds and pictures which the poets create for you in rhythmical, vivid language. If you enter into the study of narrative poetry with the spirit of high adventure and emotion that is an integral part of its origin, you will find it not a chore, but a pleasant and memorable experience.

Introduction to poetry

■ INTRODUCTION TO POETRY

Poetry was the first type of literature with which you became acquainted as a child. The nursery rhymes, the simple songs and jingles, the singing commercials—all these were an early introduction to a pleasant, rhyming language which you learned to identify as "poetry." Later you discovered that poetry not only sounds different from ordinary language, but it also looks different: each line usually begins with a capital letter and the lines are divided into stanzas instead of paragraphs. As you have progressed in your education, you have altered your early ideas about poetry; you know that not all rhymes are poetry and that not all poetry rhymes. You may also have discovered that some modern poems look very much like prose. A logical question for you to ask might be, "What *is* poetry?"

Many answers have been given to this question, some of them by recognized poets. Edgar Allan Poe refers to poetry as "the rhythmical creation of beauty." William Wordsworth calls it the "imaginative expression of strong feeling, usually rhythmical." *Webster's New World Dictionary* defines poetry as "rhythmical arrangement of words in verse, sometimes rhymed, expressing facts, ideas, or emotions in a style more concentrated, imaginative, and powerful than that of ordinary speech."

The very best way to find the answer to the question "What is poetry?" is to read many poems and to experience personally the delight and the other values that poetry can give you. Poetry consists of meaning and of sound expressed in language that has rhythm, but not necessarily rhyme. The language of poetry differs from ordinary speech in other ways: it is more concentrated; that is, it says more in fewer words. Poetic language is imaginative; it communicates ideas and impressions to the reader by presenting word pictures to him.

Poetry is intended to be read, to be heard, and to be enjoyed. Enjoyment of poetry comes through active listening to poems and to careful reading—preferably oral. Understanding the meaning of the poem is basic to an appreciation of it; and a knowledge of the form and structure of the poem—its meter, rhyme, and imagery—adds much to this appreciation. A football game is more thrilling to the spectator who understands the rules and the plays; an opera gives greater enjoyment to the listener who knows the music and the story. The same applies to appreciation of poetry.

The following sections on Versification and Imagery are intended as a reference to help you acquire a basic understanding of the technical makeup of a poem. You will gain this knowledge gradually as you read the poems and listen to your teacher's explanations. The information about various elements of poetry which precedes each section in the book and the questions following the poems will also help you to understand the mechanics of poetry. The very first step toward developing an appreciation of poetry—and the most direct one—is to read and enjoy the poems.

TYPES OF POETRY

The three main classifications of poetry are narrative, lyric, and dramatic.

A *narrative* poem is a story in poetic form.

A *lyric* poem expresses thoughts or emotions. It is so called because it was originally a song intended to be sung to the accompaniment of a lyre.

A *dramatic* poem tells a story through the actions and dialogue of the characters.

The three types of poetry are not separated in hard and fast classifications. Many of the narrative poems contain lyrical passages; and many great dramatic poems, such as Shakespeare's plays, have beautiful lyric verse.

Types of Narrative Poetry

Narrative poetry may be divided into other kinds: ballads, epics, metrical romances, and others which do not exactly fit into the above classifications.

A *ballad* is a short narrative poem in a songlike verse.

An *epic* is a long narrative poem which relates the deeds of a hero who symbolizes his nation or tribe. Examples: *The Iliad, The Odyssey, The Aeneid, Beowulf.*

A *metrical romance* is a long narrative poem about chivalry. Example: *The Idylls of the King.*

VERSIFICATION

Versification is the art of arranging words into a metrical pattern which both enhances the dramatic meaning of a poem and makes it an unforgettable combination of sound and sense.

Rhythm is the recurrence of sound or movement at regular

intervals. It is present everywhere in daily life: in the beat of the heart, the tick of the clock, the click of the wheels of a train, the beat of a riveter, the lapping of the waves. Rhythm is a basic element of poetry.

Meter in poetry is the recurrence of rhythmic patterns resulting from the arrangement of accented and unaccented syllables. If you read the following line slowly, you will hear the regular rhythmic pattern:

Quoth the raven "Nevermore."

Verse has two meanings in poetry: A line of poetry is called a verse, and metrical writing is also referred to as verse. Metrical writing has a pattern of rhythm in which the accents occur at fairly regular intervals.

A *stanza* is a division of a poem; it is composed of two or more verses (lines). A stanza of a poem may be compared to a paragraph of prose.

A *foot* (often called a *metrical foot*) is a unit of measure in a line of poetry. A foot usually consists of a combination of accented and unaccented syllables.

Patterns of Meter

In English verse there are four basic kinds of metrical feet, which are designated by the following names:

1. *Iamb (iambic)* is a foot of two syllables, the first unaccented, the second accented.

    Examples: forgive receive
    Its fleece was white as snow.

2. *Trochee (trochaic)* is a foot of two syllables, the first accented, the second unaccented.

    Examples: daughter lovely
    Mary had a little lamb.

3. *Anapest (anapestic)* is a foot of three syllables, the first two unaccented, the last accented.

    Examples: ĭntrŏdūce dĭsăppēar

            O'ĕr thĕ lānd ŏf thĕ frēe ănd thĕ hōme ŏf thĕ brāve

4. *Dactyl (dactylic)* is a foot of three syllables, the first accented, the last two unaccented.

    Examples: lōyălty yēstĕrdăy

            Hīckŏry, dīckŏry, dōck

A line of poetry is measured by the number of feet it contains. The following terms are used:

Monometer—a line of one foot
Dimeter—a line of two feet
Trimeter—a line of three feet
Tetrameter—a line of four feet
Pentameter—a line of five feet
Hexameter—a line of six feet

A line of poetry is designated by the kind and the number of its metrical feet; for example, *iambic tetrameter* means four feet of two syllables each, the first short, the second long.

Scansion

Scansion is the process of finding the prevailing meter of a line of poetry. Not all verse is regular. Poets often vary the rhythmic pattern of a verse of poetry, to achieve a desired effect, to avoid monotony, or to heighten meaning. The prevailing meter is the one which occurs most regularly. To scan poetry, follow this procedure: First, read the line naturally and listen for the accents; second, mark the accented and unaccented syllables with symbols as indicated below (or others which your teacher may specify); third, determine which metrical foot prevails in the line; fourth, count the number of feet.

NOTE: Various kinds of symbols are used to indicate the long and short syllables in scansion. In the examples in this book, the long syllable is marked ¯; the short �‿.

Examples of Scansion:

Ĭt was thĕ schōonĕr Hēspĕrŭs. *Iambic tetrameter*
  Longfellow, "The Wreck of the *Hesperus*"
Tŏ strīve, tŏ sēek, tŏ fīnd, ănd nōt tŏ yīeld. *Iambic pentameter*
  Tennyson, "Ulysses"
Dōublĕ, dōublĕ, tōil ănd trōublĕ *Trochee tetrameter*
  Shakespeare, *Macbeth*
Hāil tŏ thēe, blīthĕ spīrĭt! *Trochee trimeter*
  Shelley, "To a Skylark"
Ĭ arīse ănd ŭnbūild ĭt ăgāin. *Anapest trimeter*
  Shelley, "The Cloud"
Thĕ Ăssȳrĭăn cāme dŏwn līke ă wōlf ŏn
  thĕ fōld. *Anapest tetrameter*
  Byron, "The Destruction of Sennacherib"
Cānnŏn tŏ rīght ŏf thĕm! *Dactyl dimeter*
  Tennyson, "The Charge of the Light Brigade"
Thīs ĭs thĕ fōrĕst prĭmēvăl, thĕ mūrmŭrĭng
  pīnes ănd thĕ hēmlŏcks *Dactyl hexameter*
  Longfellow, "Evangeline"

Rhyme

Rhyme is the recurrence of similar sounds. Rhyming words usually come at the ends of lines. When rhyme is present within the line, as it occasionally is, it is called *internal rhyme*.

Example of Internal Rhyme:

> I bring fresh *showers* for the thirsting *flowers*,
>   From the seas and the streams;
> I bear light *shade* for the leaves when *laid*
>   In their noonday dreams.
>   Shelley, "The Cloud"

Rhyme is not essential to poetry, but it is used very frequently, especially in narrative poetry.

Blank verse, which is unrhymed iambic pentameter, is the poetic form used in some of the greatest literature in the English language, including Shakespeare's plays.

Free verse, a technique applied frequently in modern poetry, has no regular metrical pattern and often no rhyme.

Rhyme scheme is the rhyming pattern of a stanza or poem.

Example of Rhyme Scheme:

> The Sun came up upon the left,   a
> Out of the sea came he!   b
> And he shone bright, and on the right   c
> Went down into the sea.   b
>   Coleridge, "The Rime of the Ancient Mariner"

The prevailing meter and rhyme of this stanza are iambic tetrameter-trimeter—abcb.

Other Sound Patterns in Poetry

Repetition is often used in poetry for musical effect or for emphasis of a mood or of an idea. Sometimes lines, phrases, and stanzas are repeated throughout a poem. In the ballad the *refrain* is frequently used, sometimes as a chorus in which a group accompanies the teller of a story.

Alliteration is the repetition of consonant or vowel sounds, usually at the beginning of words. Examples:

So slender Sohrab seemed.
> Arnold, "Sohrab and Rustum"

The furrow followed free;
> Coleridge, "The Rime of the Ancient Mariner"

Onomatopoeia is a device used by poets to create a pleasing harmony of sound and meaning. Onomatopoeia is the use of words which sound somewhat like the meanings they convey. In Poe's poem, "The Bells," the words referring to the various kinds of bells suggest the sounds of the bells, such as *tinkle, tolling*. The following words are examples of onomatopoeia: *splash, crash, boom, growl, gurgle, clang, twitter, sparkle, mumble*. You can add many others to this list.

Consonance and *assonance*, like alliteration and onomatopoeia, are poetic devices used to create sounds in keeping with the content, the mood, and the desired effect of the poem. Consonance and assonance are variations of conventional rhyme. While conventional rhyme repeats combinations of vowel and consonant sounds, consonance may be recognized by the repetition only of consonants. In assonance, only vowel sounds are repeated to form the end rhyme patterns. Both devices are used, especially by modern poets who employ them to achieve a wide variety of effects.

Examples of Consonance:

grained—ground
frowned—friend
hill—hall

Examples of Assonance:

reach—scream
pale—rain
sink—ring

A *caesura* is a break in rhythm caused by a natural breath pause or employment of punctuation within the line. This makes for variety of tempo and dramatic emphasis.

Examples:

Now as I was young and easy // under the apple boughs.
Thomas, "Fern Hill"

That's my last Duchess // painted on the wall
Looking as if she were alive; // I call
That piece a wonder.
Browning, "My Last Duchess"

IMAGERY

The section on Versification discussed an important quality
of poetry—sound. Poetry consists not only of sound, pleasing though it may be; it is a combination of sound and
meaning. The poet expresses meaning through his choice
and arrangement of words, but he does not use ordinary language. He chooses words that are vivid, imaginative, and
meaningful. Through his powers of observation and his
facility with words, the poet is able to communicate his ideas
and experiences to the reader, who in turn interprets them
in relation to his own experiences. Often a certain poem
seems to speak directly to a reader when he finds in it
thoughts, emotions, and impressions which he himself has
experienced but never expressed.

The poet makes use of *imagery* to express his meaning in
a way that will arouse the imagination and the emotions of
the reader. *Imagery* is the use of language to create an impression that will appeal to any of the senses—sight, hearing, smell, taste, or touch. As an artist uses colors to present
a picture, so the poet employs words to produce an image in
the mind. These lines from Wordsworth's poem, "I Wan-
dered Lonely as a Cloud," illustrate imagery:

When all at once I saw a crowd,
A host of golden daffodils
Beside the lake, beneath the trees,
Fluttering and dancing in the breeze.

The following poem presents details which appeal to the sense of sight, smell, sound, and touch:

MEETING AT NIGHT

Robert Browning

The grey sea and the long black land;
And the yellow half-moon large and low;
And the startled little waves that leap
In fiery ringlets from their sleep,
As I gain the cove with pushing prow,
And quench its speed i' the slushy sand.

Then a mile of warm sea-scented beach;
Three fields to cross till a farm appears;
A tap at the pane, the quick sharp scratch
And blue spurt of a lighted match,
And a voice less loud, thro' its joys and fears,
Than the two hearts beating each to each!

One of the best examples of a poem using imagery which appeals to each of the senses is "The Great Lover" by Rupert Brooke. If an ambitious student will obtain a copy of this poem and read Lines 26 to 58 to the class, all of you will be able to recognize images which refer to *sight, hearing, smell, taste* and *touch.*

Figurative Language

Imagery is very often expressed through comparisons, that is, through *figurative language,* also called *figures of speech.* A figure of speech is a comparison of two things which are essentially unlike and not usually associated. By using figures of speech the poet can present images which appeal to the reader's imagination and heighten meaning. Effective figures of speech add force and beauty to language—to prose as well as to poetry.

Figurative language is also used in everyday speech. Teen-ager's language is spiced with figurative expressions, some far removed from "poetic" imagery. A person is referred to as a "square" or a "nut"; a girl is described as "catty," a man as "foxy." In expressions such as these the literal meaning is not the same as the implied meaning. Advertising in maga-zines and on television also makes use of figurative language to sell its products. It will be fun to share with the class any examples of effective figurative language you may discover in your reading or viewing.

Examples of Figures of Speech:

The following are the most frequently used figures of speech:

A *simile* is an expressed comparison between two things. The word *like, as,* or *than* is a part of a simile.

Examples:

Life is like a voyage.
The sheen of their spears was like stars on the sea.

A *metaphor* is an implied comparison.

Examples:

Life is a voyage.
The road was a ribbon of moonlight.

Though the metaphor says one thing *is* something else, it really leads the reader to make a mental comparison between the two. That is why we call the metaphor an "implied com-parison" rather than an actual one.

Note that we can convert into similes the two metaphors given above as examples, by adding the word "like" in each case:

Life is like a voyage.
The road was like a ribbon of moonlight.

With or without the word "like," the reader recognizes that life is being compared with a voyage, and the road with a ribbon shining in the moonlight.

There is much more that you will learn on the subject of metaphor from your further reading in poetry, but the foregoing will suffice by way of introduction.

A *personification* consists in giving human qualities to an object or an idea.

Examples:

> . . . the sun
> Of noon looked down, and saw not one.
> > Whittier, "Barbara Frietchie"

> This mad sea shows his teeth tonight.
> > Miller, "Columbus"

> I swung my racket at astonished oaks.
> > Untermeyer, "Swimmers"

Irony is a device by which the poet tries to convey an impression that is the opposite of what his words seem to say. We all use irony on occasion. For example, we say with mock admiration, "Brave man!" to a grown individual who has just kicked a child. The poet creates irony by choosing words that indicate clearly what his real attitude is, despite the apparent meaning of the words.

Example:

> Upon what meat doth this our Caesar feed,
> That he is grown so great?

These words of Cassius, in *Julius Caesar*, are intended as sarcasm. Cassius, one of the conspirators against Caesar, obviously means that Caesar is, in fact, no different from other men and is not "great."

Symbolism involves the use of an object, or color, or other sensuous image to represent an idea or emotion. A flag, for instance, is a symbol of a nation. Brocade and whalebone, in "Patterns," are symbols of a woman's slavery to her social code. The colors red and rose, in "The Eve of St. Agnes," are symbols of love and passion, just as white and silver are symbols of purity and innocence.

Frequent reference to the basic information contained in the foregoing introduction, in the question sections, and in the unit introductions will help the student better to understand and enjoy the poems that make up this volume. Just as driving an automobile can be more pleasurable when the driver has some technical knowledge of his machine, so, too, can the reading of poetry bring added delight when the reader can point to the specific poetic techniques that create the delightful effects. Enjoyment is the password.

The story in a narrative poem

■ THE STORY IN A NARRATIVE POEM

■ A narrative poem is a type of literature which combines a story with poetry. The story in a narrative poem may be the account of a single incident; or it may be a *plot*, that is, a plan of interrelated actions or incidents moving toward the outcome or the climax. One incident does not constitute a plot. Some kind of *conflict* occurs within the plot, but this conflict is not always physical. It may be a difference of opinion or a clash of wills, and it may be also a struggle of one person to achieve a particular goal or to solve a personal problem. Sometimes, too, the conflict may be with the forces of nature, or it may involve supernatural influences. As the conflicts build up in the story, the reader experiences *suspense*; that is, a feeling of uncertainty about what is going to happen. In most narratives the conflicts are resolved at the conclusion; but in some poems the solution is merely suggested and the details are left to the reader's own interpretation. A narrative poem is usually shorter and more compact than a short story; and the imagination of the reader is frequently challenged to supply some of the details, and sometimes even the conclusion of the story.

In this text your introduction to narrative poetry will be through quick-moving stories of action, romance, and humor.

The emphasis will be primarily on your understanding and enjoyment of the story, but your attention will be called also to the language and the sound. As you read aloud or listen to some of the poems, you will soon become alert to the stirring rhythms and the vivid words which contribute to the meaning and the enjoyment of the story.

Some of the poems included in this book may already be familiar to you; but a good poem, like a favorite song, can give you increased pleasure every time you hear or read it.

As you read and discuss the poems, think of them as stories of life experiences; laugh and sympathize with the characters; compare and contrast their outlook on life, their problems, and achievements. Enjoy the sounds and pictures which the poets create for you in rhythmical, vivid language.

If you enter into the study of narrative poetry with the spirit of high adventure and emotion that is an integral part of its origin, you will find it not a chore, but a pleasant, worthwhile experience. You will also have taken the first step toward an appreciation of poetry that will greatly enhance your life.

SWIMMERS

Louis Untermeyer

I took the crazy short-cut to the bay;
Over a fence or two and through a hedge,
Jumping a private road, along the edge
Of backyards full of drying wash it lay.
And now, the last set being played and over,
I hurried past the ruddy lakes of clover;
I swung my racket at astonished oaks,
My arm still tingling from aggressive strokes.

Tennis was over for the day—
I took the leaping short-cut to the bay.

Then the quick plunge into the cool, green dark,
The windy waters rushing past me, through me;
Filled with a sense of some heroic lark
Existing in a vigor clean and roomy.
Swiftly I rose to meet the cat-like sea
That sprang upon me with a hundred claws,
And grappled, pulled me down and played with me.
Then, held suspended in the tightening pause
When one wave grows into a toppling acre,
I dived headlong into the foremost breaker,
Pitting against a cold and turbulent strife
The feverish intensity of life.
Out of the foam I lurched and rode the wave,
Swimming, hand over hand, against the wind;
I felt the sea's vain pounding, and I grinned
Knowing I was its master, not its slave.
Back on the curving beach I stood again,
Facing the bath-house, when a group of men,
Stumbling beneath some sort of weight, went by.
I could not see the heavy thing they carried;
I only heard: "He never gave a cry—"
"Who's going to tell her?" "Yes, and they just married—"
"Such a good swimmer, too . . ." And then they passed,
Leaving the silence throbbing and aghast.

A moment there my frightened heart hung slack,
And then the rich, retarded blood came back
Singing a livelier tune; and in my pulse
Beat the great wave that endlessly exults.
Why I was there and whither I must go,
I did not care. Enough for me to know

The same persistent struggle and the glowing
Waste of all spendthrift hours, bravely showing
Life, an adventure perilous and gay,
And death, a long and vivid holiday.

CASEY AT THE BAT

Ernest Lawrence Thayer

The outlook wasn't brilliant for the Mudville nine that day:
The score stood four to two, with but one inning more to
  play,
And then when Cooney died at first, and Barrows did the
  same,
A pall-like silence fell upon the patrons of the game.

A straggling few got up to go in deep despair. The rest
Clung to that hope which springs eternal in the human
  breast;
They thought, "If only Casey could but get a whack at that—
We'd put up even money now, with Casey at the bat."

But Flynn preceded Casey, as did also Jimmy Blake,
And the former was a hoodoo, while the latter was a cake;
So upon that stricken multitude grim melancholy sat,
For there seemed but little chance of Casey getting to the
  bat.

But Flynn let drive a single, to the wonderment of all,
And Blake, the much-despisèd, tore the cover off the ball;
And when the dust had lifted, and men saw what had
  occurred,
There was Jimmy safe at second and Flynn a-hugging third.

Then from five thousand throats and more there rose a lusty
yell;
It rumbled through the valley, it rattled in the dell;
It pounded on the mountain and recoiled upon the flat,
For Casey, mighty Casey, was advancing to the bat.

There was ease in Casey's manner as he stepped into his
place;
There was pride in Casey's bearing and a smile lit Casey's
face.
And when, responding to the cheers, he lightly doffed his hat,
No stranger in the crowd could doubt 'twas Casey at the bat.

Ten thousand eyes were on him as he rubbed his hands with
dirt;
Five thousand tongues applauded when he wiped them on
his shirt;
Then while the writhing pitcher ground the ball into his hip,
Defiance flashed in Casey's eye, a sneer curled Casey's lip.

And now the leather-covered sphere came hurtling through
the air,
And Casey stood a-watching it in haughty grandeur there.
Close by the sturdy batsman the ball unheeded sped—
"That ain't my style," said Casey. "Strike one!" the umpire
said.

From the benches, black with people, there went up a
muffled roar,
Like the beating of the storm-waves on a stern and distant
shore;
"Kill him! Kill the umpire!" shouted some one on the stand;
And it's likely they'd have killed him had not Casey raised
his hand.

With a smile of Christian charity great Casey's visage shone;
He stilled the rising tumult; he bade the game go on;
He signaled to the pitcher, and once more the dun sphere
    flew;
But Casey still ignored it, and the umpire said, "Strike two!"

"Fraud!" cried the maddened thousands, and echo answered
    "Fraud!"
But one scornful look from Casey and the audience was awed.
They saw his face grow stern and cold, they saw his muscles
    strain,
And they knew that Casey wouldn't let that ball go by again.

The sneer has fled from Casey's lip, his teeth are clenched in
    hate;
He pounds with cruel violence his bat upon the plate.
And now the pitcher holds the ball, and now he lets it go,
And now the air is shattered by the force of Casey's blow.

Oh, somewhere in this favored land the sun is shining bright;
The band is playing somewhere, and somewhere hearts are
    light,
And somewhere men are laughing, and little children shout;
But there is no joy in Mudville—great Casey has struck out.

THE LABORATORY

Robert Browning

Now that I, tying thy glass-mask tightly,
May gaze thro' these faint smokes curling whitely,
As thou pliest thy trade in this devil's smithy—
Which is the poison to poison her, prithee?

He is with her; and they know that I know
Where they are, what they do; they believe my tears flow
While they laugh, laugh at me, at me fled to the drear
Empty church, to pray God in, for them!—I am here.

Grind away, moisten and mash up thy paste,
Pound at thy powder,—I am not in haste!
Better sit thus, and observe thy strange things,
Than go where men wait me and dance at the King's.

That in the mortar—you call it a gum?
Ah, the brave tree whence such gold oozings come!
And yonder soft phial, the exquisite blue,
Sure to taste sweetly,—is that poison too?

Had I but all of them, thee and thy treasures,
What a wild crowd of invisible pleasures!
To carry pure death in an earring, a casket,
A signet, a fan-mount, a filigree-basket!

Soon, at the King's, a mere lozenge to give
And Pauline should have just thirty minutes to live!
But to light a pastille, and Elise, with her head,
And her breast, and her arms, and her hands, should drop
        dead!

Quick—is it finished? The color's too grim!
Why not soft like the phial's, enticing and dim?
Let it brighten her drink, let her turn it and stir,
And try it and taste, ere she fix and prefer!

What a drop! She's not little, no minion like me—
That's why she ensnared him. This never will free
The soul from those strong, great eyes, say "no!"
To that pulse's magnificent come-and-go.

For only last night, as they whispered, I brought
My own eyes to bear on her so, that I thought
Could I keep them one half minute fixed, she would fall,
Shrivelled; she fell not; yet this does it all!

Not that I bid you spare her the pain!
Let death be felt and the proof remain;
Brand, burn up, bite into its grace—
He is sure to remember her dying face!

It is done? Take my mask off! Nay, be not morose,
It kills her, and this prevents seeing it close:
The delicate droplet, my whole fortune's fee—
If it hurts her, beside, can it ever hurt me?

Now, take all my jewels, gorge gold to your fill,
You may kiss me, old man, on my mouth if you will!
But brush this dust off me, lest horror it brings
Ere I know it—next moment I dance at the King's.

THE GLOVE AND THE LIONS

Leigh Hunt

King Francis was a hearty king, and loved a royal sport,
And one day as his lions fought, sat looking on the court;
The nobles filled the benches, with the ladies by their side,
And 'mongst them sat the Count de Lorge, with one for
   whom he sighed.

King Francis: King of France, 1515–1547.

And truly 't was a gallant thing to see that crowning show,
Valor and love; and a king above; and the royal beasts below.

Ramped and roared the lions, with horrid laughing jaws;
They bit, they glared, gave blows like bears, a wind went with
     their paws;
With wallowing might and stifled roar they rolled on one
     another,
Till all the pit with sand and mane, was in a thunderous
     smother;
The bloody foam above the bars came whizzing through the
     air,
Said Francis then, "Faith, gentlemen, we're better here than
     there."

De Lorge's love o'erheard the King, a beauteous lively dame,
With smiling lips and sharp bright eyes, which always seemed
     the same;
She thought, the Count, my lover is brave as brave can be;
He surely would do wondrous things to show his love of me;
"King, ladies, lovers, all look on; the occasion is divine;
I'll drop my glove, to prove his love; great glory will be mine."

She dropped her glove, to prove his love, then looked at him
     and smiled;
He bowed, and in a moment leaped among the lions wild:
The leap was quick, return was quick, he has regained his
     place,
Then threw the glove, but not with love, right in the lady's
     face.
"By heaven!" said Francis, "rightly done!" and he rose from
     where he sat:
"No love," quoth he, "but vanity, sets love a task like that."

THE SKATER OF GHOST LAKE

William Rose Benét

Ghost Lake's a dark lake, a deep lake and cold:
Ice black as ebony, frostily scrolled;
Far in its shadows a faint sound whirrs;
Steep stand the sentineled deep, dark firs.

A brisk sound, a swift sound, a ring-tinkle-ring;
Flit-flit,—a shadow, with a stoop and a swing,
Flies from a shadow through the crackling cold.
Ghost Lake's a deep lake, a dark lake and old!

Leaning and leaning, with a stride and a stride,
Hands locked behind him, scarf blowing wide,
Jeremy Randall skates, skates late,
Star for a candle, moon for a mate.

Black is the clear glass now that he glides,
Crisp is the whisper of long lean strides,
Swift is his swaying,—but pricked ears hark.
None comes to Ghost Lake late after dark!

Cecily only,—yes, it is she!
Stealing to Ghost Lake, tree after tree,
Kneeling in snow by the still lake side,
Rising with feet winged, gleaming, to glide.

Dust of the ice swirls. Here is his hand.
Brilliant his eyes burn. Now, as was planned,
Arm across arm twined, laced to his side,
Out on the dark lake lightly they glide.

Dance of the dim moon, a rhythmical reel,
A swaying, a swift tune,—skurr of the steel;
Moon for a candle, maid for a mate,
Jeremy Randall skates, skates late.

Black as if lacquered the wide lake lies;
Breath is a frost-fume, eyes seek eyes;
Souls are a sword-edge tasting the cold.
Ghost Lake's a deep lake, a dark lake and old!

Far in the shadows hear faintly begin
Like a string pluck-plucked of a violin,
Muffled in mist on the lake's far bound,
Swifter and swifter, a low singing sound!

Far in the shadows and faint on the verge
Of blue cloudy moonlight, see it emerge,
Flit-flit,—a phantom, with a stoop and a swing . . .
Ah, it's a night bird, burdened of wing!

Pressed close to Jeremy, laced to his side,
Cecily Culver, dizzy you glide.
Jeremy Randall sweepingly veers
Out on the dark ice far from the piers.

"Jeremy!" "Sweetheart?" "What do you fear?"
"Nothing, my darling,—nothing is here!"
"Jeremy?" "Sweetheart?" "What do you flee?"
"Something—I know not; something I see!"

Swayed to a swift stride, brisker of pace,
Leaning and leaning, they race and they race;
Ever that whirring, that crisp sound thin
Like a string pluck-plucked of a violin;

Ever that swifter and low singing sound
Sweeping behind them, winding them round;
Gasp of their breath now that chill flakes fret;
Ice black as ebony,—blacker—like jet!

Ice shooting fangs forth—sudden—like spears;
Crackling of lightning,—a roar in their ears!
Shadowy, a phantom swerves off from its prey . . .
No, it's a night bird flit-flits away!

Low-winging moth-owl, home to your sleep!
Ghost Lake's a still lake, a cold lake and deep.
Faint in its shadows a far sound whirrs.
Black stand the ranks of its sentinel firs.

THE HIGHWAYMAN

Alfred Noyes

PART ONE

The wind was a torrent of darkness among the gusty trees,
The moon was a ghostly galleon tossed upon cloudy seas,
The road was a ribbon of moonlight over the purple moor,
And the highwayman came riding—
    Riding—riding—
The highwayman came riding, up to the old inn door.

He'd a French cocked hat on his forehead, a bunch of lace at
    his chin,
A coat of the claret velvet, and breeches of brown doe-skin;
They fitted with never a wrinkle: his boots were up to the
    thigh!

And he rode with a jeweled twinkle,
  His pistol butts a-twinkle,
His rapier hilt a-twinkle, under the jeweled sky.

Over the cobbles he clattered and clashed in the dark inn
    yard,
And he tapped with his whip on the shutters, but all was
    locked and barred;
He whistled a tune to the window, and who should be wait-
    ing there
But the landlord's black-eyed daughter,
  Bess, the landlord's daughter,
Plaiting a dark red love knot into her long black hair.

And dark in the dark old inn yard a stable-wicket creaked
Where Tim the ostler listened; his face was white and
    peaked;
His eyes were hollows of madness, his hair like moldy hay,
But he loved the landlord's daughter,
  The landlord's red-lipped daughter,
Dumb as a dog he listened, and he heard the robber say—

"One kiss, my bonny sweetheart, I'm after a prize tonight,
But I shall be back with the yellow gold before the morning
    light;
Yet, if they press me sharply, and harry me through the day,
Then look for me by moonlight,
  Watch for me by moonlight,
I'll come to thee by moonlight, though hell should bar the
    way."

He rose upright in the stirrups; he scarce could reach her
    hand,
But she loosened her hair i' the casement! His face burned
    like a brand

As the black cascade of perfume came tumbling over his
    breast;
And he kissed its waves in the moonlight,
  (Oh, sweet black waves in the moonlight!)
Then he tugged at his rein in the moonlight, and galloped
    away to the West.

PART TWO

He did not come in the dawning; he did not come at noon;
And out o' the tawny sunset, before the rise o' the moon,
When the road was a gypsy's ribbon, looping the purple
    moor,
A redcoat troop came marching—
  Marching—marching—
King George's men came marching, up to the old inn door.

They said no word to the landlord, they drank his ale in-
    stead,
But they gagged his daughter and bound her to the foot of
    her narrow bed;
Two of them knelt at her casement, with muskets at their
    side!
There was death at every window;
  And hell at one dark window;
For Bess could see, through her casement, the road that *he*
    would ride.

They had tied her up to attention, with many a sniggering
    jest;
They had bound a musket beside her, with the barrel be-
    neath her breast!

"Now keep good watch!" and they kissed her.
    She heard the dead man say
Look for me by moonlight;
    Watch for me by moonlight;
I'll come to thee by moonlight, though hell should bar the
        way!

She twisted her hands behind her; but all the knots held
        good!
She writhed her hands till her fingers were wet with sweat or
        blood!
They stretched and strained in the darkness, and the hours
        crawled by like years,
Till, now, on the stroke of midnight,
    Cold on the stroke of midnight,
The tip of one finger touched it! The trigger at least was
        hers!

The tip of one finger touched it; she strove no more for the
        rest!
Up, she stood up to attention, with the barrel beneath her
        breast.
She would not risk their hearing; she would not strive again;
For the road lay bare in the moonlight;
    Blank and bare in the moonlight;
And the blood of her veins in the moonlight throbbed to her
        love's refrain.

Tlot-tlot; tlot-tlot! Had they heard it? The horse-hoofs ring-
        ing clear;
Tlot-tlot, tlot-tlot, in the distance! Were they deaf that they
        did not hear?
Down the ribbon of moonlight, over the brow of the hill,

The highwayman came riding,
   Riding,—riding!
The redcoats looked to their priming! She stood up, straight
   and still!

Tlot-tlot, in the frosty silence! *Tlot-tlot*, in the echoing night!
Nearer he came and nearer! Her face was like a light!
Her eyes grew wide for a moment; she drew one last deep
   breath,
Then her finger moved in the moonlight,
   Her musket shattered the moonlight,
Shattered her breast in the moonlight and warned him—with
   her death.

He turned; he spurred to the Westward; he did not know
   who stood
Bowed, with her head o'er the musket, drenched with her
   own red blood!
Not till the dawn he heard it, and slowly blanched to hear
How Bess, the landlord's daughter,
   The landlord's black-eyed daughter,
Had watched for her love in the moonlight, and died in the
   darkness there.

Back, he spurred like a madman, shrieking a curse to the sky,
With the white road smoking behind him, and his rapier
   brandished high!
Blood-red were his spurs i' the golden noon; wine-red was his
   velvet coat;
When they shot him down on the highway,
   Down like a dog on the highway,
And he lay in his blood on the highway, with the bunch of
   lace at his throat.

. . . . . .

And still of a winter's night, they say, when the wind is in the trees,
When the moon is a ghostly galleon tossed upon cloudy seas,
When the road is a ribbon of moonlight over the purple moor,
A highwayman comes riding—
  Riding—riding—
A highwayman comes riding, up to the old inn door.

Over the cobbles he clatters and clangs in the dark inn yard;
And he taps with his whip on the shutters, but all is locked and barred;
He whistles a tune to the window, and who should be waiting there
But the landlord's black-eyed daughter,
  Bess, the landlord's daughter,
Plaiting a dark red love knot into her long black hair.

LOCHINVAR

Sir Walter Scott

Oh, young Lochinvar is come out of the west,
Through all the wide Border his steed was the best;
And save his good broadsword he weapons had none.
He rode all unarmed, and he rode all alone.
So faithful in love, and so dauntless in war,
There never was knight like the young Lochinvar.

He stayed not for brake, and he stopped not for stone;
He swam the Eske river where ford there was none;

brake: a clump of brushwood.

But, ere he alighted at Netherby gate,
The bride had consented, the gallant came late;
For a laggard in love, and a dastard in war,
Was to wed the fair Ellen of brave Lochinvar.

So boldly he entered the Netherby hall,
'Mong bridesmen and kinsmen and brothers and all:
Then spoke the bride's father, his hand on his sword
(For the poor craven bridegroom said never a word),
"Oh, come ye in peace here, or come ye in war,
Or to dance at our bridal, young Lord Lochinvar?"

"I long wooed your daughter, my suit you denied;—
Love swells like the Solway, but ebbs like its tide;
And now I am come, with this lost love of mine
To lead but one measure, drink one cup of wine.
There are maidens in Scotland more lovely by far
That would gladly be bride to the young Lochinvar."

The bride kissed the goblet; the knight took it up:
He quaffed off the wine, and he threw down the cup.
She looked down to blush, and she looked up to sigh,
With a smile on her lips and a tear in her eye.
He took her soft hand ere her mother could bar,—
"Now tread we a measure!" said young Lochinvar.

So stately his form, and so lovely her face,
That never a hall such a galliard did grace;
While her mother did fret, and her father did fume,
And the bridegroom stood dangling his bonnet and plume;
And the bride-maidens whispered, " 'Twere better by far
To have matched our fair cousin with young Lochinvar."

Solway: part of the Irish Sea.　　　*galliard:* a lively French dance.

One touch to her hand, and one word in her ear,
When they reached the hall door and the charger stood near;
So light to the croupe the fair lady he swung,
So light to the saddle before her he sprung!
"She is won! we are gone, over bank, bush, and scaur!
They'll have fleet steeds that follow!" quoth young Lochin-
    var.

There was mounting 'mong Græmes of the Netherby clan;
Forsters, Fenwicks, and Musgraves, they rode and they ran;
There was racing and chasing on Cannobie Lee;
But the lost bride of Netherby ne'er did they see.
So daring in love, and so dauntless in war,
Have ye e'er heard of gallant like young Lochinvar?

THE INCHCAPE ROCK

Robert Southey

No stir in the air, no stir in the sea,
The ship was still as she could be;
Her sails from heaven received no motion;
Her keel was steady in the ocean.

Without either sign or sound of their shock,
The waves flowed over the Inchcape Rock;
So little they rose, so little they fell,
They did not move the Inchcape Bell.

scaur: rock cliff.
Inchcape Rock: a reef off the coast of Scotland.

The Abbot of Aberbrothok
Had placed that Bell on the Inchcape Rock;
On a buoy in the storm it floated and swung,
And over the waves its warning rung.

When the Rock was hid by the surge's swell,
The mariners heard the warning Bell;
And then they knew the perilous Rock,
And blest the Abbot of Aberbrothok.

The Sun in heaven was shining gay;
All things were joyful on that day;
The sea-birds screamed as they wheeled round,
And there was joyance in their sound.

The buoy of the Inchcape Bell was seen,
A darker speck on the ocean green:
Sir Ralph the Rover walked his deck,
And he fixed his eye on the darker speck.

He felt the cheering power of spring;
It made him whistle, it made him sing:
His heart was mirthful to excess,
But the Rover's mirth was wickedness.

His eye was on the Inchcape float:
Quoth he, "My men, put out the boat,
And row me to the Inchcape Rock,
And I'll plague the Abbot of Aberbrothok."

The boat is lowered, the boatmen row,
And to the Inchcape Rock they go;
Sir Ralph bent over from the boat,
And he cut the Bell from the Inchcape float.

Down sunk the Bell with a gurgling sound;
The bubbles rose and burst around:
Quoth Sir Ralph, "The next who comes to the Rock
Won't bless the Abbot of Aberbrothok."

Sir Ralph the Rover sailed away;
He scoured the seas for many a day;
And now, grown rich with plundered store,
He steers his course for Scotland's shore.

So thick a haze o'erspreads the sky,
They cannot see the Sun on high:
The wind hath blown a gale all day;
At evening it hath died away.

On the deck the Rover takes his stand;
So dark it is, they see no land.
Quoth Sir Ralph, "It will be lighter soon,
For there is the dawn of the rising Moon."

"Canst hear," said one, "the breakers roar?
For methinks we should be near the shore."
"Now where we are I cannot tell,
But I wish I could hear the Inchcape Bell."

They hear no sound; the swell is strong;
Though the wind hath fallen, they drift along,
Till the vessel strikes with a shivering shock:
"O Christ! it is the Inchcape Rock!"

Sir Ralph the Rover tore his hair,
He curst himself in his despair:
The waves rush in on every side;
The ship is sinking beneath the tide.

But, even in his dying fear,
One dreadful sound could the Rover hear,—
A sound as if, with the Inchcape Bell,
The Devil below was ringing his knell.

JOCK OF HAZELDEAN

Sir Walter Scott

"Why weep ye by the tide, ladie?
  Why weep ye by the tide?
I'll wed ye to my youngest son,
  And ye sall be his bride:
And ye sall be his bride, ladie,
  Sae comely to be seen"—
But aye she loot the tears down fa'
  For Jock of Hazeldean.

"Now let this wilfu' grief be done,
  And dry that cheek so pale;
Young Frank is chief of Errington
  And lord of Langley-dale;
His step is first in peaceful ha',
  His sword in battle keen"—
But aye she loot the tears down fa'
  For Jock of Hazeldean.

"A chain of gold ye sall not lack,
  Nor braid to bind your hair;
Nor mettled hound, nor managed hawk,
  Nor palfrey fresh and fair;
And you, the foremost of them a',
  Sall ride our forest-queen"—

But aye she loot the tears down fa'
    For Jock of Hazeldean.

    The kirk was deck'd at morning-tide,
    The tapers glimmered fair;
The priest and bridegroom wait the bride,
    And dame and knight are there:
They sought her baith by bower and ha';
    The ladie was not seen!
She's o'er the border and awa'
    Wi' Jock of Hazeldean.

THE YARN OF THE NANCY BELL

William Schwenck Gilbert

'Twas on the shores that round our coast
    From Deal to Ramsgate span,
That I found alone on a piece of stone
    An elderly naval man.

His hair was weedy, his beard was long,
    And weedy and long was he;
And I heard this wight on the shore recite,
    In a singular minor key:—

"Oh, I am a cook, and a captain bold,
    And the mate of the Nancy brig,
And a bo'sun tight, and a midshipmite,
    And the crew of the captain's gig."

Deal, Ramsgate: English coast towns.

And he shook his fists and he tore his hair,
  Till I really felt afraid,
For I couldn't help thinking the man had been drinking,
  And so I simply said:—

"O elderly man, it's little I know
  Of the duties of men of the sea,
And I'll eat my hand if I understand
  However you can be

"At once a cook, and a captain bold,
  And the mate of the Nancy brig,
And a bo'sun tight, and a midshipmite,
  And the crew of the captain's gig."

And he gave a hitch to his trousers, which
  Is a trick all seamen larn,
And having got rid of a thumping quid,
  He spun his painful yarn:—

" 'Twas in the good ship Nancy Bell
  That we sailed to the Indian Sea,
And there on a reef we come to grief,
  Which has often occurred to me.

"And pretty nigh all the crew was drowned
  (There was seventy-seven o' soul),
And only ten of the Nancy's men
  Said 'Here!' to the muster-roll.

"There was me and the cook and the captain bold,
  And the mate of the Nancy brig,
And the bo'sun tight, and a midshipmite,
  And the crew of the captain's gig.

"For a month we'd neither wittles nor drink,
  Till a-hungry we did feel;
So we drawed a lot, and accordin', shot
  The captain for our meal.

"The next lot fell to the Nancy's mate,
  And a delicate dish he made;
Then our appetite with the midshipmite
  We seven survivors stayed.

"And then we murdered the bo'sun tight,
  And he much resembled pig;
Then we wittled free, did the cook and me,
  On the crew of the captain's gig.

"Then only the cook and me was left,
  And the delicate question, 'Which
Of us two goes to the kettle?' arose,
  And we argued it out as sich.

"For I loved that cook as a brother, I did,
  And the cook he worshiped me;
But we'd both be blowed if we'd either be stowed
  In the other chap's hold, you see.

" 'I'll be eat if you dines off me,' says Tom;
  'Yes, that,' says I, 'you'll be:
I'm boiled if I die, my friend,' quoth I;
  And 'Exactly so,' quoth he.

"Says he, 'Dear James, to murder me
  Were a foolish thing to do,
For don't you see that you can't cook *me*,
  While I can—and will—cook *you*?'

"So he boils the water, and takes the salt
  And the pepper in portions true
(Which he never forgot), and some chopped shalot,
  And some sage and parsley too.

" 'Come here,' says he, with a proper pride,
  Which his smiling features tell;
'Twill soothing be if I let you see
  How extremely nice you'll smell.'

"And he stirred it round and round and round,
  And he sniffed at the foaming froth;
When I ups with his heels, and smothers his squeals
  In the scum of the boiling broth.

"And I eat that cook in a week or less,
  And—as I eating be
The last of his chops, why, I almost drops,
  For a wessel in sight I see!

          .   .   .   .   .   .

"And I never larf, and I never smile,
  And I never lark nor play,
But sit and croak, and a single joke
  I have—which is to say:—

" 'Oh, I am a cook, and a captain bold,
  And the mate of the Nancy brig,
And a bo'sun tight, and a midshipmite,
  And the crew of the captain's gig!' "

shalot: a type of onion.

THE CREMATION OF SAM McGEE

Robert W. Service

There are strange things done in the midnight sun
By the men who moil for gold;
The Arctic trails have their secret tales
That would make your blood run cold;
The Northern Lights have seen queer sights,
But the queerest they ever did see
Was that night on the marge of Lake Lebarge
I cremated Sam McGee.

Now Sam McGee was from Tennessee, where the cotton
blooms and blows,
Why he left his home in the South to roam 'round the Pole,
God only knows.
He was always cold, but the land of gold seemed to hold
him like a spell;
Though he'd often say in his homely way that "he'd sooner
live in hell."

On a Christmas Day we were mushing our way over the
Dawson Trail.
Talk of your cold! through the parka's fold it stabbed like a
driven nail.
If our eyes we'd close, then the lashes froze till sometimes we
couldn't see;
It wasn't much fun, but the only one to whimper was Sam
McGee.

And that very night, as we lay packed tight in our robes beneath the snow,
And the dogs were fed, and the stars o'erhead were dancing
heel and toe,

He turned to me, and "Cap," says he, "I'll cash in this trip,
    I guess;
And if I do, I'm asking that you won't refuse my last
    request."

Well, he seemed so low that I couldn't say no; then he says
    with a sort of moan:
"It's the cursèd cold, and it's got right hold till I'm chilled
    clean through to the bone.
Yet 'tain't being dead—it's my awful dread of the icy grave
    that pains;
So I want you to swear that, foul or fair, you'll cremate my
    last remains."

A pal's last need is a thing to heed, so I swore I would not
    fail;
And we started on at the streak of dawn; but God! he looked
    ghastly pale.
He crouched on the sleigh, and he raved all day of his home
    in Tennessee;
And before nightfall a corpse was all that was left of Sam
    McGee.

There wasn't a breath in that land of death, and I hurried,
    horror-driven,
With a corpse half hid that I couldn't get rid, because of a
    promise given;
It was lashed to the sleigh, and it seemed to say: "You may
    tax your brawn and brains,
But you promised true, and it's up to you to cremate those
    last remains."

Now a promise made is a debt unpaid, and the trail has its
own stern code.
In the days to come, though my lips were dumb, in my heart
how I cursed that load.
In the long, long night, by the lone firelight, while the
huskies, round in a ring,
Howled out their woes to the homeless snows—O God! how
I loathed the thing.

And every day that quiet clay seemed to heavy and heavier
grow;
And on I went, though the dogs were spent and the grub was
getting low;
The trail was bad, and I felt half mad, but I swore I would
not give in;
And I'd often sing to the hateful thing, and it hearkened
with a grin.

Till I came to the marge of Lake Lebarge, and a derelict
there lay;
It was jammed in the ice, but I saw in a trice it was called
the "Alice May."
And I looked at it, and I thought a bit, and I looked at my
frozen chum;
Then "Here," said I, with a sudden cry, "is my cre-ma-tor-
e-um."

Some planks I tore from the cabin floor, and I lit the boiler
fire;
Some coal I found that was lying around, and I heaped the
fuel higher;

The flames just soared, and the furnace roared—such a blaze
  you seldom see;
And I burrowed a hole in the glowing coal, and I stuffed in
  Sam McGee.

Then I made a hike, for I didn't like to hear him sizzle so;
And the heavens scowled, and the huskies howled, and the
  wind began to blow.
It was icy cold, but the hot sweat rolled down my cheeks, and
  I don't know why;
And the greasy smoke in an inky cloak went streaking down
  the sky.

I do not know how long in the snow I wrestled with grisly
  fear;
But the stars came out and they danced about ere again I
  ventured near;
I was sick with dread, but I bravely said: "I'll just take a peep
  inside.
I guess he's cooked, and it's time I looked"; . . . then the
  door I opened wide.

And there sat Sam, looking cold and calm, in the heart of the
  furnace roar;
And he wore a smile you could see a mile, and he said:
  "Please close that door!
It's fine in here, but I greatly fear you'll let in the cold and
  storm—
Since I left Plumtree, down in Tennessee, it's the first time
  I've been warm."

There are strange things done in the midnight sun
  By the men who moil for gold;
The Arctic trails have their secret tales

That would make your blood run cold;
The Northern Lights have seen queer sights,
   But the queerest they ever did see
Was that night on the marge of Lake Lebarge
   I cremated Sam McGee.

THE HAYSTACK IN THE FLOODS

William Morris

Had she come all the way for this,
To part at last without a kiss?
Yea, had she borne the dirt and rain
That her own eyes might see him slain
Beside the haystack in the floods?

Along the dripping leafless woods,
The stirrup touching either shoe,
She rode astride as troopers do;
With kirtle kilted to her knee,
To which the mud splash'd wretchedly;
And the wet dripp'd from every tree
Upon her head and heavy hair,
And on her eyelids broad and fair;
The tears and rain ran down her face.

By fits and starts they rode apace,
And very often was his place
Far off from her; he had to ride
Ahead, to see what might betide
When the roads cross'd; and sometimes, when
There rose a murmuring from his men,

Had to turn back with promises;
Ah me! she had but little ease;
And often for pure doubt and dread
She sobb'd, made giddy in the head
By the swift riding; while, for cold,
Her slender fingers scarce could hold
The wet reins; yea, and scarcely, too,
She felt the foot within her shoe
Against the stirrup: all for this,
To part at last without a kiss
Beside the haystack in the floods.

For when they near'd that old soak'd hay,
They saw across the only way
That Judas, Godmar, and the three
Red running lions dismally
Grinn'd from his pennon, under which
In one straight line along the ditch
They counted thirty heads.

So then,
While Robert turn'd round to his men,
She saw at once the wretched end,
And, stooping down, tried hard to rend
Her coif the wrong way from her head,
And hid her eyes; while Robert said:
"Nay, love, 'tis scarcely two to one,
At Poictiers where we made them run
So fast—why, sweet my love, good cheer,
The Gascon frontier is so near,
Nought after this."

Poictiers: a battle between the English and the French, in 1365.

But, "O," she said,
"My God! my God! I have to tread
The long way back without you; then
The court at Paris; those six men:
The gratings of the Chatelet;
The swift Seine on some rainy day
Like this, and people standing by,
And laughing, while my weak hands try
To recollect how strong men swim.
All this, or else a life with him,
For which I should be damned at last,
Would God that this next hour were past!"

He answer'd not, but cried his cry,
"St. George for Marny!" cheerily;
And laid his hand upon her rein.
Alas! no man of all his train
Gave back that cheery cry again;
And, while for rage his thumb beat fast
Upon his sword-hilt, some one cast
About his neck a kerchief long,
And bound him.

Then they went along
To Godmar; who said: "Now, Jehane,
Your lover's life is on the wane
So fast, that, if this very hour
You yield not as my paramour,
He will not see the rain leave off—
Nay, keep your tongue from gibe and scoff,
Sir Robert, or I slay you now."

Chatelet: a prison in Paris.

She laid her hand upon her brow,
Then gazed upon the palm, as though
She thought her forehead bled, and—"No,"

She said, and turn'd her head away,
As there were nothing else to say,
And everything were settled: red
Grew Godmar's face from chin to head;
"Jehane, on yonder hill there stands
My castle, guarding well my lands:
What hinders me from taking you,
And doing what I list to do
To your fair wilful body, while
Your knight lies dead?"

   A wicked smile
Wrinkled her face, her lips grew thin,
A long way out she thrust her chin:
"You know that I should strangle you
While you were sleeping; or bite through
Your throat, by God's help—ah!" she said,
"Lord Jesus, pity your poor maid!
For in such wise they hem me in,
I cannot choose but sin and sin,
Whatever happens; yet I think
They could not make me eat or drink,
And so should I just reach my rest."

"Nay, if you do not my behest,
O Jehane! though I love you well,"
Said Godmar, "would I fail to tell
All that I know?" "Foul lies," she said.
"Eh? lies, my Jehane? by God's head,
At Paris folks would deem them true!

Do you know, Jehane, they cry for you,
'Jehane the brown! Jehane the brown!
Give us Jehane to burn or drown!'—
Eh—gag me, Robert!—sweet my friend,
This were indeed a piteous end
For those long fingers, and long feet,
And long neck, and smooth shoulders sweet;
An end that few men would forget
That saw it—So, an hour yet:
Consider, Jehane, which to take
Of life or death!"

   So, scarce awake,
Dismounting, did she leave that place,
And totter some yards; with her face
Turn'd upward to the sky she lay,
Her head on a wet heap of hay,
And fell asleep: and while she slept,
And did not dream, the minutes crept
Round to the twelve again; but she,
Being waked at last, sigh'd quietly,
And strangely childlike came, and said:
"I will not." Straightway Godmar's head,
As though it hung on strong wires, turn'd
Most sharply round, and his face burn'd.

For Robert—both his eyes were dry,
He could not weep, but gloomily
He seem'd to watch the rain; yea, too,
His lips were firm; he tried once more
To touch her lips; she reach'd out, sore
And vain desire so tortured them,
The poor gray lips, and now the hem
Of his sleeve brush'd them.

With a start
Up Godmar rose, thrust them apart;
From Robert's throat he loosed the bands
Of silk and mail; with empty hands
Held out, she stood and gazed, and saw
The long bright blade without a flaw
Glide out from Godmar's sheath, his hand
In Robert's hair; she saw him bend
Back Robert's head; she saw him send
The thin steel down; the blow told well,
Right backward the knight Robert fell,
And moan'd as dogs do, being half dead,
Unwitting, as I deem; so then
Godmar turn'd grinning to his men,
Who ran, some five or six, and beat
His head to pieces at their feet.

Then Godmar turn'd again and said:
"So, Jehane, the first fitte is read!
Take note, my lady, that your way
Lies backward to the Chatelet!"
She shook her head and gazed awhile
At her cold hands with a rueful smile,
As though this thing had made her mad.

This was the parting that they had
Beside the haystack in the floods.

fitte: parts of old ballads.

QUESTIONS FOR UNDERSTANDING AND APPRECIATION

SWIMMERS

1. Is the emphasis in this poem primarily on the activity of the swimmer who is telling the story, or on the tragic accident? How does the tragedy affect the swimmer?
2. Cite words in the poem which indicate action. Quote references to the struggle between the swimmer and the sea; examples of vivid description; lines which make you feel the swimmer's love of life.
3. Express the meaning of the last stanza in your own words. Give other examples of the interest of youth in the "feverish intensity of life." How does the poem illustrate the quotation: "Life, an adventure perilous and gay"?
4. How does this poem help you to understand man's attitude toward danger? Why do people climb dangerous mountains, dive deep down into the sea?

VOCABULARY: aggressive, vigor, turbulent, strife, aghast, exult, vivid.

CASEY AT THE BAT

1. How do the spectators participate with Casey in the action of the game? Why is Casey popular with the spectators? Quote lines which indicate his effect on them.
2. Note the poet's effective use of adjectives: a *straggling* few; *stricken* multitude. List other descriptive adjectives in the poem and suggest several others to describe Casey.
3. Why has this remained a popular poem with old and young readers?
4. Why is this story more effective and more humorous as a poem than it might be as a prose short story?

VOCABULARY: eternal, melancholy, recoil, doff, tumult.

THE LABORATORY

1. This poem is an example of a dramatic monologue, a poem in which one character speaking to a silent listener gives an insight into his own character through the story he relates. What does the lady reveal about her plan, her motive, and herself?
2. What is the setting of the poem? Is character or plot the stronger element in the poem?
3. The poem can be presented as a very effective reading by one person. Do you think it could be the basis for a play, motion picture, or television drama? What added details would you include in a television presentation?

THE GLOVE AND THE LIONS

1. What sport of today could be compared with that which King Francis enjoyed in the sixteenth century? Point out descriptive details which help you to visualize the action.
2. What character trait does the lady portray by her action? Do you approve of the Count's reaction? Do you agree with the King's comment?
3. The lady is described in the poem as ". . . a beauteous lively dame, With smiling lips and sharp bright eyes, which always seemed the same." Comment on this poetic portrait.
4. Describe a modern situation in which a young lady might urge her friend to prove his love through a dangerous feat.

THE SKATER OF GHOST LAKE

1. How did this poem affect you? Would it be more effective, or less, if the mystery had been cleared? What questions would you like to ask the poet? What is your own explanation of the mystery?
2. Reread the poem to appreciate the vivid pictures and to hear the variety of sounds. Select words and phrases which express movement, sound, color, feeling.
3. After you have read, reread, and discussed the poem in class, you may wish to write your own interpretation of the tantalizing mystery.

·T H E   H I G H W A Y M A N

1. This poem has a well-developed plot. What interrelated events lead up to the tragic climax? What are the conflicts in the story? What part does Tim play, and what is his motive? Are your sympathies with Bess or the Highwayman? Who is more heroic?
2. What elements besides the plot contribute to the excitement and suspense of the poem? What is the purpose of the repetition of the words *tlot, riding,* and *marching*? What idea is implied in the last two stanzas?
3. Select words and phrases which make you experience and visualize the action of the story; for example, "his rapier hilt a-twinkle."
4. Describe Tim's thoughts as he listens in on the conversation between the highwayman and the landlord's daughter. Defend him or denounce him for notifying the police.
5. Comment on this statement: In both the poem and real life, love can prove to be a trap.

VOCABULARY: torrent, galleon, rapier, claret, ostler, harry, casement, brandish, moor.

L O C H I N V A R

1. Contrast Lochinvar and his rival by citing descriptive words which the poet applies to each of them.
2. How does the poem give the impression of hurry and excitement?

T H E   I N C H C A P E   R O C K

1. What was it that the Abbot of Aberbrothok did? How do you explain the action of Sir Ralph the Rover?
2. Explain the meaning of *poetic justice* as illustrated in this poem. (Refer to your dictionary, if necessary.)
3. What is the meaning of the last stanza? Is it dramatically satisfying?

JOCK OF HAZELDEAN

1. Why is Frank considered the more eligible suitor? How does love win over status?

VOCABULARY: kirk, taper, mettled, comely

THE YARN OF THE NANCY BELL

1. What is a yarn, and why is the poem so called?
2. How does the author succeed in making cannibalism humorous and not offensive to the reader? Do you like the poem? Why or why not?

THE CREMATION OF SAM MC GEE

1. What is meant by a "tall story"? How does this poem qualify as one? How do the realistic details heighten the effectiveness of the ending?
2. Account for Sam's reaction to the Arctic. How does his cremation become his good fortune?
3. What qualities in the poem have made it a favorite of many readers? Why did you like or dislike it?
4. Note that the rhythm and rhyme add to the pleasing effect of this poem. How does the rhyme differ from that of others you have read?

THE HAYSTACK IN THE FLOODS

1. What was your first reaction to this poem? Does it have a well-developed plot and climax? What is the relation of the first stanza to the conclusion? What details preceding the story must be imagined by the reader?
2. Cite examples in the poem of the author's skill in portraying character and in realistic description.

COMPARATIVE STUDY

1. Physical activity, romance, evil, and humor are involved in the poems in this section. From each of the four types, select one poem which you particularly enjoyed. Did the stories or the characters interest you more? Do you think the four poems you selected are likely to remain in textbooks and collections of poetry for many years? Why?

2. Point out examples of conflict in "Swimmers," "Lochinvar," and "The Haystack in the Flood."

3. "Swimmers," "Casey at the Bat," and "The Glove and the Lions" are poems with a sports background. With which of the characters' experiences can you most easily identify yourself? In which poem is the sport itself not the dominant factor in the story? What details indicate that "The Glove and the Lions" is an older poem than the others?

4. What are the obvious similarities between "Lochinvar" and "Jock of Hazeldean"? How is the reader informed of Lochinvar's character and of Jock's? What quality do both ladies possess? Write a news article for a society column describing either of these elopements.

5. In what ways can "The Highwayman," "Lochinvar," "The Inchcape Rock," and "The Skater of Ghost Lake" be compared? In which poem is the plot suggested rather than clearly presented? Which has the most vivid word pictures? the most effective sound? the most lifelike characters? the best plot?

6. Compare the plots of "The Yarn of the Nancy Bell," and "The Cremation of Sam McGee." Do you prefer stories like these or those with more believable plots? Which of the following adjectives would apply to the two poems: *delightful, ludicrous, silly, whimsical, subtle, imaginative?*

The sound of a poem

■ THE SOUND OF A POEM

■ In reading the poems in the first section of this book, your attention was focused primarily on the action and suspense of the story, but you were aware also that the pleasing sound of the words added much to the meaning and the effect of the poem. In "The Highwayman," for example, the sound of the words and the rhythm of the lines made you feel the tense excitement of the plot. In "The Skater of Ghost Lake," the sounds of the skaters expressed in rhythm helped you to experience the mystery and suspense of the story.

In this second section, you will read a variety of poems which will illustrate how sound and story combine to communicate ideas and impressions to the reader. Your enjoyment of poetry will increase as you become alert to its musical quality.

The music of poetry is achieved in a number of ways: first, through *rhythm*. The rhythm of language, like the regular sound of waves lapping on the shore, has a natural appeal to the ear. Rhythm in poetry results from a combination of accented and unaccented syllables. When the sounds of the syllables are arranged so as to occur at approximately equal intervals, the pattern of rhythm is called *meter*.

If you will read the following lines slowly, you will be able to hear the regular rhythmic pattern:

Still sits the schoolhouse by the road

Quoth the raven "Nevermore."

O'er the land of the free and the home of the brave

This is the forest primeval, the murmuring pines and the hemlocks

These regular rhythmic patterns illustrate the four kinds of meter used most frequently in English poetry—*iambic, trochee, anapest,* and *dactyl.* Very often the poet varies the rhythmic pattern in order to avoid monotony or to adapt the rhythm to the effect desired. For example, listen to the variation of meter in the following lines, in which the sound of the words reflects the suspense in the action.

And the highwayman came riding—
Riding, riding,—
And the highwayman came riding up to the old inn door.

As you progress in your study of poetry, you will learn how to find the pattern of rhythm in a line; this process is called *scansion.* Detailed information about scansion and other mechanics of poetry is included in the Introduction, page xxvi.

Another poetic device which produces effective sound is the repetition of sounds, words, and lines in a poem. The most common example of the repetition of sound is *rhyme,* which is used most often at the ends of lines; for example:

O young Lochinvar is come out of the *West.*
Through all the wide border his steed was the *best;*

The pattern of rhyme used in a stanza is called *rhyme scheme,* which is designated by letters of the alphabet. In the two lines above, the rhyme scheme is *aa,* which indicates that the end words in the first two lines of the poem rhyme; if the second end word had a different sound, the rhyme would be *ab.*

Sometimes rhyming words are used within the lines; this repetition is called *internal rhyme,* which you observed in "The Cremation of Sam McGee":

The Arctic *trails* have their secret *tales.* . . .

Another kind or repetition is called *alliteration:* consonant sounds are repeated, usually those at the beginning of lines. For example, "The Skater of Ghost Lake" has effective alliteration, as in this line:

Swifter and swifter a low singing sound . . .

This poem and "The Highwayman" illustrate another poetic device, *onomatopoeia,* that is, the use of words which suggest the meaning through their sound; in other words, sense and sound harmonize. Examples: *tlot, clatters and clangs, whirring, skurr of the steel.*

For full appreciation of the sound of poetry, oral reading is essential. To illustrate varying sound patterns conforming to the meaning and tone of the story, the poems in this section have been arranged in four separate groups. If you read many of the poems aloud, either individually or chorally, you will sense the difference in rhythm and will find pleasure in poetry as you do in music.

An old favorite, "The Pied Piper of Hamelin," has been included in this section because it illustrates many of the poetic devices related to sound.

I LOVED A LASS

George Wither

I loved a lass, a fair one,
  As fair as e'er was seen;
She was indeed a rare one,
  Another Sheba Queen;
But, fool as then I was,
  I thought she loved me too;
But now, alas! she's left me,
  Falero, lero, loo!

Her hair like gold did glister,
  Each eye was like a star,
She did surpass her sister,
  Which pass'd all others far;
She would me honey call,
  She'd—O she'd kiss me too!
But now, alas! she's left me,
  Falero, lero, loo!

Many a merry meeting
  My love and I have had;
She was my only sweeting,
  She made my heart full glad;
The tears stood in her eyes
  Like to the morning dew;
But now, alas! she's left me,
  Falero, lero, loo!

Her cheeks were like the cherry,
  Her skin was white as snow;
When she was blithe and merry

She angel-like did show;
Her waist exceeding small,
    The fives did fit her shoe;
But now, alas! she's left me,
    Falero, lero, loo!

In summer time or winter
    She had her heart's desire;
I still did scorn to stint her
    From sugar, sack, or fire;
The world went round about,
    No cares we ever knew;
But now, alas! she's left me,
    Falero, lero, loo!

To maidens' vows and swearing
    Henceforth no credit give;
You may give them the hearing,
    But never them believe;
They are as false as fair,
    Unconstant, frail, untrue;
For mine, alas! hath left me,
    Falero, lero, loo!

THE BLACKSMITH'S SERENADE

Vachel Lindsay

John Littlehouse the redhead was a large ruddy man
Quite proud to be a blacksmith, and he loved Polly Ann,
    Polly Ann.
Straightway to her window with his iron guitar he came

scorn to stint her: scorn the thought of stopping or depriving her.

Breathing like a blacksmith—his wonderful heart's flame.
Though not very bashful and not very bold
He had reached the plain conclusion his passion must be told.
And so he sang: "Awake, awake,"—this hip-hoo-ray-ious man.
"Do you like me, do you love me, Polly Ann, Polly Ann?
The rooster on my coalshed crows at break of day.
It makes a person happy to hear his roundelay.
The fido in my woodshed barks at fall of night.
He makes one feel so safe and snug. He barks exactly right.
I swear to do my stylish best and purchase all I can
Of the flummeries, flunkeries and mummeries of man.
And I will carry in the coal and the water from the spring
And I will sweep the porches if you will cook and sing.
No doubt your Pa sleeps like a rock. Of course Ma is awake
But dares not say she hears me, for gentle custom's sake.
Your sleeping father knows I am a decent honest man.
Will you wake him, Polly Ann,
And if he dares deny it I will thrash him, lash bash mash
Hash him, Polly Ann.
Hum hum hum, fee fie fo fum—
And my brawn should wed your beauty.
Do you hear me, Polly Ann, Polly Ann?"

Polly had not heard of him before, but heard him now.
She blushed behind the shutters like a pippin on the bough.
She was not overfluttered, she was not overbold.
She was glad a lad was living with a passion to be told.
But she spoke up to her mother: "Oh, what an awful
man:—
This merry merry quite contrary tricky trixy, Polly Ann,
Polly Ann.
The neighbors put their heads out of the windows. They
said:—
"What sort of turtle dove is this that seems to wake the
dead?"

Yes, in their nighties whispered this question to the night.
They did not dare to shout it. It wouldn't be right.
And so, I say, they whispered:—"Does she hear this awful
 man,
Polly Ann, Polly Ann?"

John Littlehouse the redhead sang on of his desires:
"Steel makes the wires of lyres, makes the frames of terrible
 towers
And circus chariots' tires.
Believe me, dear, a blacksmith man can feel.
I will bind you, if I can to my ribs with hoops of steel.
Do you hear me, Polly Ann, Polly Ann?"

And then his tune was silence, for he was not a fool.
He let his voice rest, his iron guitar cool.
And thus he let the wind sing, the stars sing and the grass
 sing,
The prankishness of love sing, the girl's tingling feet sing,
Her trembling sweet hands sing, her mirror in the dark sing,
Her grace in the dark sing, her pillow in the dark sing,
The savage in her blood sing, her starved little heart sing,
Silently sing.

"Yes, I hear you, Mister Man,"
To herself said Polly Ann, Polly Ann.

He shouted one great loud *"Good night,"* and laughed,
And skipped home.
And every star was winking in the wide wicked dome.
And early in the morning, sweet Polly stole away.
And though the town went crazy, she is his wife today.

THE SANDS OF DEE

Charles Kingsley

"O Mary, go and call the cattle home,
    And call the cattle home,
    And call the cattle home
  Across the sands of Dee";
The western wind was wild and dank with foam,
  And all alone went she.

The western tide crept up along the sand,
    And o'er and o'er the sand,
    And round and round the sand,
  As far as eye could see.
The rolling mist came down and hid the land:
  And never home came she.

"Oh! is it weed, or fish, or floating hair—
    A tress of golden hair,
    A drownèd maiden's hair
  Above the nets at sea?
Was never salmon yet that shone so fair
  Among the stakes on Dee."

They rowed her in across the rolling foam,
    The cruel crawling foam,
    The cruel hungry foam,
  To her grave beside the sea:
But still the boatmen hear her call the cattle home
  Across the sands of Dee.

SPANISH JOHNNY

Willa Cather

The old West, the old time,
   The old wind singing through
The red, red grass a thousand miles,
   And, Spanish Johnny, you!
He'd sit beside the water-ditch
   When all his herd was in,
And never mind a child, but sing
   To his mandolin.

The big stars, the blue night,
   The moon-enchanted plain;
The olive man who never spoke,
   But sang the songs of Spain.
His speech with men was wicked talk—
   To hear it was a sin;
But those were golden things he said
   To his mandolin.

The gold songs, the gold stars,
   The world so golden then;
And the hand so tender to a child
   Had killed so many men.
He died a hard death long ago
   Before the Road came in;
The night before he swung, he sang
   To his mandolin.

ANNABEL LEE

Edgar Allan Poe

It was many and many a year ago,
   In a kingdom by the sea
That a maiden there lived whom you may know
   By the name of *Annabel Lee*;
And this maiden she lived with no other thought
   Than to love and be loved by me.

I was a child and *she* was a child,
   In this kingdom by the sea,
But we loved with a love that was more than love—
   I and my *Annabel Lee*—
With a love that the winged seraphs of heaven
   Coveted her and me.

And this was the reason that, long ago,
   In this kingdom by the sea,
A wind blew out of a cloud, chilling
   My beautiful *Annabel Lee*;
So that her highborn kinsmen came
   And bore her away from me,
To shut her up in a sepulchre
   In this kingdom by the sea.

The angels, not half so happy in heaven,
   Went envying her and me—
Yes!—that was the reason (as all men know,
   In this kingdom by the sea)
That the wind came out of the cloud by night,
   Chilling and killing my *Annabel Lee*.

But our love it was stronger by far than the love
   Of those who were older than we—
   Of many far wiser than we—
And neither the angels in heaven above,
   Nor the demons down under the sea,
Can ever dissever my soul from the soul
   Of the beautiful *Annabel Lee*;

For the moon never beams, without bringing me dreams
   Of the beautiful *Annabel Lee*;
And the stars never rise, but I feel the bright eyes
   Of the beautiful *Annabel Lee*;
And so, all the night-tide, I lie down by the side
Of my darling—my darling—my life and my bride,
   In the sepulchre there by the sea—
   In her tomb by the sounding sea.

THE CHARGE OF THE LIGHT BRIGADE

Alfred Tennyson

The charge described in this poem occurred in 1854 at the Battle of Balaclava during the Crimean War, in which England and her allies defeated Russia. The charge resulted in great loss of life to the Light Brigade.

Half a league, half a league,
Half a league onward,
All in the valley of Death,
   Rode the six hundred.
"Forward, the Light Brigade!
Charge for the guns!" he said:

Into the valley of Death
   Rode the six hundred.

"Forward, the Light Brigade!"
Was there a man dismayed?
Not though the soldiers knew
   Some one had blundered:
Theirs not to make reply,
Theirs not to reason why,
Theirs but to do and die;—
Into the valley of Death
   Rode the six hundred.

Cannon to right of them,
Cannon to left of them,
Cannon in front of them
   Volleyed and thundered;
Stormed at with shot and shell,
Boldly they rode and well;
Into the jaws of Death,
Into the mouth of Hell
   Rode the six hundred.

Flashed all their sabers bare,
Flashed as they turned in air,
Sabering the gunners there,
Charging an army, while
   All the world wondered:
Plunged in the battery smoke,
Right through the line they broke;
Cossack and Russian
Reeled from the saber stroke
   Shattered and sundered.

Then they rode back, but not—
   Not the six hundred.

Cannon to right of them,
Cannon to left of them,
Cannon behind them
   Volleyed and thundered.
Stormed at with shot and shell,
While horse and hero fell,
They that had fought so well
Came through the jaws of Death,
Back from the mouth of Hell,
All that was left of them,
   Left of six hundred.

When can their glory fade?
O the wild charge they made!
   All the world wondered.
Honor the charge they made!
Honor the Light Brigade!
   Noble six hundred.

HOW THEY BROUGHT THE GOOD NEWS FROM GHENT TO AIX

Robert Browning

This poem has no historical basis. Browning said he wrote it at sea because he appreciated "even the fancy of a certain good horse 'York' then in my stable at home." Read aloud this stirring story and see if you can hear the horses' hoofs and feel the speed and urgency which the author succeeded so well in putting into the rhythm.

I sprang to the stirrup, and Joris, and he;
I galloped, Dirck galloped, we galloped all three;
"Good speed!" cried the watch, as the gatebolts undrew;
"Speed!" echoed the wall to us galloping through;
Behind shut the postern, the lights sank to rest
And into the midnight we galloped abreast.

Not a word to each other; we kept the great pace
Neck by neck, stride by stride, never changing our place;
I turned in my saddle and made its girths tight,
Then shortened each stirrup, and set the pique right,
Rebuckled the cheek-strap, chained slacker the bit,
Nor galloped less steadily Roland a whit.

'Twas moonset at starting; but while we drew near
Lokeren, the cocks crew and twilight dawned clear;
At Boom, a great yellow star came out to see;
At Düffeld, 'twas morning as plain as could be;
And from Mecheln church-steeple we heard the half-chime,
So, Joris broke silence with, "Yet there is time!"

At Aershot, up leaped of a sudden the sun,
And against him the cattle stood black every one,
To stare thro' the mist at us galloping past,

And I saw my stout galloper Roland at last,
With resolute shoulders, each butting away
The haze, as some bluff river headland its spray:

And his low head and crest, just one sharp ear bent back
For my voice, and the other pricked out on his track;
And one eye's black intelligence,—ever that glance
O'er its white edge at me, his own master, askance!
And the thick heavy spume-flakes which aye and anon
His fierce lips shook upwards in galloping on.

By Hasselt, Dirck groaned; and cried Joris, "Stay spur!
Your Roos galloped bravely, the fault's not in her,
We'll remember at Aix"—for one heard the quick wheeze
Of her chest, saw the stretched neck and staggering knees,
And sunk tail, and horrible heave of the flank,
As down on her haunches she shuddered and sank.

So, we were left galloping, Joris and I,
Past Looz and past Tongres, no cloud in the sky;
The broad sun above laughed a pitiless laugh,
'Neath our feet broke the brittle bright stubble like chaff
Till over by Dalhem a dome-spire sprang white,
And "Gallop," gasped Joris, "for Aix is in sight!"

"How they'll greet us!"—and all in a moment his roan
Rolled neck and croup over, lay dead as a stone;
And there was my Roland to bear the whole weight
Of the news which alone could save Aix from her fate,
With his nostrils like pits full of blood to the brim,
And with circles of red for his eye-sockets' rim.

Then I cast loose my buffcoat, each holster let fall,
Shook off both my jack-boots, let go belt and all,
Stood up in the stirrup, leaned, patted his ear,

Called my Roland his pet-name, my horse without peer;
Clapped my hands, laughed and sang, any noise, bad or good,
Till at length into Aix Roland galloped and stood.

And all I remember is—friends flocking round
As I sat with his head 'twixt my knees on the ground;
And no voice but was praising this Roland of mine,
As I poured down his throat our last measure of wine,
Which (the burgesses voted by common consent)
Was no more than his due who brought good news from
    Ghent.

THE BALLAD OF EAST AND WEST

Rudyard Kipling

The setting of this poem is the northwestern frontier of India along the
Khyber Pass, a narrow road separating India from Afghanistan, where
British troops were guarding the border against native outlaws. In the
poem, the East is represented by Kamal, the leader of the Afghans, and
the West, by the son of the English colonel.

*Oh East is East, and West is West, and never the twain
    shall meet,*
*Till Earth and Sky stand presently at God's great Judgment
    Seat;*
*But there is neither East nor West, Border, nor Breed, nor
    Birth,*
*When two strong men stand face to face, tho' they come
    from the ends of the earth!*

Kamal is out with twenty men to raise the Border side,
And he has lifted the Colonel's mare that is the Colonel's
    pride:

He has lifted her out of the stable-door between the dawn
    and the day,
And turned the calkins upon her feet, and ridden her far
    away.
Then up and spoke the Colonel's son that led a troop of the
    Guides:
"Is there never a man of all my men can say where Kamal
    hides?"
Then up and spoke Mahommed Khan, the son of the
    Ressaldar,
"If ye know the track of the morning-mist, ye know where
    his pickets are.
"At dusk he harries the Abazai—at dawn he is into Bonair,
"But he must go by Fort Bukloh to his own place to fare,
"So if ye gallop to Fort Bukloh as fast as a bird can fly,
"By the favor of God ye may cut him off, ere he win to the
    Tongue of Jagai,
"But if he be passed the Tongue of Jagai, right swiftly turn
    ye then,
"For the length and the breadth of that grisly plain is sown
    with Kamal's men.
"There is rock to the left, and rock to the right, and low,
    lean thorn between,
"And ye may hear a breech bolt snick where never a man is
    seen."
The Colonel's son has taken a horse, and a raw rough dun
    was he,
With the mouth of a bell and the heart of Hell, and the
    head of the gallows-tree.
The Colonel's son to the Fort has won, they bid him stay
    to eat—

calkins: cleats on a horse's hoofs.
Ressaldar: native Indian chief in the British army.

Who rides at the tail of a Border thief, he sits not long at his meat.

He's up and away from Fort Bukloh as fast as he can fly,

Till he was aware of his father's mare in the gut of the Tongue of Jagai,

Till he was aware of his father's mare with Kamal upon her back,

And when he could spy the white of her eye, he made the pistol crack.

He has fired once, he has fired twice, but the whistling ball went wide.

"Ye shoot like a soldier," Kamal said. "Show now if ye can ride."

It's up and over the Tongue of Jagai, as blown dust-devils go,

The dun he fled like a stag of ten, but the mare like a barren doe.

The dun he leaned against the bit and slugged his head above,

But the red mare played with the snaffle-bars, as a maiden plays with a glove.

There was rock to the left and rock to the right, and low lean thorn between,

And thrice he heard a breech-bolt snick tho' never a man was seen.

They have ridden the low moon out of the sky, their hoofs drum up the dawn,

The dun he went like a wounded bull, but the mare like a new-roused fawn.

The dun he fell at a water-course—in a woful heap fell he,

And Kamal has turned the red mare back, and pulled the rider free.

He has knocked the pistol out of his hand—small room was there to strive,

---

ten: ten points on his antlers. *snaffle-bar*: a bridle bit.

" 'Twas only by favor of mine," quoth he, "ye rode so long
 alive:
"There was not a rock for twenty miles, there was not a
 clump of tree,
"But covered a man of my own men with his rifle cocked on
 his knee.
"If I had raised my bridle-hand, as I have held it low,
"The little jackals that flee so fast, were feasting all in a row:
"If I had bowed my head on my breast, as I have held it
 high,
"The kite that whistles above us now were gorged till she
 could not fly."
Lightly answered the Colonel's son: "Do good to bird and
 beast,
"But count who come for the broken meats before thou
 makest a feast.
"If there should follow a thousand swords to carry my bones
 away,
"Belike the price of a jackal's meal were more than a thief
 could pay.
"They will feed their horse on the standing crop, their men
 on the garnered grain,
"The thatch of the byres will serve their fires when all the
 cattle are slain.
"But if thou thinkest the price be fair,—thy brethren wait
 to sup,
"The hound is kin to the jackal-spawn,—howl, dog, and call
 them up!
"And if thou thinkest the price be high, in steer and gear
 and stack,
"Give me my father's mare again, and I'll fight my own way
 back!"

byres: cow barns.

Kamal has gripped him by the hand and set him upon his feet.

"No talk shall be of dogs," said he, "when wolf and gray wolf meet.

"May I eat dirt if thou hast hurt of me in deed or breath;

"What dam of lances brought thee forth to jest at the dawn with Death?"

Lightly answered the Colonel's son: "I hold by the blood of my clan:

"Take up the mare for my father's gift—by God, she has carried a man!"

The red mare ran to the Colonel's son, and nuzzled against his breast;

"We be two strong men," said Kamal then, "but she loveth the younger best.

"So she shall go with a lifter's dower, my turquoise-studded rein,

"My broidered saddle and saddle-cloth, and silver stirrups twain."

The Colonel's son a pistol drew and held it muzzle-end,

"Ye have taken the one from a foe," said he; "will ye take the mate from a friend?"

"A gift for a gift," said Kamal straight; "a limb for the risk of a limb.

"Thy father has sent his son to me, I'll send my son to him!"

With that he whistled his only son, that dropped from a mountain-crest—

He trod the ling like a buck in spring, and he looked like a lance in rest.

"Now here is thy master," Kamal said, "who leads a troop of the Guides,

"And thou must ride at his left side as shield on shoulder rides.

ling: heather.

"Till Death or I cut loose the tie, at camp and board and
bed,

"Thy life is his—thy fate is to guard him with thy head.

"So thou must eat the White Queen's meat, and all her
foes are thine,

"And thou must harry thy father's hold for the peace of
the Border-line,

"And thou must make a trooper tough and hack thy way to
power—

"Belike they will raise thee to Ressaldar when I am hanged
in Peshawur."

They have looked each other between the eyes, and there
they have found no fault,

They have taken the Oath of the Brother-in-Blood on leav-
ened bread and salt;

They have taken the Oath of the Brother-in-Blood on fire
and fresh-cut sod,

On the hilt and the haft of the Khyber knife, and the
Wondrous Names of God.

The Colonel's son he rides the mare and Kamal's boy the
dun,

And two have come back to Fort Bukloh where there went
forth but one.

And when they drew to the Quarter-Guard, full twenty
swords flew clear—

There was not a man but carried his feud with the blood of
the mountaineer.

"Ha' done! ha' done!" said the Colonel's son, "Put up the
steel at your sides!

"Last night ye had struck at a Border thief—tonight 'tis a
man of the Guides!"

Oh East is East and West is West, and never the twain shall meet,

Till Earth and Sky stand presently at God's great Judgment Seat;

But there is neither East nor West, Border, nor Breed, nor Birth,

When two strong men stand face to face, tho' they come from the ends of the earth.

SKIPPER IRESON'S RIDE

John Greenleaf Whittier

Years after Whittier had written this poem, he learned that Ireson was innocent of the charges against him. Apparently the Skipper had shouldered the blame for refusing to stay with the sinking ship, though, in fact, the refusal had come from the mutinous crew. When they reached shore, Skipper Ireson was blamed, but he kept silent about the facts.

Of all the rides since the birth of time,
Told in story or sung in rhyme,—
On Apuleius's Golden Ass
On one-eyed Calendar's horse of brass,
Witch astride of a human back,
Islam's prophet on Al-Borák,—
The strangest ride that ever was sped
Was Ireson's, out from Marblehead!
   Old Floyd Ireson, for his hard heart,
    Tarred and feathered and carried in a cart
     By the women of Marblehead!

Apuleius's Golden Ass: an ancient Roman's famous comic story of an unusual ride.
Calendar's horse of brass: a horse in the *Arabian Nights*.
Islam's prophet on Al-Borák: Mohammed rode Al-Borák to the seven heavens.   *Marblehead:* a town near Boston.

Body of turkey, head of owl,
Wings adroop like a rained-on fowl,
Feathered and ruffled in every part,
Skipper Ireson stood in the cart.
Scores of women, old and young,
Strong of muscle, and glib of tongue,
Pushed and pulled up the rocky lane,
Shouting and singing the shrill refrain:
   "Here's Flud Oirson, fur his horrd horrt,
   Torr'd an' futherr'd an' corr'd in a corrt
      By the women o' Morble'ead!"

Wrinkled scolds with hands on hips,
Girls in bloom of cheek and lips,
Wild-eyed, free-limbed, such as chase
Bacchus round some antique vase,
Brief of skirt, with ankles bare,
Loose of kerchief and loose of hair,
With conch shells blowing and fish horns' twang,
Over and over the Mænads sang:
   "Here's Flud Oirson, fur his horrd horrt,
   Torr'd an' futherr'd an' corr'd in a corrt
      By the women o' Morble'ead!"

Small pity for him!—He sailed away
From a leaking ship in Chaleur Bay,—
Sailed away from a sinking wreck,
With his own town's people on her deck!
"Lay by! lay by!" they called to him.
Back he answered, "Sink or swim!
Brag of your catch of fish again!"
And off he sailed through the fog and rain!

Maenads: followers of Bacchus, god of wine.
Chaleur Bay: in Gulf of St. Lawrence.

Old Floyd Ireson, for his hard heart,
Tarred and feathered and carried in a cart
By the women of Marblehead!

Fathoms deep in dark Chaleur
That wreck shall lie forevermore.
Mother and sister, wife and maid,
Looked from the rocks of Marblehead
Over the moaning and rainy sea,—
Looked for the coming that might not be!
What did the winds and the sea birds say
Of the cruel captain who sailed away?—
Old Floyd Ireson, for his hard heart,
Tarred and feathered and carried in a cart
By the women of Marblehead.

Through the street, on either side,
Up flew windows, doors swung wide;
Sharp-tongued spinsters, old wives gray,
Treble lent the fish horn's bray.
Sea-worn grandsires, cripple-bound,
Hulks of old sailors run aground,
Shook head, and fist, and hat, and cane,
And cracked with curses the hoarse refrain:
"Here's Flud Oirson, fur his horrd horrt,
Torr'd an' futherr'd an' corr'd in a corrt
By the women o' Morble'ead!"

Sweetly along the Salem road
Bloom of orchard and lilac showed.
Little the wicked skipper knew
Of the fields so green and the sky so blue.
Riding there in his sorry trim,
Like an Indian idol glum and grim,

Scarcely he seemed the sound to hear
Of voices shouting, far and near:
  "Here's Flud Oirson, fur his horrd horrt,
  Torr'd an' futherr'd an' corr'd in a corrt
    By the women o' Morble'ead!"

"Hear me, neighbors!" at last he cried,—
"What to me is this noisy ride?
What is the shame that clothes the skin
To the nameless horror that lives within?
Waking or sleeping, I see a wreck,
And hear a cry from a reeling deck!
Hate me and curse me,—I only dread
The hand of God and the face of the dead!"
  Said old Floyd Ireson, for his hard heart,
  Tarred and feathered and carried in a cart
    By the women of Marblehead!

Then the wife of the skipper lost at sea
Said, "God has touched him! why should we?"
Said an old wife mourning her only son,
"Cut the rogue's tether and let him run!"
So with soft relentings and rude excuse,
Half scorn, half pity, they cut him loose,
And gave him a cloak to hide him in,
And left him alone with his shame and sin.
  Poor Floyd Ireson, for his hard heart,
  Tarred and feathered and carried in a cart
    By the women of Marblehead!

PAUL REVERE'S RIDE

Henry Wadsworth Longfellow

Listen, my children, and you shall hear
Of the midnight ride of Paul Revere,
On the eighteenth of April, in Seventy-five;
Hardly a man is now alive
Who remembers that famous day and year.
He said to his friend, "If the British march
By land or sea from the town tonight,
Hang a lantern aloft in the belfry arch
Of the North Church tower as a signal light,—
One, if by land, and two, if by sea;
And I on the opposite shore will be,
Ready to ride and spread the alarm
Through every Middlesex village and farm,
For the country folk to be up and to arm."

Then he said, "Good-night!" and with muffled oar
Silently rowed to the Charlestown shore,
Just as the moon rose over the bay,
Where swinging wide at her moorings lay
The Somerset, British man-of-war;
A phantom ship, with each mast and spar
Across the moon like a prison bar,
And a huge black hulk, that was magnified
By its own reflection in the tide.
Meanwhile, his friend, through alley and street,
Wanders and watches with eager ears,
Till in the silence around him he hears
The muster of men at the barrack door,
The sound of arms, and the tramp of feet,
And the measured tread of the grenadiers,
Marching down to their boats on the shore.

Then he climbed the tower of the Old North Church,
By the wooden stairs, with stealthy tread,
To the belfry-chamber overhead,
And startled the pigeons from their perch
On the somber rafters, that round him made
Masses and moving shapes of shade,—
By the trembling ladder, steep and tall,
To the highest window in the wall,
Where he paused to listen and look down
A moment on the roofs of the town,
And the moonlight flowing over all.

Beneath, in the churchyard, lay the dead,
In their night-encampment on the hill,
Wrapped in silence so deep and still
That he could hear, like a sentinel's tread,
The watchful night-wind, as it went
Creeping along from tent to tent,
And seeming to whisper, "All is well!"
A moment only he feels the spell
Of the place and the hour, and the secret dread
Of the lonely belfry and the dead;
For suddenly all his thoughts are bent
On a shadowy something far away,
Where the river widens to meet the bay,—
A line of black that bends and floats
On the rising tide, like a bridge of boats.

Meanwhile, impatient to mount and ride,
Booted and spurred, with a heavy stride
On the opposite shore walked Paul Revere.
Now he patted his horse's side,
Now gazed at the landscape far and near,
Then, impetuous, stamped the earth,
And turned and tightened his saddle-girth;

But mostly he watched with eager search
The belfry-tower of the Old North Church,
As it rose above the graves on the hill,
Lonely and spectral and somber and still.
And lo! as he looks, on the belfry's height
A glimmer, and then a gleam of light!
He springs to the saddle, the bridle he turns,
But lingers and gazes, till full on his sight
A second lamp in the belfry burns!

A hurry of hoofs in a village street,
A shape in the moonlight, a bulk in the dark,
And beneath, from the pebbles, in passing, a spark
Struck out by a steed flying fearless and fleet;
That was all! And yet, through the gloom and the light,
The fate of a nation was riding that night;
And the spark struck out by that steed, in his flight,
Kindled the land into flame with its heat.

He has left the village and mounted the steep,
And beneath him, tranquil and broad and deep,
Is the Mystic, meeting the ocean tides;
And under the alders, that skirt its edge
Now soft on the sand, now loud on the ledge,
Is heard the tramp of his steed as he rides.

It was twelve by the village clock
When he crossed the bridge into Medford town.
He heard the crowing of the cock,
And the barking of the farmer's dog,
And felt the damp of the river fog,
That rises after the sun goes down.

It was one by the village clock,
When he galloped into Lexington.
He saw the gilded weathercock
Swim in the moonlight as he passed,
And the meeting-house windows, blank and bare,
Gaze at him with a spectral glare,
As if they already stood aghast
At the bloody work they would look upon.

It was two by the village clock,
When he came to the bridge in Concord town.
He heard the bleating of the flock,
And the twitter of birds among the trees,
And felt the breath of the morning breeze
Blowing over the meadows brown.
And one was safe and asleep in his bed
Who at the bridge would be first to fall,
Who that day would be lying dead,
Pierced by a British musket-ball.

You know the rest.   In the books you have read,
How the British Regulars fired and fled,—
How the farmers gave them ball for ball,
From behind each fence and farm-yard wall,
Chasing the red-coats down the lane,
Then crossing the fields to emerge again
Under the trees at the turn of the road,
And only pausing to fire and load.

So through the night rode Paul Revere;
And so through the night went his cry of alarm
To every Middlesex village and farm,—

A cry of defiance and not of fear,
A voice in the darkness, a knock at the door,
And a word that shall echo forevermore!
For, borne on the night-wind of the Past,
Through all our history, to the last,
In the hour of darkness and peril and need,
The people will waken and listen to hear
The hurrying hoof-beats of that steed,
And the midnight message of Paul Revere.

A RUNNABLE STAG

John Davidson

When the pods went pop on the broom, green broom,
    And apples began to be golden skinned,
We harbour'd a stag in the Priory coomb,
    And we feather'd his trail up-wind, up-wind,
    We feather'd his trail up-wind—
        A stag of warrant, a stag, a stag,
        A runnable stag, a kingly crop,
        Brow, bay and tray and three on top,
        A stag, a runnable stag.

Then the huntsman's horn rang yap, yap, yap,
    And 'Forwards' we heard the harbourer shout;
But 'twas only a brocket that broke a gap
    In the breechen underwood, driven out,
    From the underwood antler'd out,
        By warrant and might of the stag, the stag,
        The runnable stag, whose lordly mind
        Was bent on sleep, though beamed and tined
        He stood, a runnable stag.

coomb: a narrow ravinelike valley.

So we tufted the covert till afternoon
  With Tinkerman's Pup and Bell-of-the-North;
And hunters were sulky and hounds out of tune
  Before we tufted the right stag forth,
  Before we tufted him forth,
      The stag of warrant, the wily stag,
      The runnable stag with his kingly crop,
      Brow, bay and tray and three on top,
      The royal and runnable stag.

It was Bell-of-the-North and Tinkerman's Pup
  That stuck to the scent till the copse was drawn.
'Tally ho! tally ho!' and the hunt was up,
  The tufters whipped and the pack laid on,
  The resolute pack laid on,
      And the stag of warrant away at last,
      The runnable stag, the same, the same,
      His hoofs on fire, his horns like flame,
      A stag, a runnable stag.

'Let your gelding be: if you check or chide
  He stumbles at once and you're out of the hunt;
For three hundred gentlemen, able to ride,
  On hunters accustom'd to bear the brunt,
  Accustomed to bear the brunt,
      Are after the runnable stag, the stag,
      The runnable stag with his kingly crop,
      Brow, bay and tray and three on top,
      The right, the runnable stag.'

By perilous paths in coomb and dell,
  The heather, the rocks, and the river-bed,
The pace grew hot, for the scent lay well,
  And the runnable stag goes right ahead,
  The quarry went right ahead—

Ahead, ahead, and fast and far;
His antler'd crest, his cloven hoof,
Brow, bay and tray and three aloof,
The stag, the runnable stag.

For a matter of twenty miles and more,
By the densest hedge and the highest wall,
Through herds of bullocks he baffled the lore
Of harbourer, huntsman, hounds and all,
Of harbourer, hounds and all—
The stag of warrant, the wily stag,
For twenty miles, and five and five,
He ran, and he never was caught alive,
This stag, this runnable stag.

When he turn'd at bay in the leafy gloom,
In the emerald gloom where the brook ran deep
He heard in the distance the rollers boom,
And he saw in a vision of peaceful sleep,
A stag of warrant, a stag, a stag,
A runnable stag in a jewell'd bed,
Under the sheltering ocean dead,
A stag, a runnable stag.

So a fateful hope lit up his eye,
And he open'd his nostrils wide again.
And he toss'd his branching antlers high
As he headed the hunt down the Charlock glen
As he raced down the echoing glen—
For five miles more, the stag, the stag,
For twenty miles, and five and five,
Not to be caught now, dead or alive,
The stag, the runnable stag.

Three hundred gentlemen, able to ride,
   Three hundred horses as gallant and free,
Beheld him escape on the evening tide,
   Far out till he sank in the Severn Sea,
   Till he sank in the depths of the sea—
      The stag, the buoyant stag, the stag
      That slept at last in a jewell'd bed
      Under the sheltering ocean spread,
      The stag, the runnable stag.

DANNY DEEVER

Rudyard Kipling

In this dramatic poem Kipling presents one of his famous pictures of soldiers in India, which was then a part of the British Empire. The cockney dialect adds to the realistic portrayal of Danny Deever.

"What are the bugles blowin' for?" said Files-on-Parade.
"To turn you out, to turn you out," the Color Sergeant said.
"What makes you look so white, so white?" said Files-on-
    Parade.
"I'm dreadin' what I've got to watch," the Color Sergeant
    said.
   For they're hangin' Danny Deever, you can 'ear the dead
    march play,
   The regiment's in 'ollow square—they're hangin' him today;
   They've taken of his buttons off an' cut his stripes away,
   An' they're hangin' Danny Deever in the mornin'.

"What makes the rear-rank breathe so 'ard?" said Files-on-
    Parade.
"It's bitter cold, it's bitter cold," the Color Sergeant said.

"What makes that front-rank man fall down?" says Files-on-
   Parade.
"A touch o' sun, a touch o' sun," the Color Sergeant said.
   They are hangin' Danny Deever, they are marchin' of 'im
      round,
   They 'ave 'alted Danny Deever by 'is coffin on the ground;
   An' 'e'll swing in 'arf a minute for a sneakin', shootin'
      hound—
   O they're hangin' Danny Deever in the mornin'!

" 'Is cot was right-'and cot to mine," said Files-on-Parade.
" 'E's sleepin' out an' far tonight," the Color Sergeant said.
"I've drunk 'is beer a score o' times," said Files-on-Parade.
" 'E's drinkin' bitter beer alone," the Color Sergeant said.
   They are hangin' Danny Deever, you must mark 'im to 'is
      place,
   For 'e shot a comrade sleepin'—you must look 'im in the
      face;
   Nine 'undred of 'is county an' the regiment's disgrace,
   While they're hangin' Danny Deever in the mornin'.

"What's that so black agin the sun?" said Files-on-Parade.
"It's Danny fightin' 'ard fur life," the Color Sergeant said.
"What's that that whimpers over 'ead?" said Files-on-Parade.
"It's Danny's soul that's passin' now," the Color Sergeant
      said.
   For they're done with Danny Deever, you can 'ear the
      quickstep play,
   The regiment's in column, an' they're marchin' us away;
   Ho! the young recruits are shakin', an' they'll want their
      beer today,
   After hangin' Danny Deever in the mornin'.

O WHAT IS THAT SOUND?

W. H. Auden

O what is that sound which so thrills the ear
   Down in the valley drumming, drumming?
Only the scarlet soldiers, dear,
      The soldiers coming.

O what is that light I see flashing so clear
   Over the distance brightly, brightly?
Only the sun on their weapons, dear,
      As they step lightly.

O what are they doing with all that gear;
   What are they doing this morning, this morning?
Only their usual maneuvers, dear,
      Or perhaps a warning.

O why have they left the road down there;
   Why are they suddenly wheeling, wheeling?
Perhaps a change in the orders, dear;
      Why are you kneeling?

O haven't they stopped for the doctor's care;
   Haven't they reined their horses, their horses?
Why, they are none of them wounded, dear,
      None of these forces.

O is it the parson they want with white hair;
   Is it the parson, is it, is it?
No, they are passing his gateway, dear,
      Without a visit.

O it must be the farmer who lives so near;
    It must be the farmer so cunning, so cunning?
They have passed the farm already, dear,
            And now they are running.

O where are you going? Stay with me here!
    Were the vows you swore me deceiving, deceiving?
No, I promised to love you, dear,
            But I must be leaving.

O it's broken the lock and splintered the door,
    O it's the gate where they're turning, turning;
Their feet are heavy on the floor
            And their eyes are burning.

THE PIED PIPER OF HAMELIN

A Child's Story

Robert Browning

An old legend about cheating magicians may be the basis of this poem,
which Browning wrote to please Willie Macready—the Willy referred
to in the last stanza—who was the son of a famous actor. The poet's
skill in combining story, picture, and sound created a poem which
continues to delight readers.

Hamelin Town's in Brunswick,
    By famous Hanover city;
The river Weser, deep and wide,
Washes its wall on the southern side;
A pleasanter spot you never spied;

Brunswick: a section in Western Germany.

But, when begins my ditty,
Almost five hundred years ago,
To see the townsfolk suffer so
    From vermin, was a pity.

Rats!
They fought the dogs and killed the cats,
    And bit the babies in the cradles,
And ate the cheese out of the vats,
    And licked the soup from the cooks' own ladles,
Split open the kegs of salted sprats,
Made nests inside men's Sunday hats,
And even spoiled the women's chats
    By drowning their speaking
    With shrieking and squeaking
In fifty different sharps and flats.

At last the people in a body
    To the Town Hall came flocking:
" 'Tis clear," cried they, "our Mayor's a noddy;
    And as for our Corporation—shocking
To think we buy gowns lined with ermine
For dolts that can't or won't determine
What's best to rid us of our vermin!
You hope, because you're old and obese,
To find in the furry civic robe ease?
Rouse up, sirs! Give your brains a racking
To find the remedy we're lacking
Or, sure as fate, we'll send you packing!"
At this the Mayor and the Corporation
Quaked with a mighty consternation.

Corporation: governing body of the city.

An hour they sat in council,
   At length the Mayor broke silence:
"For a guilder I'd my ermine gown sell,
   I wish I were a mile hence!
It's easy to bid one rack one's brain—
I'm sure my poor head aches again,
I've scratched it so, and all in vain.
Oh for a trap, a trap, a trap!"
Just as he said this, what should hap
At the chamber door but a gentle tap?
"Bless us," cried the Mayor, "what's that?"
(With the Corporation as he sat,
Looking little though wondrous fat;
Nor brighter was his eye, nor moister
Than a too-long-opened oyster,
Save when at noon his paunch grew mutinous
For a plate of turtle green and glutinous)
"Only a scraping of shoes on the mat?
Anything like the sound of a rat
Makes my heart go pit-a-pat!"

"Come in!"—the Mayor cried, looking bigger:
And in did come the strangest figure!
His queer long coat from heel to head
Was half of yellow and half of red,
And he himself was tall and thin,
With sharp blue eyes, each like a pin,
And light loose hair, yet swarthy skin,
No tuft on cheek nor beard on chin,
But lips where smiles went out and in;
There was no guessing his kith and kin:
And nobody could enough admire
The tall man and his quaint attire.

Quoth one: "It's as my great-grandsire,
Starting up at the Trump of Doom's tone,
Had walked this way from his painted tombstone!"

He advanced to the council-table:
And, "Please your honors," said he, "I'm able,
By means of a secret charm, to draw
   All creatures living beneath the sun
   That creep or swim or fly or run,
After me so as you never saw!
And I chiefly use my charm
On creatures that do people harm,
The mole and toad and newt and viper;
And people call me the Pied Piper."
(And here they noticed round his neck
   A scarf of red and yellow stripe,
To match with his coat of the self-same cheque;
   And at the scarf's end hung a pipe;
And his fingers, they noticed, were ever straying
As if impatient to be playing
Upon this pipe, as low it dangled
Over his vesture so old-fangled.)
"Yet," said he, "poor piper as I am,
In Tartary I freed the Cham,
   Last June, from his huge swarm of gnats;
I eased in Asia the Nizam
   Of a monstrous brood of vampire-bats:
And as for what your brain bewilders,
   If I can rid your town of rats
Will you give me a thousand guilders?"
"One? fifty thousand!"—was the exclamation
Of the astonished Mayor and Corporation.

Trump of Doom's tone: Judgment Day trumpet.
Cham: an Asiatic ruler.   *Nizam:* a native ruler in India.

Into the street the Piper stept,
   Smiling first a little smile,
As if he knew what magic slept
   In his quiet pipe the while;
Then, like a musical adept,
To blow the pipe his lips he wrinkled
And green and blue his sharp eyes twinkled,
Like a candle-flame where salt is sprinkled;
And ere three shrill notes the pipe uttered,
You heard as if an army muttered;
And the muttering grew to a grumbling;
And the grumbling grew to a mighty rumbling;
And out of the houses the rats came tumbling.
Great rats, small rats, lean rats, brawny rats,
Brown rats, black rats, gray rats, tawny rats,
Grave old plodders, gay young friskers,
   Fathers, mothers, uncles, cousins,
Cocking tails and pricking whiskers,
   Families by tens and dozens,
Brothers, sisters, husbands, wives—
Followed the Piper for their lives.
From street to street he piped advancing,
And step for step they followed dancing,
Until they came to the river Weser,
   Wherein all plunged and perished!
—Save one who, stout as Julius Cæsar,
Swam across and lived to carry
   (As he, the manuscript he cherished)
To Rat-land home his commentary:
Which was, "At the first shrill notes of the pipe,
I heard a sound as of scraping tripe,
And putting apples, wondrous ripe,
Into a cider-press's gripe:

And a moving away of pickle-tub-boards,
And a leaving ajar of conserve-cupboards,
And a drawing the corks of train-oil-flasks,
And a breaking the hoops of butter-casks:
And it seemed as if a voice
　(Sweeter far than by harp or by psaltery
Is breathed) called out, "Oh rats, rejoice!
　The world is grown to one vast drysaltery!
So munch on, munch on, take your nuncheon,
Breakfast, supper, dinner, luncheon!'
And just as a bulky sugar-puncheon,
All ready staved, like a great sun shone
Glorious scarce an inch before me,
Just as methought it said, 'Come, bore me!'
—I found the Weser rolling o'er me."

You should have heard the Hamelin people
Ringing the bells till they rocked the steeple.
"Go," cried the Mayor, "and get long·poles,
Poke out the nests and block up the holes!
　Consult with carpenters and builders,
And leave in our town not even a trace
Of the rats!"—when suddenly, up the face
Of the Piper perked in the market-place,
　With a, "First, if you please, my thousand guilders!"

A thousand guilders! The Mayor looked blue;
So did the Corporation too.
For council dinners made rare havoc
With Claret, Moselle, Vin-de-Grace, Hock;
And half the money would replenish
Their cellar's biggest butt with Rhenish.
To pay this sum to a wandering fellow
With a gipsy coat of red and yellow!

"Beside," quoth the Mayor with a knowing wink,
"Our business was done at the river's brink;
We saw with our eyes the vermin sink,
And what's dead can't come to life, I think.
So, friend, we're not the folks to shrink
From the duty of giving you something for drink,
And a matter of money to put in your poke;
But as for the guilders, what we spoke
Of them, as you very well know, was in joke.
Beside, our losses have made us thrifty.
A thousand guilders! Come, take fifty!"

The Piper's face fell, and he cried,
"No trifling! I can't wait, beside!
I've promised to visit by dinner time
Bagdad, and accept the prime
Of the Head-Cook's pottage, all he's rich in,
For having left, in the Caliph's kitchen,
Of a nest of scorpions no survivor:
With him I proved no bargain-driver,
With you, don't think I'll bate a stiver!
And folks who put me in a passion
May find me pipe after another fashion."

"How?" cried the Mayor, "d'ye think I brook
Being worse treated than a Cook?
Insulted by a lazy ribald
With idle pipe and vesture piebald?
You threaten us, fellow? Do your worst,
Blow your pipe there till you burst!"

Once more he stept into the street
   And to his lips again

stiver: small Dutch coin.

Laid his long pipe of smooth straight cane;
And ere he blew three notes (such sweet
Soft notes as yet musician's cunning
    Never gave the enraptured air)
There was a rustling that seemed like a bustling
Of merry crowds justling at pitching and hustling;
Small feet were pattering, wooden shoes clattering,
Little hands clapping and little tongues chattering,
And, like fowls in a farm-yard when barley is scattering,
Out came the children running.
All the little boys and girls,
With rosy cheeks and flaxen curls,
And sparkling eyes and teeth like pearls,
Tripping and skipping, ran merrily after
The wonderful music with shouting and laughter.

The Mayor was dumb, and the Council stood
As if they were changed into blocks of wood,
Unable to move a step, or cry
To the children merrily skipping by,
—Could only follow with the eye
That joyous crowd at the Piper's back.
But how the Mayor was on the rack,
And the wretched Council's bosoms beat,
As the Piper turned from the High Street
To where the Weser rolled its waters
Right in the way of their sons and daughters!
However, he turned from South to West,
And to Koppelberg Hill his steps addressed,
And after him the children pressed;
Great was the joy in every breast.
"He never can cross that mighty top!
He's forced to let the piping drop,
And we shall see our children stop!"

When, lo, as they reached the mountain-side,
A wondrous portal opened wide,
As if a cavern was suddenly hollowed;
And the Piper advanced and the children followed,
And when all were in to the very last,
The door in the mountain-side shut fast.
Did I say all? No! One was lame,
   And could not dance the whole of the way;
And in after years, if you would blame
   His sadness, he was used to say,—
"It's dull in our town since my playmates left!
I can't forget that I'm bereft
Of all the pleasant sights they see,
Which the Piper also promised me.
For he led us, he said, to a joyous land,
Joining the town and just at hand,
Where waters gushed and fruit-trees grew
And flowers put forth a fairer hue,
And everything was strange and new;
The sparrows were brighter than peacocks here,
And their dogs outran our fallow deer,
And honey-bees had lost their stings,
And horses were born with eagles' wings:
And just as I became assured
My lame foot would be speedily cured,
The music stopped and I stood still,
And found myself outside the hill,
Left alone against my will,
To go now limping as before,
And never hear of that country more!"

Alas, alas for Hamelin!
   There came into many a burgher's pate

A text which says that heaven's gate
Opes to the rich at as easy rate
As the needle's eye takes a camel in!
The Mayor sent East, West, North, and South,
To offer the Piper, by word of mouth,
Wherever it was men's lot to find him,
Silver and gold to his heart's content,
If he'd only return the way he went,
And bring the children behind him.
But when they saw 'twas a lost endeavor,
And Piper and dancers were gone forever,
They made a decree that lawyers never
Should think their records dated duly
If, after the day of the month and year,
These words did not as well appear,
"And so long after what happened here
On the Twenty-second of July,
Thirteen hundred and seventy-six:"
And the better in memory to fix
The place of the children's last retreat,
They called it, the Pied Piper's Street—
Where any one playing on pipe or tabor
Was sure for the future to lose his labor.
Nor suffered they hostelry or tavern
To shock with mirth a street so solemn;
But opposite the place of the cavern
They wrote the story on a column,
And on the great church-window painted
The same, to make the world acquainted
How their children were stolen away,
And there it stands to this very day.
And I must not omit to say
That in Transylvania there's a tribe

Of alien people who ascribe
The outlandish ways and dress
On which their neighbors lay such stress,
To their fathers and mothers having risen
Out of some subterraneous prison
Into which they were trepanned
Long time ago in a mighty band
Out of Hamelin town in Brunswick land,
But how or why, they don't understand.

So, Willy, let me and you be wipers
Of scores out with all men—especially pipers!
And, whether they pipe us free from rats or from mice,
If we've promised them aught, let us keep our promise!

trepanned: trapped.

QUESTIONS FOR UNDERSTANDING AND APPRECIATION

A. I LOVED A LASS

1. What attitude does the man express about the lass he loved and about women generally? Is he concerned about his broken romance?

2. A narrative poem tells a story; a lyric poem expresses emotions. Both narrative and lyric qualities are often combined in a poem. What is the simple narrative in this poem, and what are its lyrical features?

3. What effect does the refrain serve? Point out examples of comparisons.

THE BLACKSMITH'S SERENADE

1. Do you think that John and Polly Ann are likely to live happily? What qualities has John which please Polly Ann?

2. Realistic writing presents life as it really is; romantic, presents a more glamorous, adventurous picture of life. In what ways is this poem both realistic and romantic?

3. Cite examples of alliteration and onomatopoeia. What other poetic device adds to the musical effect of the poem?

B. THE SANDS OF DEE

1. Summarize the poem in one sentence. Compare your summary with the poem to illustrate how poetic language and musical rhythm transform a simple incident into a beautiful poem.

2. Point out examples of effective repetition, of mystery, of personification (human qualities applied to an inanimate object).

93

SPANISH JOHNNY

1. What is your opinion of Spanish Johnny? How does his character seem contradictory?
2. Notice the repetition of sounds, words, and lines. How does this repetition help to create an image of Johnny for the reader?

ANNABEL LEE

1. Does the name, Annabel Lee, seem to be better suited for this poem than that of Poe's wife, Virginia? Why? What is the poetic term for a word that harmonizes in sound with its meaning?
2. Quote lines which express the following ideas: the characteristics of Annabel Lee; her death; the poet's reasoning about his loss; the triumph of the poet's love over death; his consolation.

C. CHARGE OF THE LIGHT BRIGADE

1. How and why did Tennyson "honor the Light Brigade"? Was this honor a lasting one? Explain.
2. Which of these phrases expresses most exactly the central thought of the poem: the price of an error in war; courage in the face of great odds; the horrors of war?
3. How does the poet create a feeling of excitement and urgency in the sound of the poem?
4. Scan a stanza and give the name of the kind of meter.

HOW THEY BROUGHT THE GOOD NEWS FROM GHENT TO AIX

1. Which word in the title is most descriptive of the content of the poem? Is the "good news" explained to the reader?
2. How many riders are there at the beginning and end of the ride? How long does it last?
3. Browning succeeds in making the reader hear the sound of the horses and feel the urgency of horse and rider. The regular, galloping rhythm and onomatopoeic words combine to pro-

duce the effect of the poem. Choose lines and words which are especially effective.

THE BALLAD OF EAST AND WEST

1. State and explain the underlying idea of the poem.
2. Why does the Colonel's son pursue Kamal? Describe their meeting. How are their characteristics similar? Why do they admire each other? How are their difficulties settled?
3. Why is the theme of the poem especially applicable today? Is the relationship between East and West different today from what it was in Kipling's time? Explain.
4. Find examples of internal rhyme in the poem. How does it affect your sense of rapid action?

SKIPPER IRESON'S RIDE

1. Do you think the poem would have been more effective if it had told the exact historical facts? Why?
2. Note the last three lines of each stanza which serve as a refrain. In which of the stanzas is dialect used?
3. Read aloud the descriptions of the women of Marblehead. Which words of Skipper Ireson's cause a change in the attitude of the women? What does the Skipper consider his greatest punishment?
4. Do you agree that this was "the strangest ride that ever was sped"? Do you sympathize with Skipper Ireson?

PAUL REVERE'S RIDE

1. What was the purpose of this ride? How does the poem illustrate the effectiveness of literature to keep alive historical events? Name another literary work which has had a similar effect. What is known about Paul Revere besides his famous ride? (Refer to library references to supplement your information.)
2. Explain the last six lines of the poem.

3. Mention other incidents in American history to which the following lines could refer:

The fate of a nation was riding that night.

A cry of defiance and not of fear

In the hour of darkness and peril and fear

A RUNNABLE STAG

1. Why does this poem arouse your sympathies? What do you find yourself hoping for as the poem develops? Explain the ending of the poem.
2. Why are stories about chases so fascinating? Recall other thrilling chases you have read about, or seen at the movies or on television.
3. How does the rhythm of this poem contribute to the excitement?
4. Pick out all the words and phrases that appeal to you for their sounds or for the mental pictures they call forth. What is the effect of the refrains?
5. Find examples of alliteration, onomatopoeia. What is the rhyme scheme? Scan some of the lines.

D. DANNY DEEVER

1. How is the reader acquainted with the details about Danny Deever? What was his crime and his punishment? How do his comrades feel about him? Do you sympathize with him?
2. What contradictory statements are made by the Color-Sergeant? Is there any explanation for his remarks? Do the last three lines indicate heartlessness in the young recruits? Explain.
3. After reading the poem in class, scan a stanza of it to find the predominant meter. Is it regular or irregular? What relation has the sound of the poem to the story?

O WHAT IS THAT SOUND?

1. By what device does the poet get the reader into the mood of the poem? What effect has the repetition?
2. Write your own interpretation of the poem and compare yours with other students' explanations.
3. The quality of *universality* may be applied to many works of literature; that is, ideas expressed can apply to people widely separated in circumstances, time, and place. How can you apply this poem to historical events of recent and past times?

E. THE PIED PIPER OF HAMELIN

1. This amusing poem with its ingenious rhyme and pleasing rhythm continues to delight each new generation. Do you think the story or the sound contributes more to the enjoyment? Or both story and sound together?
2. Read aloud stanzas seven and twelve to observe the contrast in sound; note how the sound harmonizes with the sense of the stanzas. Select onomatopoeic words in each stanza.
3. What is the moral of the poem? Do you think the last four lines add to the effect of the poem? Why?

VOCABULARY: mutinous, glutinous, newt, viper, psaltery, commentary, puncheon, swarthy, obese, tawny, pate, burgher.

COMPARATIVE STUDY

1. The poems in this section have been grouped to illustrate variations in sound and the relation of the sound of a poem to its story and meaning. Select an adjective to describe the kind of rhythm in each of the groups—A, B, C, D. (See table of contents.) Does each adjective relate also to the type of stories told in the poems? In which group of poems does the story harmonize most effectively with the meaning of the poem?
2. To illustrate variations in rhythmic patterns, select four class committees to prepare choral readings of poems from each of the four groups.
3. Which of the love poems in Group A did you like best?
4. Is there similarity in the plots of "The Sands of Dee," "Spanish Johnny," and "Annabel Lee"?
5. The six poems in Group C are based on rides. Which has the most stirring rhythm? the most interesting story? Which poem celebrates a group endeavor rather than an individual's? Which poem has no historical basis? Which is historically inaccurate? Which rider is best known in history? Which of the five poems is most effective in making the reader participate in the ride?
6. What poetic device is used by the authors of "Danny Deever" and "O What Is That Sound?" to convey a feeling of urgency? Which plot is merely suggested?
7. Select lines from "The Pied Piper of Hamelin" which illustrate variations in rhythmic sounds.
8. Quote an example from any of the poems to illustrate the following: alliteration; refrain; onomatopoeia; regular rhythm in a line of poetry.

Imagery

■ IMAGERY

■ In this section, a third element of poetry, *imagery*, is given major emphasis. The poet often expresses his ideas and impressions through an *image*; that is, he presents a picture to the mind through details which appeal to one or more of the five senses: sight, hearing, touch, taste, and smell. Two of the poems you have read—"The Highwayman" and "The Skater of Ghost Lake"—illustrate the use of imagery combined with effective sound and exciting plots. You will agree that the two poems appeal to the ear, the imagination, and the interest of the reader.

Note the use of imagery in these two poems:

The landlord's blackeyed daughter . . .
Plaiting a dark red love-knot into her long black hair—Sight

A stable wicket creaked—Sound

Black is the clear glass now that he glides,—Sight
Crisp is the whisper of long lean strides,—Sound and Sight

The black cascade of perfume came tumbling over his breast—Smell

FIGURES OF SPEECH

Very often the poet expresses his imagery in *figures of speech*, also referred to as *figurative language*, which is an unusual way of expressing meaning in order to add force or vividness. Figurative language is commonly used in everyday speech. Expressions such as these may not be poetic, but they do add force to the idea: tired as a dog, mad as a wet hen, a fish story, skeleton in the closet, hard as nails, cool as a cucumber. Note that in each of these expressions there is a comparison expressed or implied.

The three figures of speech most frequently used in poetry are *simile*, *metaphor*, and *personification*. Each is a kind of comparison.

His hair like moldy hay—Simile
Ice black as ebony—Simile

The moon was a ghostly galleon—Metaphor
Breath is a frost-fume—Metaphor

I swung my racket at the astonished oaks.—Personification
The heavens scowled.—Personification

Metaphor and simile are alike with one exception: a simile expresses the comparison with *like* or *as*; a metaphor is an implied comparison. Personification refers to a human being; it attributes human qualities to an inanimate object or idea. In the examples above, the *heavens* and the *oaks* are given qualities of human beings (*astonished* and *scowled*).

Your identification of figurative language and your appreciation of imagery will develop with experience in reading and hearing poetry. Poetry not only sounds different from ordinary speech; it has vivid, imaginative language which adds force and beauty to the meaning.

(See the Introduction, page xxxi, for a more detailed explanation of imagery and figurative language.)

ANGUS McGREGOR

Lew Sarett

Angus McGregor lies brittle as ice,
With snow tucked up to his jaws,
Somewhere tonight where the hemlocks moan
And crack in the wind like straws.

Angus went cruising the woods last month,
With a blanket-roll on his back,
With never an ax, a dirk, a gun,
Or a compass in his pack.

"The hills at thirty below have
      teeth;
McGregor," I said, "you're daft
To tackle the woods like a simple child."
But he looked at me and laughed.

He flashed his teeth in a grin and said:
"The earth is an open book;
I've followed the woods for forty years,
I know each cranny and crook.

"I've battled her weather, her winds, her brutes,
I've stood with them toe to toe;
I can beat them back with my naked fist
And answer them blow for blow."

Angus McGregor sleeps under the stars,
With an icicle gripped in his hand,
Somewhere tonight where the grim-lipped peaks
Brood on a haggard land.

Oh, the face of the moon is dark tonight,
And dark the gaunt wind's sigh;
And the hollow laughter troubles me
In the wild wolves' cry.

PATTERNS

Amy Lowell

I walk down the garden paths,
And all the daffodils
Are blowing, and the bright blue squills.
I walk down the patterned garden-paths
In my stiff, brocaded gown.
With my powdered hair and jeweled fan,
I too am a rare
Pattern, as I wander down
The garden paths.

My dress is richly figured,
And the train
Makes a pink and silver stain
On the gravel, and the thrift
Of the borders.
Just a plate of current fashion,
Tripping by in high-heeled, ribboned shoes.
Not a softness anywhere about me,
Only whalebone and brocade.
And I sink on a seat in the shade
Of a lime-tree. For my passion
Wars against the stiff brocade.
The daffodils and squills

Flutter in the breeze
As they please.
And I weep;
For the lime-tree is in blossom
And one small flower has dropped upon my bosom.

And the plashing of waterdrops
In the marble fountain
Comes down the garden-paths.
The dripping never stops.
Underneath my stiffened gown
Is the softness of a woman bathing in a marble basin,
A basin in the midst of hedges grown
So thick, she cannot see her lover hiding,
But she guesses he is near,
And the sliding of the water
Seems the stroking of a dear
Hand upon her.
What is Summer in a fine brocaded gown!
I should like to see it lying in a heap upon the ground.
All the pink and silver crumpled up on the ground.

I would be the pink and silver as I ran along the paths,
And he would stumble after,
Bewildered by my laughter.
I should see the sun flashing from his sword-hilt and the
    buckles on his shoes.
I would choose
To lead him in a maze along the patterned paths,
A bright and laughing maze for my heavy-booted lover.
Till he caught me in the shade,
And the buttons of his waistcoat bruised my body as he
    clasped me,

Aching, melting, unafraid,
With the shadows of the leaves and the sundrops,
And the plopping of the waterdrops,
All about us in the open afternoon—
I am very like to swoon
With the weight of this brocade,
For the sun sifts through the shade.

Underneath the fallen blossom
In my bosom,
Is a letter I have hid.
It was brought to me this morning by a rider from the
    Duke.
"Madam, we regret to inform you that Lord Hartwell
Died in action Thursday se'nnight."
As I read it in the white, morning sunlight,
The letters squirmed like snakes.
"Any answer, Madam?" said my footman.
"No," I told him.
"No, no answer.
See that the messenger takes some refreshment."
And I walked into the garden,
Up and down the patterned paths,
In my stiff, correct brocade.
The blue and yellow flowers stood up proudly in the sun,
Each one.
I stood upright too,
Held rigid to the pattern
By the stiffness of my gown.
Up and down I walked,
Up and down.

In a month he would have been my husband.
In a month, here, underneath this lime,
We would have broke the pattern;
He for me, and I for him,
He as Colonel, I as Lady,
On this shady seat.
He had a whim
That sunlight carried blessing.
And I answered, "It shall be as you have said."
Now he is dead.

In Summer and in Winter I shall walk
Up and down
The patterned garden paths
In my stiff, brocaded gown.
The squills and daffodils
Will give place to pillared roses, and to asters, and to snow.
I shall go
Up and down,
In my gown.
Gorgeously arrayed,
Boned and stayed.
And the softness of my body will be guarded from embrace
By each button, hook, and lace.
For the man who should loose me is dead,
Fighting with the Duke in Flanders,
In a pattern called a war.
Christ! What are patterns for?

THE DESTRUCTION OF SENNACHERIB

George Gordon, Lord Byron

In the seventh century B.C., Jerusalem was besieged by the Assyrian army led by King Sennacherib. Though the Jewish army was greatly outnumbered by the Assyrians, Jerusalem was saved. The full account of the siege is told in II Kings, 19 : 35–37. Read aloud Byron's beautiful, poetic account of this event.

The Assyrian came down like the wolf on the fold,
And his cohorts were gleaming in purple and gold;
And the sheen of their spears was like stars on the sea,
When the blue wave rolls nightly on deep Galilee.

Like the leaves of the forest when Summer is green,
That host with their banners at sunset were seen:
Like the leaves of the forest when Autumn hath blown,
That host on the morrow lay withered and strown.

For the Angel of Death spread his wings on the blast,
And breathed in the face of the foe as he passed;
And the eyes of the sleepers waxed deadly and chill,
And their hearts but once heaved, and for ever grew still!

And there lay the steed with his nostril all wide,
But through it there rolled not the breath of his pride;
And the foam of his gasping lay white on the turf,
And cold as the spray of the rock-beating surf.

And there lay the rider distorted and pale,
With the dew on his brow and the rust on his mail:
And the tents were all silent, the banners alone,
The lances unlifted, the trumpet unblown.

And the widows of Ashur are loud in their wail,
And the idols are broke in the temple of Baal;
And the might of the Gentile, unsmote by the sword,
Hath melted like snow in the glance of the Lord!

THE LADY OF SHALOTT

Alfred, Lord Tennyson

This melodious poem is based on the legends of King Arthur's Court, about which Tennyson wrote twelve tales in a series, *The Idylls of the King*. One of these poems, "Lancelot and Elaine," is a longer, more elaborate account of this legend about the Lady and Sir Lancelot.

PART I

On either side the river lie
Long fields of barley and of rye,
That clothe the wold and meet the sky;
And thro' the field the road runs by
   To many-tower'd Camelot;
And up and down the people go,
Gazing where the lilies blow
Round an island there below,
   The island of Shalott.

Willows whiten, aspens quiver,
Little breezes dusk and shiver
Thro' the wave that runs for ever
By the island in the river
   Flowing down to Camelot.

Ashur: Assyria.   *Baal*: a god of the Assyrians.
wold: meadowland.   *Camelot*: place of King Arthur's Court.

Four gray walls, and four gray towers,
Overlook a space of flowers,
And the silent isle imbowers
    The Lady of Shalott.

By the margin, willow-veil'd
Slide the heavy barges trail'd
By slow horses; and unhail'd
The shallop flitteth silken-sail'd
    Skimming down to Camelot:
But who hath seen her wave her hand?
Or at the casement seen her stand?
Or is she known in all the land,
    The Lady of Shalott?

Only reapers, reaping early
In among the bearded barley,
Hear a song that echoes cheerly
From the river winding clearly,
    Down to tower'd Camelot:
And by the moon the reaper weary,
Piling sheaves in uplands airy,
Listening, whispers " 'Tis the fairy
    Lady of Shalott."

PART II

There she weaves by night and day
A magic web with colors gay.
She has heard a whisper say,
A curse is on her if she stay
    To look down to Camelot.

shallop: a small open boat.

She knows not what the curse may be,
And so she weaveth steadily,
And little other care hath she,
   The Lady of Shalott.

And moving thro' a mirror clear
That hangs before her all the year,
Shadows of the world appear.
There she sees the highway near
   Winding down to Camelot:
There the river eddy whirls,
And there the surly village-churls,
And the red cloaks of market girls,
   Pass onward from Shalott.

Sometimes a troop of damsels glad,
An abbot on an ambling pad,
Sometimes a curly shepherd-lad,
Or long-hair'd page in crimson clad,
   Goes by to tower'd Camelot:
And sometimes thro' the mirror blue
The knights come riding two and two:
She hath no loyal knight and true,
   The Lady of Shalott.

But in her web she still delights
To weave the mirror's magic sights,
For often thro' the silent nights
A funeral, with plumes and lights
   And music, went to Camelot:
Or when the moon was overhead,
Came two young lovers lately wed;
"I am half sick of shadows," said
   The Lady of Shalott.

PART III

A bow-shot from her bower-eaves,
He rode between the barley-sheaves,
The sun came dazzling thro' the leaves,
And flamed upon the brazen greaves
    Of bold Sir Lancelot.
A red-cross knight for ever kneel'd
To a lady in his shield,
That sparkled on the yellow field,
    Beside remote Shalott.

The gemmy bridle glitter'd free,
Like to some branch of stars we see
Hung in the golden Galaxy.
The bridle bells rang merrily
    As he rode down to Camelot:
And from his blazon'd baldric slung
A mighty silver bugle hung,
And as he rode his armor rung,
    Beside remote Shalott.

All in the blue unclouded weather
Thick-jewel'd shone the saddle-leather,
The helmet and the helmet-feather
Burn'd like one burning flame together,
    As he rode down to Camelot.
As often thro' the purple night,
Below the starry clusters bright,
Some bearded meteor, trailing light,
    Moves over still Shalott.

greaves: leg armor.
Golden Galaxy: the Milky Way, of which our earth is a part.
baldric: a sword belt worn over one shoulder and across the chest.

His broad clear brow in sunlight glow'd;
On burnish'd hooves his war-horse trode;
From underneath his helmet flow'd
His coal-black curls as on he rode,
   As he rode down to Camelot.
From the bank and from the river
He flash'd into the crystal mirror,
"Tirra lirra," by the river
   Sang Sir Lancelot.

She left the web, she left the loom,
She made three paces thro' the room,
She saw the water-lily bloom,
She saw the helmet and the plume,
   She look'd down to Camelot.
Out flew the web and floated wide;
The mirror crack'd from side to side;
"The curse is come upon me," cried
   The Lady of Shalott.

PART IV

In the stormy east-wind straining,
The pale yellow woods were waning,
The broad stream in his banks complaining,
Heavily the low sky raining
   Over tower'd Camelot;
Down she came and found a boat
Beneath a willow left afloat,
And round about the prow she wrote
   The Lady of Shalott.

And down the river's dim expanse
Like some bold seër in a trance,
Seeing all his own mischance—
With a glassy countenance
   Did she look to Camelot.
And at the closing of the day
She loosed the chain, and down she lay;
The broad stream bore her far away,
   The Lady of Shalott.

Lying, robed in snowy white
That loosely flew to left and right—
The leaves upon her falling light—
Thro' the noises of the night
   She floated down to Camelot.
And as the boat-head wound along
The willowy hills and fields among,
They heard her singing her last song,
   The Lady of Shalott.

Heard a carol, mournful, holy,
Chanted loudly, chanted lowly,
Till her blood was frozen slowly,
And her eyes were darken'd wholly,
   Turn'd to tower'd Camelot.
For ere she reach'd upon the tide
The first house by the water-side,
Singing in her song she died,
   The Lady of Shalott.

Under tower and balcony,
By garden-wall and gallery,
A gleaming shape she floated by,
Dead-pale between the houses high,

Silent into Camelot.
Out upon the wharfs they came,
Knight and burgher, lord and dame,
And round the prow they read her name,
  The Lady of Shalott.

Who is this? and what is here?
And in the lighted palace near
Died the sound of royal cheer;
And they cross'd themselves for fear,
  All the knights at Camelot:
But Lancelot mused a little space;
He said, "She has a lovely face;
God in his mercy lend her grace,
  The Lady of Shalott."

THE EVE OF ST. AGNES

John Keats

"The Eve of St. Agnes" is an outstanding example of Keats' ability to combine a narrative with rich, vivid imagery and effective rhythm. The poem is written in Spenserian stanza—nine iambic lines with a definite rhyme scheme—a form devised by the poet Spenser. The story is based on the old legend that girls who perform certain rituals on St. Agnes' Eve, January 20, will be permitted a vision of their future husbands. St. Agnes, the patron of young girls, was martyred in the fourth century.

St. Agnes' Eve—Ah, bitter chill it was!
The owl, for all his feathers, was a-cold;
The hare limp'd trembling through the frozen grass,
And silent was the flock in woolly fold:
Numb were the Beadsman's fingers, while he told
His rosary, and while his frosted breath,
Like pious incense from a censer old,
Seem'd taking flight for heaven, without a death,
Past the sweet Virgin's picture, while his prayer he saith.

His prayer he saith, this patient, holy man;
Then takes his lamp, and riseth from his knees
And back returneth, meagre, barefoot, wan,
Along the chapel aisle by slow degrees:
The sculptured dead, on each side, seem to freeze,
Emprison'd in black, purgatorial rails:
Knights, ladies, praying in dumb orat'ries,
He passeth by; and his weak spirit fails
To think how they may ache in icy hoods and mails.

Northward he turneth through a little door,
And scarce three steps, ere Music's golden tongue

Beadsman: person who offers prayers for the dead.
orat'ries: small chapels for private prayer.   *mails:* coats of armor.

Flatter'd to tears this aged man and poor;
But no—already had his death-bell rung;
The joys of all his life were said and sung:
His was harsh penance on St. Agnes' Eve:
Another way he went, and soon among
Rough ashes sat he for his soul's reprieve,
And all night kept awake, for sinners' sake to grieve.

That ancient Beadsman heard the prelude soft;
And so it chanced, for many a door was wide,
From hurry to and fro. Soon, up aloft,
The silver, snarling trumpets 'gan to chide:
The level chambers, ready with their pride,
Were glowing to receive a thousand guests:
The carvèd angels, ever eager-eyed,
Stared, where upon their heads the cornice rests,
With hair blown back, and wings put crosswise on their
    breasts.

At length burst in the argent revelry,
With plume, tiara, and all rich array,
Numerous as shadows haunting fairily
The brain, new-stuff'd, in youth, with triumphs gay
Of old romance. These let us wish away,
And turn, sole-thoughted, to one Lady there,
Whose heart had brooded, all that wintry day,
On love, and wing'd St. Agnes' saintly care,
As she had heard old dames full many times declare.

They told her how, upon St. Agnes' Eve,
Young virgins might have visions of delight,
And soft adorings from their loves receive

argent revelry: gay groups of merrymakers.

Upon the honey'd middle of the night,
If ceremonies due they did aright;
As, supperless to bed they must retire,
And couch supine their beauties, lily white;
Nor look behind, nor sideways, but require
Of Heaven with upward eyes for all that they desire.

Full of this whim was thoughtful Madeline:
The music, yearning like a God in pain,
She scarcely heard: her maiden eyes divine,
Fix'd on the floor, saw many a sweeping train
Pass by—she heeded not at all: in vain
Came many a tiptoe, amorous cavalier,
And back retired; not cool'd by high disdain,
But she saw not: her heart was otherwhere;
She sigh'd for Agnes' dreams, the sweetest of the year.

She danced along with vague, regardless eyes,
Anxious her lips, her breathing quick and short:
The hallow'd hour was near at hand: she sighs
Amid the timbrels, and the throng'd resort
Of whisperers in anger, or in sport;
Mid looks of love, defiance, hate, and scorn,
Hoodwink'd with faery fancy; all amort,
Save to St. Agnes and her lambs unshorn,
And all the bliss to be before to-morrow morn.

So, purposing each moment to retire,
She linger'd still. Meantime, across the moors,
Had come young Porphyro, with heart on fire
For Madeline. Beside the portal doors,
Buttress'd from moonlight, stands he, and implores
All saints to give him sight of Madeline,

amort: as if dead.

But for one moment in the tedious hours,
That he might gaze and worship all unseen;
Perchance speak, kneel, touch, kiss—in sooth such things
    have been.

He ventures in: let no buzz'd whisper tell:
All eyes be muffled, or a hundred swords
Will storm his heart, Love's fev'rous citadel:
For him, those chambers held barbarian hordes,
Hyena foemen, and hot-blooded lords,
Whose very dogs would execrations howl
Against his lineage: not one breast affords
Him any mercy, in that mansion foul,
Save one old beldame, weak in body and in soul.

Ah, happy chance! the aged creature came,
Shuffling along with ivory-headed wand,
To where he stood, hid from the torch's flame,
Behind a broad hall-pillar, far beyond
The sound of merriment and chorus bland:
He startled her; but soon she knew his face,
And grasp'd his fingers in her palsied hand,
Saying, "Mercy, Porphyro! hie thee from this place;
They are all here to-night, the whole bloodthirsty race!

"Get hence! get hence! there's dwarfish Hildebrand;
He had a fever late, and in the fit
He cursèd thee and thine, both house and land:
Then there's that old Lord Maurice, not a whit
More tame for his gray hairs—Alas me! flit!
Flit like a ghost away."—"Ah, Gossip dear,
We're safe enough; here in this armchair sit,
And tell me how"—"Good Saints! not here, not here;
Follow me, child, or else these stones will be thy bier."

He follow'd through a lowly archèd way,
Brushing the cobwebs with his lofty plume;
And as she mutter'd "Well-a—well-a-day!"
He found him in a little moonlight room,
Pale, latticed, chill, and silent as a tomb.
"Now tell me where is Madeline," said he,
"O tell me, Angela, by the holy loom
Which none but secret sisterhood may see,
When they St. Agnes' wool are weaving piously."

"St. Agnes! Ah! it is St. Agnes' Eve—
Yet men will murder upon holy days:
Thou must hold water in a witch's sieve,
And be liege-lord of all the Elves and Fays,
To venture so: it fills me with amaze
To see thee, Porphyro!—St. Agnes' Eve!
God's help! my lady fair the conjuror plays
This very night: good angels her deceive!
But let me laugh awhile, I've mickle time to grieve."

Feebly she laugheth in the languid moon,
While Porphyro upon her face doth look,
Like puzzled urchin on an agèd crone
Who keepeth closed a wond'rous riddlebook,
As spectacled she sits in chimney nook.
But soon his eyes grew brilliant, when she told
His lady's purpose; and he scarce could brook
Tears, at the thought of those enchantments cold,
And Madeline asleep in lap of legends old.

When they St. Agnes' wool are weaving piously: In honor of St. Agnes,
   the symbol of innocence, two lambs were slain on the eve of her feast.
   The wool was woven into clothes for the poor.
mickle: much.

Sudden a thought came like a full-blown rose,
Flushing his brow, and in his pained heart
Made purple riot: then doth he propose
A stratagem, that makes the beldame start:
"A cruel man and impious thou art:
Sweet lady, let her pray, and sleep, and dream
Along with her good angels, far apart
From wicked men like thee. Go, go! I deem
Thou canst not surely be the same that thou didst seem."

"I will not harm her, by all saints I swear,"
Quoth Porphyro: "O may I ne'er find grace
When my weak voice shall whisper its last prayer,
If one of her soft ringlets I displace,
Or look with ruffian passion in her face:
Good Angela, believe me by these tears;
Or I will, even in a moment's space,
Awake, with horrid shout, my foemen's ears,
And beard them, though they be more fanged than wolves
    and bears."

"Ah! why wilt thou affright a feeble soul?
A poor, weak, palsy-stricken, churchyard thing,
Whose passing-bell may ere the midnight toll;
Whose prayers for thee, each morn and evening,
Were never missed." Thus plaining, doth she bring
A gentler speech from burning Porphyro;
So woeful, and of such deep sorrowing,
That Angela gives promise she will do
Whatever he shall wish, betide her weal or woe.

Which was, to lead him, in close secrecy,
Even to Madeline's chamber, and there hide

Him in a closet, of such privacy
That he might see her beauty unespied,
And win perhaps that night a peerless bride,
While legioned fairies paced the coverlet,
And pale enchantment held her sleepy-eyed.
Never on such a night have lovers met,
Since Merlin paid his Demon all the monstrous debt.

"It shall be as thou wishest," said the Dame:
"All cates and dainties shall be stored there
Quickly on this feast-night: by the tambour frame
Her own lute thou wilt see: no time to spare,
For I am slow and feeble, and scarce dare
On such a catering trust my dizzy head.
Wait here, my child, with patience; kneel in prayer
The while. Ah! thou must needs the lady wed,
Or may I never leave my grave among the dead."

So saying she hobbled off with busy fear.
The lover's endless minutes slowly pass'd;
The Dame return'd, and whisper'd in his ear
To follow her; with agèd eyes aghast
From fright of dim espial. Safe at last,
Through many a dusky gallery, they gain
The maiden's chamber, silken, hush'd and chaste;
Where Porphyro took covert, pleased amain.
His poor guide hurried back with agues in her brain.

Her falt'ring hand upon the balustrade,
Old Angela was feeling for the stair,
When Madeline, St. Agnes' charmèd maid,

Merlin: King Arthur's magician, whose spells finally brought about his
    own death.   *cates:* food delicacies.
tambour frame: embroidery hoops, in a drumlike shape.
amain: greatly

Rose, like a mission'd spirit, unaware:
With silver taper's light, and pious care,
She turn'd, and down the agèd gossip led
To a safe level matting. Now prepare,
Young Porphyro, for gazing on that bed;
She comes, she comes again, like ring-dove fray'd and fled.

Out went the taper as she hurried in;
Its little smoke, in pallid moonshine, died:
She closed the door, she panted, all akin
To spirits of the air, and visions wide:
No uttered syllable, or, woe betide!
But to her heart, her heart was voluble,
Paining with eloquence her balmy side;
As though a tongueless nightingale should swell
Her throat in vain, and die, heart-stifled in her dell.

A casement high and triple arch'd there was,
All garlanded with carven imag'ries
Of fruits, and flowers, and bunches of knotgrass,
And diamonded with panes of quaint device,
Innumerable of stains and splendid dyes,
As are the tiger-moth's deep-damask'd wings;
And in the midst, 'mong thousand heraldries,
And twilight saints, and dim emblazonings,
A shielded scutcheon blush'd with blood of queens and
    kings.

Full on this casement shone the wintry moon,
And threw warm gules on Madeline's fair breast,
As down she knelt for heaven's grace and boon;

fray'd: frightened, alarmed.
heraldries: coats of arms.
gules: parallel red lines used in designs of coats of arms.

Rose-bloom fell on her hands, together prest,
And on her silver cross soft amethyst,
And on her hair a glory, like a saint:
She seem'd a splendid angel, newly drest,
Save wings, for heaven:—Porphyro grew faint;
She knelt, so pure a thing, so free from mortal taint.

Anon his heart revives: her vespers done,
Of all its wreathèd pearls her hair she frees;
Unclasps her warmèd jewels one by one;
Loosens her fragrant bodice; by degrees
Her rich attire creeps rustling to her knees:
Half-hidden, like a mermaid in sea-weed,
Pensive awhile she dreams awake, and sees,
In fancy, fair St. Agnes in her bed,
But dares not look behind, or all the charm is fled.

Soon, trembling in her soft and chilly nest,
In sort of wakeful swoon, perplex'd she lay,
Until the poppied warmth of sleep oppress'd
Her soothèd limbs, and soul fatigued away;
Flown, like a thought, until the morrow-day;
Blissfully haven'd both from joy and pain;
Clasp'd like a missal where swart Paynims pray;
Blinded alike from sunshine and from rain,
As though a rose should shut, and be a bud again.

Stol'n to this paradise, and so entranced,
Porphyro gazed upon her empty dress,
And listen'd to her breathing, if it chanced
To wake into a slumberous tenderness;
Which when he heard, that minute did he bless,

missal: prayerbook.
Paynims: pagans.

And breathed himself: then from the closet crept,
Noiseless as fear in a wide wilderness,
And over the hush'd carpet, silent, stept,
And 'tween the curtains peep'd, where, lo!—how fast she
  slept.

Then by the bed-side, where the faded moon
Made a dim, silver twilight, soft he set
A table, and, half anguish'd, threw thereon
A cloth of woven crimson, gold, and jet:—
O for some drowsy Morphean amulet!
The boisterous, midnight, festive clarion,
The kettle-drum, and far-heard clarionet,
Affray his ears, though but in dying tone:—
The hall-door shuts again, and all the noise is gone.

And still she slept an azure-lidded sleep,
In blanchèd linen, smooth, and lavender'd,
While he from forth the closet brought a heap
Of candied apple, quince, and plum, and gourd;
With jellies soother than the creamy curd,
And lucent syrops, tinct with cinnamon;
Manna and dates, in argosy transferr'd
From Fez; and spiced dainties, every one,
From silken Samarcand to cedar'd Lebanon.

These delicates he heap'd with glowing hand
On golden dishes and in baskets bright
Of wreathèd silver: sumptuous they stand
In the retirèd quiet of the night,
Filling the chilly room with perfume light.—

amulet: a charm against evil luck; in this case, from Morpheus, god
  of sleep.   *argosy:* a large ancient sailing ship.

"And now, my love, my seraph fair, awake!
Thou art my heaven, and I thine eremite:
Open thine eyes, for meek St. Agnes' sake,
Or I shall drowse beside thee, so my soul doth ache."

Thus whispering, his warm, unnervèd arm
Sank in her pillow. Shaded was her dream
By the dusk curtains:—'twas a midnight charm
Impossible to melt as icèd stream:
The lustrous salvers in the moonlight gleam;
Broad golden fringe upon the carpet lies:
It seem'd he never, never could redeem
From such a steadfast spell his lady's eyes;
So mused awhile, entoil'd in woofèd phantasies.

Awakening up, he took her hollow lute,—
Tumultuous,—and, in chords that tenderest be,
He play'd an ancient ditty, long since mute,
In Provence call'd "La belle dame sans merci:"
Close to her ear touching the melody;—
Wherewith disturb'd, she utter'd a soft moan:
He ceased—she panted quick—and suddenly
Her blue affrayèd eyes wide open shone:
Upon his knees he sank, pale as smooth-sculptured stone.

Her eyes were open, but she still beheld,
Now wide awake, the vision of her sleep:
There was a painful change, that nigh expell'd
The blisses of her dream so pure and deep:
At which fair Madeline began to weep,
And moan forth witless words with many a sigh;

eremite: a hermit.
woofèd phantasies: fantasies interwoven like threads in weaving.
"La belle dame sans merci": "The beautiful lady without mercy." See
    page 157 for Keats' poem with this title.

While still her gaze on Porphyro would keep;
Who knelt, with joinèd hands and piteous eye,
Fearing to move or speak, she look'd so dreamingly.

"Ah, Porphyro!" said she, "but even now
Thy voice was at sweet tremble in mine ear,
Made tuneable with every sweetest vow;
And those sad eyes were spiritual and clear:
How changed thou art! how pallid, chill, and drear!
Give me that voice again, my Porphyro,
Those looks immortal, those complainings dear!
Oh leave me not in this eternal woe,
For if thou diest, my Love, I know not where to go."

Beyond a mortal man impassion'd far
At these voluptuous accents, he arose,
Ethereal, flush'd, and like a throbbing star
Seen 'mid the sapphire heaven's deep repose;
Into her dream he melted, as the rose
Blendeth its odour with the violet,—
Solution sweet: meantime the frost-wind blows
Like Love's alarum pattering the sharp sleet
Against the window-panes; St. Agnes' moon hath set.

'Tis dark: quick pattereth the flaw-blown sleet:
"This is no dream, my bride, my Madeline!"
'Tis dark: the icèd gusts still rave and beat:
"No dream, alas! alas! and woe is mine!
Porphyro will leave me here to fade and pine.—
Cruel! what traitor could thee hither bring?
I curse not, for my heart is lost in thine,
Though thou forsakest a deceivèd thing;—
A dove forlorn and lost with sick unprunèd wing."

"My Madeline! sweet dreamer! lovely bride!
Say, may I be for aye thy vassal blest?
Thy beauty's shield, heart-shaped and vermeil dyed?
Ah, silver shrine, here will I take my rest
After so many hours of toil and quest,
A famish'd pilgrim,—saved by miracle.
Though I have found, I will not rob thy nest
Saving of thy sweet self; if thou think'st well
To trust, fair Madeline, to no rude infidel.

"Hark! 'tis an elfin storm from faery land,
Of haggard seeming, but a boon indeed:
Arise—arise! the morning is at hand:—
The bloated wassailers will never heed:—
Let us away, my love, with happy speed;
There are no ears to hear, or eyes to see,—
Drown'd all in Rhenish and the sleepy mead:
Awake! arise! my love, and fearless be,
For o'er the southern moors I have a home for thee."

She hurried at his words, beset with fears,
For there were sleeping dragons all around,
At glaring watch, perhaps, with ready spears—
Down the wide stairs a darkling way they found.—
In all the house was heard no human sound.
A chain-droop'd lamp was flickering by each door;
The arras, rich with horseman, hawk, and hound,
Flutter'd in the besieging wind's uproar;
And the long carpets rose along the gusty floor.

vermeil: bright red.
of haggard seeming: wild-looking.
Drown'd all in Rhenish and the sleepy mead: drowned in red wine and
    a drink made of honey.
arras: tapestry.

They glide, like phantoms, into the wide hall;
Like phantoms to the iron porch they glide,
Where lay the Porter, in uneasy sprawl,
With a huge empty flagon by his side:
The wakeful bloodhound rose, and shook his hide,
But his sagacious eye an inmate owns:
By one, and one, the bolts full easy slide:—
The chains lie silent on the footworn stones;—
The key turns, and the door upon its hinges groans;

And they are gone: aye, ages long ago
These lovers fled away into the storm.
That night the Baron dreamt of many a woe,
And all his warrior-guests, with shade and form
Of witch, and demon, and large coffin-worm,
Were long be-nightmared. Angela the old
Died palsy-twitched, with meager face deform;
The Beadsman, after thousand aves told,
For aye unsought for slept among his ashes cold.

QUESTIONS FOR UNDERSTANDING AND APPRECIATION

1. The plot of a narrative involves conflict. What was Angus McGregor's opponent? Why was Angus unafraid of this opponent? Was he foolhardy or brave in this lack of fear? Why?
2. This poem has many figures of speech. Find the comparisons in the following lines and decide whether each is a simile, metaphor, or personification: 1, 9, 11, 14, 26.
3. Select imagery which appeals to the senses of sound, sight, touch, and hearing.

PATTERNS

1. In this poem the speaker in a monologue describes the pattern of her life and reveals the conflict between her real self and the outward appearance of herself as represented by her "stiff, brocaded gown." Quote lines in which she expresses her feeling about this gown. Cite other lines which indicate that the gown is not typical of the lady's real personality.
2. How was the pattern of her life about to be changed? Why was it not changed? What are the feelings expressed in the last stanza? What mood does the last line of the poem indicate?
3. The poem is written in free verse. How does this differ from forms used in most of the other poems you have read?
4. List examples of effective imagery, of alliteration, and of exact use of words.
5. The author of this poem, Amy Lowell, belonged to a group of writers, called the Imagists, who advocated the presenta-

tion of precise, sharp images in poetry. Give examples of these characteristics in "Patterns."
6. Could the poem itself be thought of as a set of patterns? Explain.

THE DESTRUCTION OF SENNACHERIB

1. The poem presents a series of quickly changing pictures. Identify them. If you were an artist, could you sketch the scenes described by Byron?
2. How do the first two stanzas contrast with the others? How many similes can you identify?
3. The sound of the poem also contributes to its appeal. Byron uses a pattern of meter which is not found very frequently in narrative poems. Scan the first two stanzas to find which metric form predominates. What is the rhyme scheme?

THE LADY OF SHALOTT

1. A romantic story, musical sound, and beautiful imagery are combined to create this artistic poem. It illustrates all the characteristics of narrative poetry which have been discussed in the first three sections of this book. Does the story predominate in this poem, or the sound and imagery?
2. Part I is a description of the island and the surrounding country. Cite details which describe the scene. By what means is the presence of the Lady of Shalott known to the reapers?
3. In Part II the scene shifts to the Lady in the tower. What is her daily occupation? How is she acquainted with the outside world? What prompts her to say, "I am half-sick of shadows"?
4. Part III presents Sir Lancelot's coming and its effect upon the Lady. Note the description of the famous knight. How does the Lady react to Sir Lancelot's image in her crystal mirror?
5. Part IV gives the tragic conclusion to the story. Describe the Lady's coming to Camelot. What are Lancelot's words about her? Had he seen her previously?

6. What is your reaction to the poem and the characters? Can you visualize the characters and the scenes presented? What is the meaning of the expression, "living in an ivory tower"? How does it apply to the poem?

THE EVE OF ST. AGNES

1. What were the rituals required for the fulfillment of the legend of St. Agnes' Eve? How does Madeline succeed in carrying out the rites? Why is secrecy essential? How does the plot conclude for the lovers, Angela, the Beadsman, the Baron, the guests?

2. This poem is famous for its excellent imagery. List details in the first two stanzas which convey a feeling of intense cold. In the five stanzas following the one which begins with the line, "Then by the bed-side, where the faded moon . . . ," select examples of imagery appealing to the senses—sight, smell, taste, touch, hearing. Give examples of simile, metaphor, personification.

3. List effective words and phrases which Keats uses to describe the following: persons, sensations, actions, food, architectural and decorative details.

4. One of the most attractive things about this poem is the set of contrasts that Keats develops: age and youth; cold and warmth; love and hate; the spirit and the flesh; the real and the unreal. Reread the poem and trace these contrasts, picking out the lines or stanzas that reveal them.

5. How is the medieval setting of the poem conveyed to the reader?

6. Scan a stanza and give the rhyme scheme and prevailing meter. What is the name of this stanza form?

7. What qualities make this a great poem?

VOCABULARY: censer, oratories, purgatorial, mails, revelry, requite, cavalier, timbrel, citadel, meager, wassailer, sumptuous, boon, cornice, voluble, treachery, phantasy, moor, flagon, affray, clarion, phantom, sagacious, ague, lineage, conjurer, vassal. Add to this list any other words which are unfamiliar to you, and give their meanings.

COMPARATIVE STUDY

1. "Patterns" and "Angus McGregor" are modern poems; "The Destruction of Sennacherib" and "The Lady of Shalott" were written in the nineteenth century. Each poem has effective imagery. Point out differences in language and in imagery between the old and new poems. How are the tone and imagery of the poems in keeping with the stories?
2. Which of the two modern poems is written in the traditional form? Which is more musical? Which has the more clearly defined plot?
3. Compare "The Destruction of Sennacherib" and "The Lady of Shalott" as to plot, imagery, sound. Which do you consider the greater poem? Why? What qualities in these poems have made them literary classics?
4. Quote an example from any of the poems you have read in this text to illustrate each of the following: simile, metaphor, personification, imagery appealing to specific senses.
5. Both "The Lady of Shalott" and "The Eve of St. Agnes" present a fully rounded story to the reader. Is one of the poems richer in imagery than the other? If so, which one? Explain. Discuss the differences in musical effect gained in each poem. To which of these poems do you think a reader would acquire more attachment as the years went on? Explain.
6. "Patterns" is a dramatic monologue. In this poem, the author must suit his imagery to the character of the speaker. In "The Eve of St. Agnes," the imagery is presented by a person outside the action of the poem. In what way does this change the nature of the imagery in each poem?
7. In the five poems which you have just read in this section, cite examples of how the imagery advances the action of the poem.

Setting and mood

■ SETTING AND MOOD

■ The *setting* of a narrative poem is the background in which the story occurs: the time, place, scenery, manner of life, general environment in which the characters live. In some narrative poems the setting is the focal point of the action. "The Cremation of Sam McGee," for example, tells a story in which the plot is based upon the effect of the Arctic cold upon a man from Tennessee. In "Angus McGregor" the cold weather and the locale are also very important to the action of the poem.

Very often the setting is related to the prevailing *mood* of the poem, which is the state of mind or emotion which pervades the poem and its characters. For instance, you can readily feel the tense mood which surrounds the characters in "Danny Deever" and in "O What Is That Sound?" and the fearful, mysterious experiences of the two skaters at Ghost Lake.

In this section you will read other poems which illustrate the effect of setting and mood upon the characters of a narrative poem and, finally, upon the reader himself.

THE COURTIN'

James Russell Lowell

God makes sech nights, all white an' still
    Fur 'z you can look or listen,
Moonshine an' snow on field an' hill,
    All silence an' all glisten.

Zekle crep' up quite unbeknown
    An' peeked in thru the winder,
An' there sot Huldy all alone,
    'ith no one nigh to hender.

A fireplace filled the room's one side
    With half a cord o' wood in—
There warn't no stoves (tell comfort died)
    To bake ye to a puddin'.

The wa'nut logs shot sparkles out
    Towards the pootiest, bless her,
An' leetle flames danced all about
    The chiny on the dresser.

Agin the chimbley crook-necks hung,
    An' in amongst 'em rusted
The ole queen's-arm thet gran'ther Young
    Fetched back f'om Concord busted.

The very room, coz she was in,
    Seemed warm f'om floor to ceilin',
An' she looked full ez rosy agin
    Ez the apples she was peelin'.

crook-necks: squash.

'Twas kin' o' kingdom-come to look
   On sech a blessed cretur;
A dogrose blushin' to a brook
   Ain't modester nor sweeter.

He was six foot o' man, A 1,
   Clear grit an' human natur';
None couldn't quicker pitch a ton
   Nor dror a furrer straighter.

He'd sparked it with full twenty gals,
   He'd squired 'em, danced 'em, druv 'em,
Fust this one, an' then thet, by spells—
   All is, he couldn't love 'em.

But long o' her his veins 'ould run
   All crinkly like curled maple;
The side she breshed fell full o' sun
   Ez a south slope in Ap'il.

She thought no v'ice hed sech a swing
   Ez hisn in the choir;
My! when he made Ole Hunderd ring
   She *knowed* the Lord was nigher.

An' she'd blush scarlit, right in prayer,
   When her new meetin'-bunnet
Felt somehow thru' its crown a pair
   O' blue eyes sot upun it.

Thet night, I tell ye, she looked *some*!
   She seemed to 've gut a new soul,
For she felt sartin-sure he'd come,
   Down to her very shoe-sole.

She heered a foot, an' knowed it tu,
   A-raspin' on the scraper,—
All ways to once her feelin's flew
   Like sparks in burnt-up paper.

He kin' o' l'itered on the mat,
   Some doubtfle o' the sekle;
His heart kep' goin' pity-pat,
   But hern went pity Zekle.

An' yit she gin her cheer a jerk
   Ez though she wished him furder,
An' on her apples kep' to work,
   Parin' away like murder.

"You want to see my Pa, I s'pose?"
   "Wal . . . no . . . I come dasignin' "—
"To see my Ma? She's sprinklin' clo'es
   Agin tomorrer's i'nin'."

To say why gals act so or so,
   Or don't, 'ould be presumin';
Mebby to mean *yes* an' say *no*
   Comes nateral to women.

He stood a spell on one foot fust,
   Then stood a spell on t'other,
An' on which one he felt the wust
   He couldn't ha' told ye nuther.

Says he, "I'd better call agin";
   Says she, "Think likely, Mister";
Thet last word pricked him like a pin,
   An' . . . Wal, he up an' kist her.

When Ma bimeby upon 'em slips,
    Huldy sot pale ez ashes,
All kin' o' smily roun' the lips
    An' teary roun' the lashes.

For she was jes' the quiet kind
    Whose naturs never vary,
Like streams that keep a summer mind
    Snowhid in Jenoory.

The blood clost roun' her heart felt glued
    Too tight for all expressin',
Tell mother see how metters stood,
    An' gin 'em both her blessin'.

Then her red come back like the tide
    Down to the Bay o' Fundy,
An' all I know is they was cried
    In meetin' come nex' Sunday.

IN SCHOOL-DAYS

John Greenleaf Whittier

Still sits the schoolhouse by the road,
    A ragged beggar sunning;
Around it still the sumachs grow,
    And blackberry vines are running.

Within, the master's desk is seen,
    Deep scarred by raps official;
The warping floor, the battered seats,
    The jack-knife's carved initial;

The charcoal frescos on its wall;
  Its door's worn sill, betraying
The feet that, creeping slow to school,
  Went storming out to playing!

Long years ago a winter sun
  Shone over it at setting;
Lit up its western window-panes,
  And low eaves' icy fretting.

It touched the tangled golden curls,
  And brown eyes full of grieving,
Of one who still her steps delayed
  When all the school were leaving.

For near her stood the little boy
  Her childish favor singled:
His cap pulled low upon a face
  Where pride and shame were mingled.

Pushing with restless feet the snow
  To right and left, he lingered;—
As restlessly her tiny hands
  The blue-checked apron fingered.

He saw her lift her eyes; he felt
  The soft hand's light caressing,
And heard the tremble of her voice,
  As if a fault confessing.

"I'm sorry that I spelt the word:
  I hate to go above you,
Because,"—the brown eyes lower fell,—
  "Because, you see, I love you!"

Still memory to a gray-haired man
  That sweet child-face is showing.
Dear girl! the grasses on her grave
  Have forty years been growing!

He lives to learn, in life's hard school,
  How few who pass above him
Lament their triumph and his loss,
  Like her,—because they love him.

SPANISH WATERS

John Masefield

Spanish waters, Spanish waters, you are ringing in my ears,
Like a slow sweet piece of music from the gray forgotten
    years;
Telling tales, and beating tunes, and bringing weary thoughts
    to me
Of the sandy beach at Muertos, where I would that I could
    be.

There's a surf breaks on Los Muertos, and it never stops to
    roar,
And it's there we came to anchor, and it's there we went
    ashore,
Where the blue lagoon is silent amid snags of rotting trees,
Dropping like the clothes of corpses cast up by the seas.

We anchored at Los Muertos when the dipping sun was red,
We left her half-a-mile to sea, to west of Nigger Head;

Muertos: islands off the Cuban coast.

And before the mist was on the Cay, before the day was
    done,
We were all ashore on Muertos with the gold that we had
    won.

We bore it through the marshes in a half-score battered
    chests,
Sinking, in the sucking quagmires to the sunburn on our
    breasts,
Heaving over tree-trunks, gasping, damning at the flies and
    heat,
Longing for a long drink, out of silver, in the ship's cool
    lazareet.

The moon came white and ghostly as we laid the treasure
    down,
There was gear there'd make a beggarman as rich as Lima
    Town,
Copper charms and silver trinkets from the chests of Spanish
    crews,
Gold doubloons and double moydores, louis d'ors and
    ortagues,

Clumsy yellow-metal earrings from the Indians of Brazil,
Uncut emeralds out of Rio, bezoar stones from Guayaquil,
Silver, in the crude and fashioned, pots of old Arica bronze,
Jewels from the bones of Incas desecrated by the Dons.

We smoothed the place with mattocks, and we took and
    blazed the tree,

Cay: a bay dotted with little islands.   *lazareet:* storeroom of a ship.
double moydores, louis d'ors, and ortagues: gold coins of different values.
bezoar stones: stones (often found in the bodies of animals) thought to
  be antidotes for poisons.
Incas: ancient South American Indians.   *Dons:* Spanish nobles.

Which marks yon where the gear is hid that none will ever
    see,
And we laid aboard the ship again, and south away we steers,
Through the loud surf of Los Muertos which is beating in
    my ears.

I'm the last alive that knows it. All the rest have gone their
    ways
Killed, or died, or come to anchor in the old Mulatas Cays,
And I go singing, fiddling, old and starved and in despair,
And I know where all that gold is hid, if I were only there.

It's not the way to end it all. I'm old and nearly blind,
And an old man's past's a strange thing, for it never leaves his
    mind.
And I see in dreams, awhiles, the beach, the sun's disc dip-
    ping red,
And the tall ship, under topsails, swaying in past Nigger
    Head.

I'd be glad to step ashore there. Glad to take a pick and go
To the lone blazed coco-palm tree in the place no others
    know,
And lift the gold and silver that has mouldered there for years
By the loud surf of Los Muertos which is beating in my ears.

THE LISTENERS

Walter de la Mare

"Is there anybody there?" said the Traveller,
    Knocking on the moonlit door;
And his horse in the silence champed the grasses
    Of the forest's ferny floor:
And a bird flew up out of the turret,
    Above the Traveller's head:
And he smote upon the door again a second time;
    "Is there anybody there?" he said.
But no one descended to the Traveller;
    No head from the leaf-fringed sill
Leaned over and looked into his grey eyes,
    Where he stood perplexed and still.
But only a host of phantom listeners
    That dwelt in the lone house then
Stood listening in the quiet of the moonlight
    To that voice from the world of men:
Stood thronging the faint moonbeams on the dark stair,
    That goes down to the empty hall,
Hearkening in an air stirred and shaken
    By the lonely Traveller's call.
And he felt in his heart their strangeness,
    Their stillness answering his cry,
While his horse moved, cropping the dark turf,
    'Neath the starred and leafy sky;
For he suddenly smote on the door, even
    Louder, and lifted his head:—
"Tell them I came, and no one answered,
    That I kept my word," he said.
Never the least stir made the listeners,
    Though every word he spake

Fell echoing through the shadowiness of the still house
  From the one man left awake:
Ay, they heard his foot upon the stirrup,
  And the sound of iron on stone,
And how the silence surged softly backward,
  When the plunging hoofs were gone.

THE HOST OF THE AIR

William Butler Yeats

"The gods of ancient Ireland, the Sidhe, still ride the country as of old. The Sidhe have much to do with the wind. When the country people see the leaves whirling on the road they bless themselves, because they believe the Sidhe to be passing by. If anyone becomes too much interested in them and sees them overmuch, he loses all interest in ordinary things. They are said to steal brides just after their marriage, and sometimes in a blast of wind. The story in the poem is founded on an old Gaelic ballad."—William Butler Yeats.

O'Driscoll drove with a song,
The wild duck and the drake,
From the tall and the tufted reeds
Of the drear Hart Lake.

And he saw how the reeds grew dark
At the coming of night tide,
And dreamed of the long dim hair
Of Bridget his bride.

He heard while he sang and dreamed
A piper piping away,
And never was piping so sad,
And never was piping so gay.

And he saw young men and young girls
Who danced on a level place
And Bridget his bride among them,
With a sad and a gay face.

The dancers crowded about him,
And many a sweet thing said,
And a young man brought him red wine
And a young girl white bread.

But Bridget drew him by the sleeve,
Away from the merry bands,
To old men playing at cards
With a twinkling of ancient hands.

The bread and the wine had a doom,
For these were the host of the air;
He sat and played in a dream
Of her long dim hair.

He played with the merry old men
And thought not of evil chance,
Until one bore Bridget his bride
Away from the merry dance.

He bore her away in his arms,
The handsomest young man there,
And his neck and his breast and his arms
Were drowned in her long dim hair.

O'Driscoll scattered the cards
And out of his dream awoke:
Old men and young men and young girls
Were gone like a drifting smoke;

But he heard high up in the air
A piper piping away,
And never was piping so sad,
And never was piping so gay.

"A MAN WAS DRAWING NEAR TO ME"

Thomas Hardy

On that gray night of mournful drone,
Apart from aught to hear, to see,
I dreamt not that from shires unknown
   In gloom, alone,
   By Halworthy,
A man was drawing near to me.

I'd no concern at anything,
No sense of coming pull-heart play;
Yet, under the silent outspreading
   Of even's wing
   Where Otterham lay,
A man was riding up my way.

I thought of nobody—not of one,
But only of trifles—legends, ghosts—
Though, on the moorland dim and dun
   That travellers shun
   About these coasts,
The man had passed Tresparret Posts.

Halworthy, Otterham, etc.: The proper names have no significance other
than to create suspense.

There was no light at all inland,
Only the seaward pharos-fire,
Nothing to let me understand
   That hard at hand
   By Hennett Byre
The man was getting nigher and nigher.

There was a rumble at the door,
A draught disturbed the drapery,
And but a minute passed before,
   With gaze that bore
   My destiny,
The man revealed himself to me.

DANIEL WEBSTER'S HORSES

Elizabeth Coatsworth

If when the wind blows
Rattling the trees,
Clicking like skeletons'
Elbows and knees,

You hear along the road
Three horses pass—
Do not go near the dark
Cold window glass.

If when the first snow lies
Whiter than bones
You see the mark of hoofs
Cut to the stones,

Hoofs of three horses
Going abreast—
Turn about, turn about,
A closed door is best!

Upright in the earth
Under the sod
They buried three horses
Bridled and shod,

Daniel Webster's horses—
He said as he grew old,
"Flesh, I loved riding,
Shall I not love it, cold?

"Shall I not love to ride
Bone astride bone,
When the cold wind blows
And snow covers stone?

"Bury them on their feet
With bridle and bit.
They were fine horses—
See their shoes fit."

THE RAVEN

Edgar Allan Poe

Once upon a midnight dreary, while I pondered, weak and
    weary,
Over many a quaint and curious volume of forgotten lore—
While I nodded, nearly napping, suddenly there came a
    tapping,
As of someone gently rapping, rapping at my chamber door:
" 'Tis some visitor," I muttered, "tapping at my chamber
    door—
        Only this and nothing more."

Ah, distinctly I remember it was in the bleak December;
And each separate dying ember wrought its ghost upon the
    floor.
Eagerly I wished the morrow;—vainly I had sought to borrow
From my books surcease of sorrow—sorrow for the lost
    Lenore—
For the rare and radiant maiden whom the angels name
    Lenore—
        Nameless *here* for evermore.

And the silken, sad, uncertain rustling of each purple curtain
Thrilled me—filled me with fantastic terrors never felt before;
So that now, to still the beating of my heart, I stood repeat-
    ing,
" 'Tis some visitor entreating entrance at my chamber door—
Some late visitor entreating entrance at my chamber door;—
        This it is and nothing more."

Presently my soul grew stronger; hesitating then no longer,
"Sir," said I, "or Madam, truly your forgiveness I implore;
But the fact is I was napping, and so gently you came rap-
    ping,

And so faintly you came tapping, tapping at my chamber
     door,
That I scarce was sure I heard you"—here I opened wide the
     door;—
          Darkness there and nothing more.

Deep into that darkness peering, long I stood there wonder-
     ing, fearing,
Doubting, dreaming dreams no mortal ever dared to dream
     before;
But the silence was unbroken, and the stillness gave no token,
And the only word there spoken was the whispered word,
     "Lenore!"
This I whispered, and an echo murmured back the word,
     "Lenore!"
          Merely this and nothing more.

Back into the chamber turning, all my soul within me burn-
     ing,
Soon again I heard a tapping somewhat louder than before.
"Surely," said I, "surely that is something at my window
     lattice;
Let me see, then, what thereat is, and this mystery explore—
Let my heart be still a moment and this mystery explore;—
          'Tis the wind and nothing more!"

Open here I flung the shutter, when, with many a flirt and
     flutter
In there stepped a stately Raven of the saintly days of yore.
Not the least obeisance made he; not a minute stopped or
     stayed he;
But, with mien of lord or lady, perched above my chamber
     door—
Perched upon a bust of Pallas just above my chamber door—
          Perched, and sat, and nothing more.

Pallas: Minerva, goddess of wisdom.

Then this ebony bird beguiling my sad fancy into smiling,
By the grave and stern decorum of the countenance it wore,
"Though thy crest be shorn and shaven, thou," I said, "art
    sure no craven,
Ghastly grim and ancient Raven wandering from the Nightly
    shore—
Tell me what thy lordly name is on the Night's Plutonian
    shore!"
          Quoth the Raven, "Nevermore."

Much I marvelled this ungainly fowl to hear discourse so
    plainly,
Though its answer little meaning—little relevancy bore;
For we cannot help agreeing that no living human being
Ever yet was blessed with seeing bird above his chamber
    door—
Bird or beast upon the sculptured bust above his chamber
    door,
          With such name as "Nevermore."

But the Raven, sitting lonely on the placid bust, spoke only
That one word, as if his soul in that one word he did outpour.
Nothing farther then he uttered—not a feather then he
    fluttered—
Till I scarcely more than muttered, "Other friends have
    flown before—
On the morrow *he* will leave me, as my hopes have flown
    before."
          Then the bird said, "Nevermore."

Startled at the stillness broken by reply so aptly spoken,
"Doubtless," said I, "what it utters is its only stock and store,
Caught from some unhappy master whom unmerciful Dis-
    aster

Plutonian: referring to Pluto, ancient Greek god of the dark underworld.

Followed fast and followed faster till his songs one burden
    bore—
Till the dirges of his Hope that melancholy burden bore
      Of 'Never—nevermore.' "

But the Raven still beguiling all my fancy into smiling,
Straight I wheeled a cushioned seat in front of bird and bust
    and door;
Then, upon the velvet sinking, I betook myself to linking
Fancy unto fancy, thinking what this ominous bird of yore—
What this grim, ungainly, ghastly, gaunt, and ominous bird
    of yore
      Meant in croaking "Nevermore."

This I sat engaged in guessing, but no syllable expressing
To the fowl whose fiery eyes now burned into my bosom's
    core;
This and more I sat divining, with my head at ease reclining
On the cushion's velvet lining that the lamplight gloated o'er,
But whose velvet violet lining with the lamplight gloating
    o'er,
      She shall press, ah, nevermore!

Then, methought, the air grew denser, perfumed from an
    unseen censer
Swung by Seraphim whose foot-falls tinkled on the tufted
    floor.
"Wretch," I cried, "thy God hath lent thee—by these angels
    he hath sent thee
Respite—respite and nepenthe from thy memories of Lenore;
Quaff, oh quaff this kind nepenthe and forget this lost
    Lenore!"
      Quoth the Raven, "Nevermore."

nepenthes: drugs that cause forgetfulness.

"Prophet!" said I, "thing of evil! prophet still, if bird or
   devil!—

Whether Tempter sent, or whether tempest tossed thee here
   ashore,

Desolate yet all undaunted, on this desert land enchanted—
On this home by Horror haunted—tell me truly, I implore—
Is there—*is* there balm in Gilead?—tell me—tell me, I im-
   plore!"

>   Quoth the Raven, "Nevermore."

"Prophet!" said I, "thing of evil!—prophet still, if bird or
   devil!

By that Heaven that bends above us—by that God we both
   adore—

Tell this soul with sorrow laden if, within the distant Aidenn,
It shall clasp a sainted maiden whom the angels name
   Lenore—

Clasp a rare and radiant maiden whom the angels name
   Lenore."

>   Quoth the Raven, "Nevermore."

"Be that word our sign of parting, bird or fiend!" I shrieked,
   upstarting—

"Get thee back into the tempest and the Night's Plutonian
   shore!

Leave no black plume as a token of that lie thy soul hath
   spoken!

Leave my loneliness unbroken!—quit the bust above my door!
Take thy beak from out my heart, and take thy form from
   off my door!"

>   Quoth the Raven, "Nevermore."

balm in Gilead: a healing lotion; comfort, consolation.
Aidenn: Eden, Paradise.

And the Raven, never flitting, still is sitting, *still* is sitting
On the pallid bust of Pallas just above my chamber door;
And his eyes have all the seeming of a demon's that is dream-
　　ing,
And the lamp-light o'er him streaming throws his shadow on
　　the floor;
And my soul from out that shadow that lies floating on the
　　floor
　　　　Shall be lifted—nevermore!

LA BELLE DAME SANS MERCI

John Keats

The French title means "Beautiful Lady without Mercy." Old ballads
and romances often used the theme of a sorceress bewitching a mortal.

O what can ail thee, knight-at-arms,
　　Alone and palely loitering?
The sedge has wither'd from the lake,
　　And no birds sing.

O what can ail thee, knight-at-arms!
　　So haggard and so woe-begone?
The squirrel's granary is full,
　　And the harvest's done.

I see a lily on thy brow
　　With anguish moist and fever-dew,
And on thy cheeks a fading rose
　　Fast withereth too.

I met a lady in the meads,
    Full beautiful—a faery's child,
Her hair was long, her foot was light,
    And her eyes were wild.

I made a garland for her head,
    And bracelets too, and fragrant zone;
She look'd at me as she did love,
    And made sweet moan.

I set her on my pacing steed
    And nothing else saw all day long,
For sidelong would she bend, and sing
    A faery's song.

She found me roots of relish sweet,
    And honey wild and manna-dew,
And sure in language strange she said,
    "I love thee true."

She took me to her elfin grot,
    And there she wept and sigh'd full sore;
And there I shut her wild, wild eyes
    With kisses four.

And there she lulléd me asleep,
    And there I dream'd—Ah! woe betide!
The latest dream I ever dream'd
    On the cold hill's side.

zone: belt, girdle.
elfin grot: a cavern of elves.

I saw pale kings and princes too,
  Pale warriors, death-pale were they all:
They cried—"La belle Dame sans Merci
  Hath thee in thrall!"

I saw their starved lips in the gloam
  With horrid warning gapéd wide,
And I awoke and found me here
  On the cold hill's side.

And this is why I sojourn here
  Alone and palely loitering,
Though the sedge is wither'd from the lake,
  And no birds sing.

QUESTIONS FOR UNDERSTANDING AND APPRECIATION

THE COURTIN'

1. What details in the poem help you to visualize the characters and the setting? Quote lines which make Huldy and Zekle seem very real people.
2. The poem illustrates *local color*, that is, the mannerisms, dress, speech, and customs of a particular region. Give examples of local color in the poem.
3. What observation is made about women? Do you agree?
4. Cite examples of similes, and show how they conform with the setting of the poem.

IN SCHOOL DAYS

1. Cite details which indicate that the setting of the poem is an old country school. Why is the first word in the poem significant? Select examples of description which help you to visualize the school and the two children. Identify the figure of speech in the first two lines.
2. What observation about life is expressed in the last stanza? Do you agree with it?
3. How do you explain the continued appeal of this simple poem?
4. Suggested theme: A paragraph comparing the school described in the poem with your elementary school.
5. You may have observed that your parents and other older people love to reminisce occasionally about their childhood and their school days. Why do you think they find pleasure in doing so?

VOCABULARY: warp, fresco, lament.

SPANISH WATERS

1. Who is telling the story, and what is his expressed wish? Do you think Los Muertos was as appealing to the old seaman when he first saw it? Is it characteristic of old people to glamorize the places associated with their youth?

2. Quote: a line which could apply to other aged persons; description of the treasure; description of the old seaman; a nostalgic wish; an onomatopoeic line.

3. Write an imaginary ending to the poem, entitled "The Return to Los Muertos." Select a class committee to read the themes and to select the best to be read to the class.

THE LISTENERS

1. As you read or listen to the poem, you will experience the mysterious mood which the poet has created through the music of the words and the description of the setting. Can your imagination supply answers to the following questions: Who was the Traveller? Why is he returning to the lone house? Who is the *Them* to whom he refers? Who are the Listeners?

2. Write your own interpretation of the poem, and compare your explanation with your classmates' versions.

3. Select examples of alliteration, of onomatopoeia.

THE HOST OF THE AIR

1. This poem, as the poet's headnote makes clear, is based on a legend of ancient Ireland about the Sidhe, gods of the air, who were believed to be associated with the wind. Sometimes in a gust of wind they were supposed to steal away brides after marriage. How does the author create a real and a magical quality at the same time?

2. Is the contraction expressed in the last stanza applicable to any personal experience in which sadness and gladness are intermingled?

"A MAN WAS DRAWING NEAR TO ME"

1. Visualize the setting in which the speaker awaits the "man." Would the suspense be greater if the names of the places were familiar to you?

2. Cite examples of words that build up the mood; of alliteration.

3. Would you like more explanation following the climax? If so, write your own conclusion in a stanza imitating the rhythm and rhyme of the poem.

DANIEL WEBSTER'S HORSES

1. How does the author create a tense mood in the very first stanza? Note that the last four stanzas explain the mystery presented in the first four stanzas. What is the explanation?

2. Who was Daniel Webster? What interest of his is indicated in the poem?

3. To which of the senses does the poem particularly appeal in the first two stanzas? in the third?

THE RAVEN

1. Setting and mood, sound and imagery—all are exemplified in this well-known poem. What is the setting, and how does it conform with the mood of the poem? Can you visualize the room? Describe it.

2. The sound emphasizes the mood of the poem. What is the meter? the rhyme scheme? What rhyme is used in each stanza?

3. The poem is an unusual example of the effective use of words. Give examples of onomatopoeia, of alliteration, of words which build up the melancholy mood of the poem.

4. What is your interpretation of the poem? What questions does the speaker ask of the raven? What is the reply? What means does the speaker use to find "surcease from sorrow"? What does the raven probably symbolize? After reading the poem, refer to Poe's biography and decide whether the poem relates to a personal grief.

VOCABULARY: surcease, obeisance, decorum, relevancy, ominous, censer, seraphim

LA BELLE DAME SANS MERCI

1. Give the setting of the story, and how is it in keeping with the mood? Show how the description of the knight also harmonizes with the mood of the poem.

2. What are the two questions the knight is asked? The rest of the poem answers them. Describe his experiences.

3. Select word pictures and descriptive details which help to create the haunting atmosphere.

COMPARATIVE STUDY

1. Which poems in this section did you enjoy most? Which are most successful in creating a mood which you can experience with the characters? Which have well-defined plots, and which merely a suggested plot? Do you prefer to imagine the ending of a story or to have it presented to you?

2. The sound of a poem contributes greatly to the mood and its effect on the reader. What poetic devices do poets use to produce this effective sound? Give specific examples from "The Raven" and "Daniel Webster's Horses."

3. Point out any comparisons that you can in the following sets of poems (setting, mood, characters, sound, plot, suspense):

"The Listeners" and "A Man Was Drawing Near to Me"
"In School Days" and "The Courtin' "
"La Belle Dame Sans Merci" and "The Host of the Air"
"The Raven" and "Spanish Waters"

The ballad

■ THE BALLAD

■ A narrative poem, as you have seen, combines story, sound, and imagery. One of these elements may be more pronounced than the others; for example, the imagery in narrative poetry is often not so prominent as the story and sound.

In addition to these three elements, a poem has structure; it is arranged according to a pattern. A poet may be compared to an architect who is developing an idea for a building. Just as he must choose a design adapted to the function of his building, so also the poet selects a pattern to fit his purpose. A narrative poem may be written in the form of a simple story in verse or an elaborate epic. The kind of poem, the length and number of stanzas, the type of rhyme and rhythm—all these make up the *structure* of the poem.

THE LIMERICK

The structure of a poem may be illustrated by the *limerick,* a five-line poem which follows a definite pattern in rhyme and rhythm. The subject is usually light and nonsensical, for which a short stanza is well-suited. You may wish to imitate the structure of the limericks below by writing an original humorous verse.

A foolish young fellow named Hyde
In a funeral procession was spied.
When asked, "Who is dead?"
He giggled and said,
"I don't know. I just came for the ride."

There was a young lady of Lynn
Who was so uncommonly thin
That when she essayed
To drink lemonade
She slipped through the straw and fell in.

There are various kinds of narrative poems. One type, the *ballad*, will serve as a good introduction to your later study of many other forms in which poems are written.

BALLADS

A *ballad* is a short, simple narrative poem, originally intended to be sung; in other words, a story in song. *Folk ballads* have been handed down to us anonymously from the past. *Literary ballads*, also called *imitation ballads*, were written by known authors in the style of the folk ballad.

Ballads have appealed to people throughout the ages, probably because the ballad is a form of poetry which pleasingly combines story and song. Today there is an enthusiastic interest in singing, listening to, and composing ballads. Folk singers are reviving some of the old ballads; and through the media of radio, television, and recordings, these songs are bringing entertainment to modern listeners. If you enjoy singing and listening to folk songs, your study of the ballad should be an enjoyable experience.

Old Folk Ballads

The old ballads originated in England and Scotland, some of them as early as the fourteenth and fifteenth centuries. The authors of the ballads are unknown. As the name implies, these poems were "ballads of the folk," and they may have been composed as a group activity by members of a family or clan or by people gathered in a social or work situation. It is likely that some of the ballads were originally composed by individual singers.

The themes and plots of the ballads represented the ideals, beliefs, fears, and tragedies of the group. Generally the stories were sad rather than humorous. The plots of the ballads were usually related to local happenings known to the people who listened to and participated in the singing. When a minstrel sang a ballad, it is very likely that the group would join in for the chorus. Folk singing, often accompanied by dancing, provided entertainment and recreation as it does in our own day.

The old English and Scottish folk ballads were sung and passed down from generation to generation before they were recorded in written form. As the ballads were sung, changes were often made in the original; new verses were added, and others omitted. As a result, several versions of the same ballad often exist. The popular poem, "Barbara Allen," is an example.

Many of these old ballads were brought to the United States by immigrants from the British Isles; and some of these songs are still sung in their original form, especially in remote mountain regions of South and East. Excellent collections of these old ballads have been compiled. Since the revival of folk singing, an even greater effort is being made to keep alive the melodies and words of these old songs which reflect the lives and spirit of those who composed them. Collectors and publishers go to remote regions to seek out residents who remember the words and the melodies taught them by their ancestors, and sometimes on-the-spot recordings are made. Modern Americans who hear and sing the songs can share in the legends and the music of past generations.

Characteristics of Old Ballads

—The author is unknown.
—The story is simple and direct, often based on only one incident told in condensed form with very little detail.
—The poem usually ends abruptly at the story's climax.
—The story is often told as a dialogue between the characters.
—Repetition of a line or lines is often used in ballads. Sometimes a technique called "incremental repetition" is employed to add to the suspense of the story and build up to a final "punch line" or climax. In incremental repetition, a phrase or line is repeated with some words added or changed. "Lord Randal" is an example.
—Dialect is commonly used in the English and Scottish ballads.
—The usual subjects of ballads are warfare; romance—often tragic; supernatural happenings; exploits of a hero; domestic conflicts.
—The characters represent basic traits: faith, love, loyalty, cowardice, revenge, treachery.
—The most commonly used ballad stanza consists of four lines, the first and third line usually having four feet, and the second and fourth three feet of two syllables each in iambic meter; that is, the first syllable unaccented and the second accented. The second and fourth lines rhyme.

Example:

"I cast my net into the tide	a
Before I made for home:	b
Too heavy for my hands to raise.	c
I drew it through the foam."	b

—Sigerson, "A Ballad of Marjorie"

—Note that the first and third lines are called *iambic tetrameter*, that is, four feet in which an unaccented sound is followed by an accented sound. The second and fourth lines are *iambic trimeter*—three feet. (See page 203.)

Reading Ballads

Your first experience in reading the old ballads may present a challenge to you, but it should also be fun. In some of these poems, Old English and Scottish dialect is used, along with unusual spelling; and as a result, you may find some difficulty in pronouncing and understanding the words. However, you will soon learn to decipher the meanings if you pronounce the words according to the sounds of the letters and if you refer to the glossary for explanation. Some of the old ballads in this text are rewritten in modern English; but others, such as "Sir Patrick Spence," would lose much of their rhythmic effect without the Old English words.

Your enjoyment of the ballads will be greatly increased if you read them aloud or listen to them. Remember, these poems were originally sung or recited, and their effect is lost in silent reading. Under your teacher's direction, you will find varied ways of making the ballad come to life for you—choral reading by selected members of the class, total class participation, and perhaps an occasional folk-sing by students who can accompany the songs with a guitar. Excellent recordings of many of the ballads are available to help you get into the spirit of the old folk singers as you listen to their dramatic stories.

You may wish to start your study of old ballads with a class reading of this old tragic poem, which is typical of the old ballads in many ways: the old spelling, the use of dialogue and repetition, the lack of details and the abrupt ending, the musical meter. You will then wish to discuss Lord Randal's tragedy.

LORD RANDAL

Anonymous

"O where hae ye been, Lord Randal, my son?
O where hae ye been, my handsome young man?"—
"I hae been to the wild wood; mother, make my bed soon,
For I'm weary wi' hunting, and fain wad lie down."

"Where gat ye your dinner, Lord Randal, my son?
Where gat ye your dinner, my handsome young man?"—
"I dined wi' my true-love; mother, make my bed soon,
For I'm weary wi' hunting, and fain wad lie down."

"What gat ye to your dinner, Lord Randal, my son?
What gat ye to your dinner, my handsome young man?"
"I gat eels boil'd in broo'; mother, make my bed soon,
For I'm weary wi' hunting, and fain wad lie down."

"What became of your bloodhounds, Lord Randal, my son?
What became of your bloodhounds, my handsome young
    man?"—
"O they swell'd and they died; mother, make my bed soon,
For I'm weary wi' hunting, and fain wad lie down."

"O I fear ye are poison'd, Lord Randal, my son!
O I fear ye are poison'd, my handsome young man!"—
"O yes! I am poison'd; mother, make my bed soon,
For I'm sick at the heart, and I fain wad lie down."

SIR PATRICK SPENCE

Anonymous

This old Scottish poem is concise, rhythmic, and dramatic—a classic example of the folk ballad. The plot is probably based on an actual event in 1290, when nobles were sent on a voyage to Norway to bring back the Princess Margaret, the daughter of the King of Scotland. According to most accounts, the voyage ended in a disastrous shipwreck.

The king sits in Dumferling toune,
   Drinking the blude-reid wine:
"O whar will I get guid sailor,
   To sail this schip of mine?"

Up and spak an eldern knicht,
   Sat at the kings richt kne:
"Sir Patrick Spence is the best sailor
   That sails upon the se."

The king has written a braid letter,
   And signd it wi his hand,
And sent it to Sir Patrick Spence,
   Was walking on the sand.

The first line that Sir Patrick red,
   A loud lauch lauched he;
The next line that Sir Patrick red,
   The teir blinded his ee.

"O wha is this has don this deid,
   This ill deid don to me,
To send me out this time o' the yeir,
   To sail upon the se!

Dumferling toune: a town not far from Edinburgh, Scotland.
braid: broad.   *lauched:* laughed. ("gh" is often found as "ch" in Scottish dialect.)

"Mak hast, mak hast, my mirry men all,
   Our guid schip sails the morne:"
"O say na sae, my master deir,
   For I feir a deadlie storme.

"Late late yestreen I saw the new moone,
   Wi the auld moone in hir arme,
And I feir, I feir, my deir master,
   That we will cum to harme."

O our Scots nobles wer richt laith
   To weet their cork-heild schoone;
Bot lang owre a' the play wer playd,
   Thair hats they swam aboone.

O lang, lang may their ladies sit,
   Wi thair fans into their hand,
Or eir they se Sir Patrick Spence
   Cum sailing to the land.

O lang, lang may the ladies stand,
   Wi thair gold kems in their hair,
Waiting for thair ain deir lords,
   For they'll se thame na mair.

Haf owre, haf owre to Aberdour,
   It's fiftie fadom deip,
And thair lies guid Sir Patrick Spence,
   Wi the Scots lords at his feit.

---

laith: loath, unwilling.   *schoone*: shoes.
Thair hats they swam aboone: Their hats floated on the waves. They
  had drowned.   *kems*: combs.   *owre*: over.

LORD ULLIN'S DAUGHTER

Thomas Campbell

A chieftain, to the Highlands bound,
    Cries, "Boatman, do not tarry!
And I'll give thee a silver pound
    To row us o'er the ferry."—

"Now who be ye, would cross Lochgyle,
    This dark and stormy water?"
"Oh, I'm the chief of Ulva's isle,
    And this Lord Ullin's daughter.—

"And fast before her father's men
    Three days we've fled together,
For should he find us in the glen,
    My blood would stain the heather.

"His horsemen hard behind us ride;
    Should they our steps discover,
Then who will cheer my bonny bride
    When they have slain her lover?"

Out spoke the hardy Highland wight,
    "I'll go, my chief—I'm ready:—
It is not for your silver bright,
    But for your winsome lady:

"And by my word! the bonny bird
    In danger shall not tarry;
So though the waves are raging white
    I'll row you o'er the ferry."—

wight: man.

By this the storm grew loud apace,
   The water-wraith was shrieking;
And in the scowl of heaven each face
   Grew dark as they were speaking.

But still as wilder blew the wind,
   And as the night grew drearer,
Adown the glen rode armèd men,
   Their trampling sounded nearer.—

"O haste thee, haste!" the lady cries,
   "Though tempests round us gather;
I'll meet the raging of the skies,
   But not an angry father."—

The boat has left a stormy land,
   A stormy sea before her,—
When, oh! too strong for human hand,
   The tempest gather'd o'er her.—

And still they row'd amidst the roar
   Of waters fast prevailing:
Lord Ullin reach'd that fatal shore,
   His wrath was changed to wailing.

For, sore dismay'd, through storm and shade,
   His child he did discover:—
One lovely hand she stretch'd for aid,
   And one was round her lover.

"Come back! come back!" he cried in grief,
   "Across this stormy water:
And I'll forgive your Highland chief,
   My daughter!—oh, my daughter!"—

wraith: ghost, specter.

'Twas vain: the loud waves lash'd the shore,
    Return or aid preventing:—
The waters wild went o'er his child,
    And he was left lamenting.

THE WRECK OF THE *HESPERUS*

Henry Wadsworth Longfellow

It was the schooner *Hesperus*,
    That sailed the wintry sea;
And the skipper had taken his little daughtèr,
    To bear him company.

Blue were her eyes as the fairy-flax,
    Her cheeks like the dawn of day,
And her bosom white as the hawthorn buds,
    That ope in the month of May.

The skipper he stood beside the helm,
    His pipe was in his mouth,
And he watched how the veering flaw did blow
    The smoke now West, now South.

Then up and spake an old Sailòr,
    Had sailed to the Spanish Main,
"I pray thee, put into yonder port,
    For I fear a hurricane.

"Last night, the moon had a golden ring,
   And tonight no moon we see!"
The skipper, he blew a whiff from his pipe,
   And a scornful laugh laughed he.

Colder and colder blew the wind,
   A gale from the Northeast,
The snow fell hissing in the brine,
   And the billows frothed like yeast.

Down came the storm, and smote amain
   The vessel in its strength;
She shuddered and paused, like a frighted steed,
   Then leaped her cable's length.

"Come hither! come hither! my little daughter,
   And do not tremble so;
For I can weather the roughest gale
   That ever wind did blow."

He wrapped her warm in his seaman's coat
   Against the stinging blast;
He cut a rope from a broken spar,
   And bound her to the mast.

"O father! I hear the church bells ring;
   Oh, say, what may it be?"
" 'Tis a fog bell on a rock-bound coast!"—
   And he steered for the open sea.

"O father! I hear the sound of guns;
   Oh, say, what may it be?"
"Some ship in distress, that cannot live
   In such an angry sea!"

"O father! I see a gleaming light;
  Oh, say, what may it be?"
But the father answered never a word,
  A frozen corpse was he.

Lashed to the helm, all stiff and stark,
  With his face turned to the skies,
The lantern gleamed through the gleaming snow
  On his fixed and glassy eyes.

Then the maiden clasped her hands and prayed
  That savèd she might be;
And she thought of Christ, who stilled the wave,
  On the Lake of Galilee.

And fast through the midnight dark and drear,
  Through the whistling sleet and snow,
Like a sheeted ghost, the vessel swept
  Tow'rds the reef of Norman's Woe.

And ever the fitful gusts between
  A sound came from the land;
It was the sound of the trampling surf
  On the rocks and the hard sea-sand.

The breakers were right beneath her bows,
  She drifted a dreary wreck,
And a whooping billow swept the crew
  Like icicles from her deck.

She struck where the white and fleecy waves
  Looked soft as carded wool,
But the cruel rocks, they gored her side
  Like the horns of an angry bull.

Her rattling shrouds, all sheathed in ice,
  With the masts went by the board;
Like a vessel of glass, she strove and sank,
  Ho! ho! the breakers roared!

At daybreak, on the bleak sea-beach,
  A fisherman stood aghast,
To see the form of a maiden fair,
  Lashed close to a drifting mast.

The salt sea was frozen on her breast,
  The salt tears in her eyes;
And he saw her hair, like the brown seaweed,
  On the billows fall and rise.

Such was the wreck of the *Hesperus*,
  In the midnight and the snow!
Christ save us all from a death like this,
  On the reef of Norman's Woe!

THE WIFE OF USHER'S WELL

Anonymous

There lived a wife at Usher's Well,
  And a wealthy wife was she;
She had three stout and stalwart sons,
  And sent them o'er the sea.

They hadna been a week from her,
  A week but barely ane,

Whan word came to the carline wife
   That her three sons were gane.

They hadna been a week from her,
   A week but barely three,
Whan word came to the carline wife
   That her sons she'd never see.

"I wish the wind may never cease,
   Nor fashes in the flood,
Till my three sons come hame to me,
   In earthly flesh and blood."

It fell about the Martinmas,
   When nights are lang and mirk,
The carline wife's three sons came hame,
   And their hats were o' the birk.

It neither grew in syke nor ditch,
   Nor yet in ony sheugh;
But at the gates o' Paradise,
   That birk grew fair eneugh.

"Blow up the fire, my maidens,
   Bring water from the well;
For a' my house shall feast this night,
   Since my three sons are well."

And she has made to them a bed,
   She's made it large and wide,
And she's taen her mantle her about,
   Sat down at the bedside.

carline: old lady.   *gane:* gone.   *fashes:* troubles.
birk: birch.   *syke:* a marsh.   *sheugh:* furrow, ditch.

Up then crew the red, red cock,
    And up and crew the gray;
The eldest to the youngest said,
    " 'Tis time we were away."

The cock he hadna crawd but once,
    And clapped his wings at a',
When the youngest to the eldest said,
    "Brother, we must awa',

"The cock doth craw, the day doth daw,
    The channerin' worm doth chide;
Gin we be mist out o' our place,
    A sair pain we maun bide.

"Fare ye weel, my mother dear!
    Fareweel to barn and byre!
And fare ye weel, the bonny lass,
    That kindles my mother's fire!"

FAREWELL TO BARN AND STACK AND TREE

A. E. Housman

"Farewell to barn and stack and tree,
    Farewell to Severn shore.
Terence, look your last at me,
    For I come home no more.

channerin': fretting.   *byre*: stable.
Severn: river in West England.

"The sun burns on the half-mown hill,
   By now the blood is dried;
And Maurice amongst the hay lies still
   And my knife is in his side.

"My mother thinks us long away;
   'Tis time the field were mown.
She had two sons at rising day,
   To-night she'll be alone.

"And here's a bloody hand to shake,
   And oh, man, here's good-bye;
We'll sweat no more on scythe and rake,
   My bloody hands and I.

"I wish you strength to bring you pride,
   And a love to keep you clean,
And I wish you luck, come Lammastide,
   At racing on the green.

"Long for me the rick will wait,
   And long will wait the fold,
And long will stand the empty plate,
   And dinner will be cold."

Lammastide: church festival, August 1. (Juliet, in Shakespeare's play,
   was born at Lammastide.)
rick: hay stack.

JOHNNIE ARMSTRONG

Anonymous

This poem recounts the fate of John Armstrong, a powerful outlaw knight, who robbed and plundered along the Scottish border. In 1530 King James sent an army to rid the country of him. The ballad gives one version of the historical incident.

There dwelt a man in fair Westmoreland,
    Johnnie Armstrong men did him call;
He had neither lands nor rents coming in
    Yet he kept eight score men in his hall.

He had horse and harness for them all,
    Goodly steeds were all milk-white;
O the golden bands about their necks,
    And their weapons, they were all alike.

News then was brought unto the king
    That there was such a one as he,
That livèd like a bold outlaw,
    And robbèd all the north country.

The king he wrote a letter then,
    A letter which was large and long;
He signèd it with his own hand,
    And he promised to do him no wrong.

When this letter came Johnnie unto,
    His heart was as blythe as birds on the tree:
"Never was I sent for before any king,
    My father, my grandfather, nor none but me.

"And if we go the king before,
    I would we went most orderly;
Every man of you shall have his scarlet cloak,
    Laced with silver laces three.

"Every one of you shall have his velvet coat,
    Laced with silver lace so white;
O the golden bands about your necks,
    Black hats, white feathers, all alike."

By the morrow morning at ten of the clock,
    Towards Edinborough gone was he,
And with him all his eight score men;
    Good Lord, it was a goodly sight for to see!

When Johnnie came before the king,
    He fell down on his knee;
"O pardon, my sovereign liege," he said,
    "O pardon my eight score men and me."

"Thou shalt have no pardon, thou traitor strong,
    For thy eight score men nor thee;
For tomorrow morning by ten of the clock,
    Both thou and them shall hang on the gallow-tree."

But Johnnie looked over his left shouldèr,
    Good Lord, what a grievous look looked he!
Saying, "Asking grace of a graceless face—
    Why, there is none for you nor me."

But Johnnie had a bright sword by his side,
    And it was made of the mettle so free,

That had not the king stept his foot aside,
   He had smitten his head from his fair body.

Saying, "Fight on, my merry men all,
   And see that none of you be ta'en;
For rather than men shall say we were hanged,
   Let them report how we were slain."

Then, God knows, fair Edinborough rose,
   And so beset poor Johnnie round,
That four score and ten of Johnnie's best men
   Lay gasping all upon the ground.

Then like a madman Johnnie laid about,
   And like a madman then fought he,
Until a false Scot came Johnnie behind,
   And ran him through the fair body.

Saying, "Fight on, my merry men all,
   And see that none of you be ta'en
I will lay me down for to bleed a while,
   Then I'll rise and fight with you again."

News then was brought to young Johnnie Armstrong,
   As he stood by his nurse's knee,
Who vowed if e'er he lived for to be a man,
   On the treacherous Scots revenged he'd be.

ROBIN HOOD'S DEATH
AND BURIAL

Anonymous

When Robin Hood and Little John
 Down a down, a down, a down,
Went o'er yon bank of broom,
 Said Robin Hood bold to Little John,
"We have shot for many a pound,
 Hey, down, a down, a down.

"But I am not able to shoot one shot more,
 My broad arrows will not flee;
But I have a cousin lives down below,
 Please God, she will bleed me."

Now Robin he is to fair Kirkly gone,
 As fast as he can win;
But before he came there, as we do hear,
 He was taken very ill.

And when that he came to fair Kirkly-hall,
 He knockd all at the ring,
But none was so ready as his cousin herself
 For to let bold Robin in.

"Will you please to sit down, cousin Robin," she said,
 "And drink some beer with me?"
"No I will neither eat nor drink,
 Till I am blooded by thee."

"Well, I have a room, cousin Robin," she said,
 "Which you did never see,

And if you please to walk therein,
　　You blooded by me shall be."

She took him by the lily-white hand,
　　And led him to a private room,
And there she blooded bold Robin Hood,
　　While one drop of blood would run down.

She blooded him in a vein of the arm,
　　And locked him up in the room;
Then did he bleed all the live-long day,
　　Until the next day at noon.

He then bethought him of a casement there,
　　Thinking for to get down;
He was so weak he could not leap,
　　He could not get him down.

He then bethought him of his bugle-horn,
　　Which hung low down to his knee;
He set his horn unto his mouth,
　　And blew out weak blasts three.

Then Little John, when hearing him,
　　As he sat under a tree,
"I fear my master is now near dead,
　　He blows so wearily."

Then Little John to fair Kirkly is gone,
　　As fast as he can dree;
But when he came to Kirkly-hall,
　　He broke locks two or three:

can dree: is able.

Until he came bold Robin to see,
    Then he fell on his knee;
"A boon, a boon," cries Little John,
    "Master, I beg of thee."

"What is that boon," said Robin Hood,
    "Little John, [thou] begs of me?"
"It is to burn fair Kirkly-hall,
    And all their nunnery."

"Now nay, now nay," quoth Robin Hood,
    "That boon I'll not grant thee;
I never hurt woman in all my life,
    Nor men in woman's company.

"I never hurt fair maid in all my time,
    Nor at mine end shall it be;
But give me my bent bow in my hand,
    And a broad arrow I'll let flee
And where this arrow is taken up,
    There shall my grave digged be.

"Lay me a green sod under my head,
    And another at my feet;
And lay my bent bow by my side,
    Which was my music sweet;
And make my grave of gravel and green,
    Which is most right and meet.

"Let me have length and breadth enough,
    With a green sod under my head;
That they may say, when I am dead,
    Here lies bold Robin Hood."

These words they readily granted him,
   Which did bold Robin please:
And there they buried bold Robin Hood,
   Within the fair Kirkleys.

THE BALLAD OF THE HARP-WEAVER

Edna St. Vincent Millay

"Son," said my mother,
   When I was knee-high,
"You've need of clothes to cover you,
   And not a rag have I.

"There's nothing in the house
   To make a boy breeches,
Nor shears to cut a cloth with
   Nor thread to take stitches.

"There's nothing in the house
   But a loaf-end of rye,
And a harp with a woman's head
   Nobody will buy."
   And she began to cry.

That was in the early fall.
   When came the late fall,
"Son," she said, "the sight of you
   Makes your mother's blood crawl,—

"Little skinny shoulder-blades
   Sticking through your clothes!
And where you'll get a jacket from
   God above knows!

"It's lucky for me, lad,
   Your daddy's in the ground,
And can't see the way I let
   His son go around!"
   And she made a queer sound.

That was in the late fall.
   When the winter came,
I'd not a pair of breeches
   Nor a shirt to my name.

I couldn't go to school,
   Or out of doors to play.
And all the other little boys
   Passed our way.

"Son," said my mother,
   "Come, climb into my lap,
And I'll chafe your little bones
   While you take a nap."

And, oh, but we were silly
   For half an hour or more,
Me with my long legs
   Dragging on the floor,

A-rock-rock-rocking
   To a mother-goose rhyme!

Oh, but we were happy
  For half an hour's time!

But there was I, a great boy,
  And what would folks say
To hear my mother singing me
  To sleep all day,
  In such a daft way?

Men say the winter
  Was bad that year;
Fuel was scarce,
  And food was dear.

A wind with a wolf's head
  Howled about our door,
And we burned up the chairs
  And sat upon the floor.

All that was left us
  Was a chair we couldn't break,
And the harp with a woman's head
  Nobody would take,
  For song or pity's sake.

The night before Christmas
  I cried with the cold,
I cried myself to sleep
  Like a two-year-old.

And in the deep night
  I felt my mother rise,
And stare down upon me
  With love in her eyes.

I saw my mother sitting
   On the one good chair,
A light falling on her
   From I couldn't tell where,

Looking nineteen,
   And not a day older,
And the harp with a woman's head
   Leaned against her shoulder.

Her thin fingers, moving
   In the thin, tall strings,
Were weav-weav-weaving
   Wonderful things.

Many bright threads,
   From where I couldn't see,
Were running through the harp-strings
   Rapidly,

And gold threads whistling
   Through my mother's hand.
I saw the web grow
   And the pattern expand.

She wove a child's jacket,
   And when it was done
She laid it on the floor
   And wove another one.

She wove a red cloak
   So regal to see,
"She's made it for a king's son,"

I said, "and not for me."
But I knew it was for me.

She wove a pair of breeches
    Quicker than that!
She wove a pair of boots
    And a little cocked hat.

She wove a pair of mittens,
    She wove a little blouse,
She wove all night
    In the still, cold house.

She sang as she worked,
    And the harp-strings spoke;
Her voice never faltered,
    And the thread never broke.
    And when I awoke—

There sat my mother
    With the harp against her shoulder,
Looking nineteen
    And not a day older,

A smile about her lips,
    And a light about her head,
And her hands in the harp-strings
    Frozen dead.

And piled up beside her
    And toppling to the skies,
Were the clothes of a king's son,
    Just my size.

JESSE JAMES

American Myth

A Design in Red and Yellow for a Nickel Library

William Rose Benét

Jesse James was a two-gun man,
 (Roll on, Missouri!)
Strong-arm chief of an outlaw clan.
 (From Kansas to Illinois!)
He twirled an old Colt forty-five,
 (Roll on, Missouri!)
They never took Jesse James alive.
 (Roll, Missouri, roll!)

Jesse James was King of the Wes';
 (Cataracks in the Missouri!)
He'd a di'mon' heart in his lef' breas';
 (Brown Missouri rolls!)
He'd a fire in his heart no hurt could stifle;
 (Thunder, Missouri!)
Lion eyes an' a Winchester rifle.
 (Missouri, roll down!)

Jesse James rode a pinto hawse;
Come at night to a water-cawse;
Tetched with the rowel that pinto's flank;
She sprung the torrent from bank to bank.

Jesse rode through a sleepin' town;
Looked the moonlit street both up an' down;
Crack-crack-crack, the street ran flames
An' a great voice cried, "I'm Jesse James!"

Hawse an' afoot they're after Jess!
    (Roll on, Missouri!)
Spurrin' an' spurrin'—but he's gone Wes'.
    (Brown Missouri rolls!)
He was ten foot tall when he stood in his boots;
    (Lightnin' light the Missouri!)
More'n a match fer sich galoots.
    (Roll, Missouri, roll!)

Jesse James rode outa the sage;
Roun' the rocks come the swayin' stage;
Straddlin' the road a giant stan's
An' a great voice bellers, "Throw up yer han's!"

Jesse raked in the di'mon' rings,
The big gold watches an' the yuther things;
Jesse divvied 'em then an' thar
With a cryin' child had lost her mar.

The U. S. troopers is after Jess;
    (Roll on, Missouri!)
Their hawses sweat foam, but he's gone Wes';
    (Hear Missouri roar!)
He was broad as a b'ar, he'd a ches' like a drum,
    (Wind an' rain through Missouri!)
An' his red hair flamed like Kingdom Come.
    (Missouri down to the sea!)

Jesse James all alone in the rain
Stopped an' stuck up the Eas'-boun' train;
Swayed through the coaches with horns an' a tail,
Lit out with the bullion an' the registered mail.

Jess made 'em all turn green with fright,
Quakin' in the aisles in the pitch-black night;
An' he give all the bullion to a pore ole tramp
Campin' nigh the cuttin' in the dirt an' damp.

The whole U. S. is after Jess;
    (Roll on, Missouri!)
The son-of-a-gun, if he ain't gone Wes';
    (Missouri to the Sea!)
He could chaw cold iron an' spit blue flame;
    (Cataracks down the Missouri!)
He rode on a catamount he'd larned to tame.
    (Hear that Missouri roll!)

Jesse James rode into a Bank;
Give his pinto a tetch on the flank;
Jumped the teller's window with an awful crash;
Heaved up the safe an' twirled his mustache;

He said, "So long, boys!" He yelped, "So long!
Feelin' porely to-day—I ain't feelin' strong!"
Rode right through the wall agoin' crack-crack-crack,—
Took the safe home to Mother in a gunny-sack.

They're creepin', they're crawlin', they're stalkin' Jess;
    (Roll on, Missouri!)
They's a rumor he's gone much further Wes';
    (Roll, Missouri, roll!)
They's word of a cayuse hitched to the bars
    (Ruddy clouds on Missouri!)
Of a golden sunset that busts into stars.
    (Missouri, roll down!)

Jesse James rode hell fer leather;
He was a hawse an' a man together;
In a cave in a mountain high up in air
He lived with a rattlesnake, a wolf, an' a bear.

Jesse's heart was as sof' as a woman;
Fer guts an' stren'th he was sooper-human;
He could put six shots through a woodpecker's eye
And take in one swaller a gallon o' rye.

They sought him here an' they sought him there,
 (Roll on, Missouri!)
But he strides by night through the ways of the air,
 (Brown Missouri rolls!)
They say he was took an' they say he is dead;
 (Thunder, Missouri!)
But he ain't—he's a sunset overhead!
 (Missouri down to the sea!)

Jesse James was a Hercules.
When he went through the woods he tore up the trees.
When he went on the plains he smoked the groun'
An' the hull lan' shuddered fer miles aroun'.

Jesse James wore a red bandanner
That waved on the breeze like the Star Spangled Banner;
In seven states he cut up dadoes.
He's gone with the buffler an' the desperadoes.

Yes, Jesse James was a two-gun man
 (Roll on, Missouri!)
The same as when this song began;
 (From Kansas to Illinois!)

An' when you see a sunset bust into flames
  (Lightnin' light the Missouri!)
Or a thunderstorm blaze—that's Jesse James!
  (Hear that Missouri roll!)

BINNORIE

Anonymous

Romance, tragedy, and revenge are combined in this old ballad, which
is often titled "The Twa Sisters." Various refrains are used in other
versions, such as "Bow down . . . I'll be true to my love and my love'll
be true to me."

There were two sisters sat in a bower;
  Binnorie, O Binnorie!
There came a knight to be their wooer,
  By the bonnie milldams o' Binnorie.

He courted the eldest with glove and ring
But he loved the youngest above everything.

The eldest she was vexèd sair
And greatly envied her sister fair.

Upon a morning fair and clear,
She cried upon her sister dear:

"O sister, sister, take my hand,
And we'll see our father's ships to land."

She's taken her by the lily hand,
And led her down to the river-strand.

The youngest stood upon a stone,
The eldest came and pushed her in.

"O sister, sister, reach your hand!
And you shall be heir of half my land."

"O sister, I'll not reach my hand,
And I'll be heir of all your land."

"O sister, reach me but your glove!
And sweet Williàm shall be your love."

"Sink on, nor hope for hand or glove!
And sweet Williàm shall be my love!"

Sometimes she sank, sometimes she swam,
Until she came to the miller's dam.

Out then came the miller's son,
And saw the fair maid floating in.

"O father, father, draw your dam!
There's either a mermaid or a swan."

The miller hastened and drew his dam,
And there he found a drowned womàn.

You could not see her waist so small,
Her girdle with gold was broidered all.

You could not see her lily feet,
Her golden fringes were so deep.

You could not see her yellow hair
For the strings of pearls that were twisted there.

You could not see her fingers small,
With diamond rings they were covered all.

And by there came a harper fine,
To harp to the king when he should dine.

And when he looked that lady on,
He sighed and made a heavy moan.

He's made a harp of her breast-bone,
Whose sound would melt a heart of stone.

He's taken three locks of her yellow hair,
And with them strung his harp so rare.

He went into her father's hall,
And there was the court assembled all.

He laid his harp upon a stone,
And straight it began to play alone.

"O yonder sits my father, the King,
And yonder sits my mother, the Queen;

"And yonder stands my brother Hugh,
And by him my William, sweet and true."

But the last tune that the harp played then—
    Binnorie, O Binnorie!
Was, "Woe to my sister, false Helèn!"
    By the bonnie milldams o' Binnorie.

BARBARA ALLEN

Anonymous

Of all the old ballads that we have inherited from the British Isles,
"Barbara Allen" is probably the most widely and frequently sung today.
Many versions exist, with variations in some details; but the character
of Barbara Allen is basically the same in all the songs.

It was in and about the Martinmas time,
   When the green leaves were a-falling,
That Sir John Graeme in the west country
   Fell in love with Barbara Allen.

He sent his man down through the town,
   To the place where she was dwelling,
"O haste and come to my master dear,
   Gin ye be Barbara Allen."

O hooly, hooly rose she up,
   To the place where he was lying,
And when she drew the curtain by—
   "Young man, I think you're dying."

"O it's I'm sick, and very, very sick,
   And 'tis a' for Barbara Allen."
"O the better for me ye's never be,
   Tho' your heart's blood were a-spilling.

"O dinna ye mind, young man," said she,
   "When ye was in the tavern a-drinking,
That ye made the health gae round and round,
   And slighted Barbara Allen."

He turn'd his face unto the wall,
   And death was with him dealing:

"Adieu, adieu, my dear friends all,
    And be kind to Barbara Allen."

And slowly, slowly raise she up,
    And slowly, slowly left him;
And sighing, said she cou'd not stay,
    Since death of life had reft him.

She had not gane a mile but twa,
    When she heard the dead-bell ringing,
And every jow that the dead-bell geid,
    It cry'd, Woe to Barbara Allen.

"O mother dear, O mak my bed,
    An' mak it saft an' narrow;
My love has died for me to-day,
    I'll die for him to-morrow."

A BALLAD OF MARJORIE

Dora Sigerson

"What ails you that you look so pale,
    O fisher of the sea?"
" 'Tis for a mournful tale I own,
    Fair maiden Marjorie."

"What is the dreary tale to tell,
    O toiler of the sea?"
"I cast my net into the waves,
    Sweet maiden Marjorie.

jow: stroke, clang.   *geid:* gave.

"I cast my net into the tide
  Before I made for home:
Too heavy for my hands to raise,
  I drew it through the foam."

"What saw you that you look so pale,
  Sad searcher of the sea?"
"A dead man's body from the deep
  My haul had brought to me!"

"And was he young, and was he fair?"
  "Oh, cruel to behold!
In his white face the joy of life
  Not yet was grown a-cold."

"Oh, pale you are, and full of prayer
  For one who sails the sea."
"Because the dead looked up and spoke,
  Poor maiden Marjorie."

"What said he, that you seem so sad,
  O fisher of the sea?"
(Alack! I know it was my love,
  Who fain would speak to me!)

"He said: 'Beware a woman's mouth—
  A rose that bears a thorn.'"
"Ah, me! these lips shall smile no more
  That gave my lover scorn."

"He said: 'Beware a woman's eyes;
  They pierce you with their death.'"
"Then falling tears shall make them blind
  That robbed my dear of breath."

"He said: 'Beware a woman's hair—
    A serpent's coil of gold.'"
"Then will I shear the cruel locks
    That crushed him in their fold."

"He said: 'Beware a woman's heart
    As you would shun the reef.'"
"So let it break within my breast,
    And perish of my grief."

"He raised his hands; a woman's name
    Thrice bitterly he cried.
My net had parted with the strain;
    He vanished in the tide."

"A woman's name; What name but mine,
    O fisher of the sea?"
"A woman's name, but not your name,
    Poor maiden Marjorie."

QUESTIONS FOR UNDERSTANDING AND APPRECIATION

LORD RANDAL

1. Who are the two characters who carry on the dialogue in this ballad? What is the story that unfolds? What conflict do you imagine lies behind the events in the story?
2. How does this ballad differ in form from most ballads?
3. Trace the "incremental repetition" through the five stanzas. What is the effect of the repetition and of the final variation?

SIR PATRICK SPENCE

1. Notice how swiftly the plot moves: the King's request; the old knight's suggestion; Sir Patrick's first reaction and his later response to the king's request; the tragic climax and the final scene. What decision of Sir Patrick's would have changed the course of events? Why does he decide as he does?
2. What is your opinion of the character of Sir Patrick and of the King?
3. Cite an example of superstition. Point out descriptive details, such as "blude-reid wine."
4. In what respects is the poem a typical old ballad?

LORD ULLIN'S DAUGHTER

1. Explain the reason for the chieftain's haste to elope with his bride. Describe their flight. What details make the tragedy seem very real?
2. Why may this poem be called an imitation ballad? Is the form (rhyme and meter) exactly the same as that of "Sir Patrick Spence"?

THE WRECK OF THE *HESPERUS*

1. Is the father to blame for the tragedy? Explain. Do you feel as sorry for him as for his daughter? What details present the tragedy very realistically?
2. Select descriptive details which present images through the sense of sound, sight, and touch. Give an example of simile, onomatopoeia.
3. Discuss the poem's theme of misplaced confidence.

THE WIFE OF USHER'S WELL

1. State the simple plot in one sentence.
2. Select lines or phrases which indicate the mother's feeling for her sons; lines which show busy activity in the home. Cite an example of suspense, of superstition.
3. Can you suggest an explanation for the last two lines? As in other ballads, the emotions are implied rather than expressed. Do you think that the reasons for the mother's grief and joy are evident without explanation? How can you infer the brothers' regret at leaving home?
4. Scan the first two stanzas and give meter and rhyme scheme.

FAREWELL TO BARN AND STACK AND TREE

1. Write a one-sentence summary of the plot. To whom is the poem addressed? Why is the speaker leaving? Name the objects mentioned in the last stanza. How does the picture in this stanza make you feel? What wish has the speaker for Terence?
2. Explain why this poem is a good example of an imitation ballad.
3. As an extra assignment, use your imagination to fill in the missing details which will more fully explain the plot, and write a short dialogue between the two brothers.

JOHNNIE ARMSTRONG

1. State briefly the incidents leading to the tragedy. What is learned of the character of Johnnie Armstrong and of the king? What indication is there that Johnnie's death will be avenged?

2. Cite an example of bravery, of pathos, of treachery.
3. Suggested topic for an imaginative theme: Young Johnnie Seeks Revenge.

ROBIN HOOD'S DEATH AND BURIAL

1. What was the direct cause of Robin Hood's death? Is there any explanation of the motive for his cousin's action? What is Little John's suggestion and Robin's reply?
2. Based on your previous knowledge of Robin Hood and on this poem, discuss his character.

THE BALLAD OF THE HARP-WEAVER

1. How does the poet succeed in making the plot believable in spite of its magical note? State the plot briefly.
2. On occasion the poet adds a fifth line to a stanza. What effect does this have? Do you find any instances of alliteration? If so, where?
3. What happens to the mother at the close of the poem? How is she described?

JESSE JAMES

1. Look up the meaning of *myth*, and explain why the author probably used the subtitle, "An American Myth." The second subtitle, "A Design in Black and Yellow," refers to inexpensive weekly publications of sensational stories, similar in quality to today's comic books. What idea does the author seem to convey with this subtitle?
2. What qualities are attributed to Jesse James in the poem? Does the poet idealize Jesse James? Explain the reference: "Jesse James was a Hercules."
3. Shakespeare said:

"The evil that men do lives after them;
The good is oft interred with their bones."

Does this quotation apply to Jesse James? Is it generally applicable to people in everyday life?

BINNORIE

1. Could this poem be made into a successful play? What human emotions are blended in this poem which are often portrayed in drama?
2. Quote lines which give the older sister's motive for envying the younger; which indicate the social position of the sisters; which give the knight's attitude toward the sisters.
3. What part does the harp play in the plot? How was it made? Why is the last line a strong ending?

BARBARA ALLEN

1. This ballad was referred to by Samuel Pepys in his *Diary* for January 2, 1666, and it continues to be a favorite of folk singers today. How do you account for its continued popularity?
2. The various versions of the ballad have different titles, such as "Bonny Barbara Allen," and "Barbara Allen's Cruelty." Do you think Barbara should be described as *bonny* or as *cruel*?
3. Do you think Barbara's attitude toward Sir John was justified? Did she love him? What aroused her conscience to feel regret? Is the conclusion too abrupt?

A BALLAD OF MARJORIE

1. Would you like to know more about Marjorie's story? Why does the ending surprise Marjorie as well as the reader? How do you think she reacted to the fisherman's account of her lover's death?
2. What four qualities does the fisherman refer to in his account of the dead man's last words? Identify the figure of speech in these comparisons. What poetic device is exemplified in the words *maiden Marjorie*?

COMPARATIVE STUDY

1. Summarize the similarities and differences between the old ballads and those written by known authors. Select one poem of each type and point out the similarities.

2. "Sir Patrick Spence" and "The Wreck of the *Hesperus*" have striking similarities; for example, note these lines:

   "Up and spak an eldern knicht"

   and

   "Then up and spoke an old sailor."

   Find other similarities in individual lines, and also in the story and the structure of the poems. With which characters do you sympathize more? Which do you consider the more artistic of the two poems? Why?

3. "The Wreck of the *Hesperus*" and "Lord Ullin's Daughter" are based on similar tragic events. How are the fathers of the two girls involved in the tragedies? Which poem has the greater element of suspense? of pathos?

4. Point out comparisons between "The Wife of Usher's Well" and "Farewell to Barn and Stack and Tree," with respect to the mothers' losses, to the boys' departures. In which poem is there a greater element of suspense? Which has more descriptive details and a more clearly defined plot?

5. What are the similarities and differences in the plots and the characters of the poems about the three outlaws—Johnnie Armstrong, Robin Hood, and Jesse James? Notice that Benét's ballad makes the character come alive through realistic descriptive phrases; cite several examples.

6. Do you prefer the imitation ballads, "A Ballad of Marjorie" and "The Ballad of the Harp-Weaver," to "Binnorie" and "Barbara Allen"? Explain your choices. How do the imitation ballads differ from the older ones? Does one present a clearer picture of the characters?

7. Are "The Ballad of the Harp-Weaver" and "A Ballad of Marjorie" good examples of the imitation ballad? Why?

Character portraits

■ CHARACTER PORTRAITS

■ Literature has many values for you. Primarily, it offers pleasure and enlarges the scope of your own life by presenting new dimensions beyond your personal experience. One of the chief values of literature is its portrayal of human nature. Though many narrative poems are short and compact, they often present portraits of the characters in the stories. In some of the poems the stories are merely suggested and the characters not sharply outlined; in others, the action overshadows the characters, and you are given only quick snapshots of them.

The poems included in this section of the book present clear-cut portraits of fictitious and historical characters. Some of these characters you will admire; a few you will pity; and others may give you inspiration. Acquaintance with them can widen and deepen your knowledge of human nature and give you a better understanding of other people and of yourself. Through insight into the thoughts, feelings, and motives of the characters, you can gain a more sympathetic approach to the problems of people in real life and a greater appreciation of their accomplishments.

These poems are arranged so that there are many bases for comparison and contrast among the characters. Discussion about their problems and achievements can provide interesting, worthwhile class activities.

MAUD MULLER

John Greenleaf Whittier

Maud Muller on a summer's day
Raked the meadow sweet with hay.

Beneath her torn hat glowed the wealth
Of simple beauty and rustic health.

Singing, she wrought, and her merry glee
The mock-bird echoed from his tree.

But when she glanced to the far-off town,
White from its hill-slope looking down,

The sweet song died, and a vague unrest
And a nameless longing filled her breast,

A wish, that she hardly dared to own,
For something better than she had known.

The Judge rode slowly down the lane,
Smoothing his horse's chestnut mane.

He drew his bridle in the shade
Of the apple-trees, to greet the maid,

And asked a draught from the spring that flowed
Through the meadow across the road.

She stooped where the cool spring bubbled up,
And filled for him her small tin cup,

And blushed as she gave it, looking down
On her feet so bare and her tattered gown.

"Thanks!" said the Judge; "a sweeter draught
From a fairer hand was never quaffed."

He spoke of the grass and flowers and trees,
Of the singing birds and the humming bees;

Then talked of the haying, and wondered whether
The cloud in the west would bring foul weather.

And Maud forgot her brier-torn gown,
And her graceful ankles bare and brown;

And listened, while a pleased surprise
Looked from her long-lashed hazel eyes.

At last, like one who for delay
Seeks a vain excuse, he rode away.

Maud Muller looked and sighed: "Ah me!
That I the Judge's bride might be!

"He would dress me up in silks so fine,
And praise and toast me at his wine.

"My father should wear a broadcloth coat;
My brother should sail a painted boat.

"I'd dress my mother so grand and gay,
And the baby should have a new toy each day.

"And I'd feed the hungry and clothe the poor,
And all should bless me who left our door."

The Judge looked back as he climbed the hill,
And saw Maud Muller standing still.

"A form more fair, a face more sweet
Ne'er hath it been my lot to meet.

"And her modest answer and graceful air
Show her wise and good as she is fair.

"Would she were mine, and I today,
Like her, a harvester of hay:

"No doubtful balance of rights and wrongs,
Nor weary lawyers with endless tongues,

"But low of cattle and song of birds,
And health and quiet and loving words."

But he thought of his sisters proud and cold
And his mother vain of her rank and gold.

So, closing his heart, the Judge rode on,
And Maud was left in the field alone.

But the lawyers smiled that afternoon,
When he hummed in court an old love-tune;

And the young girl mused beside the well
Till the rain on the unraked clover fell.

He wedded a wife of richest dower,
Who lived for fashion as he for power.

Yet oft, in his marble hearth's bright glow,
He watched a picture come and go;

And sweet Maud Muller's hazel eyes
Looked out in their innocent surprise.

Oft, when the wine in his glass was red,
He longed for the wayside well instead;

And closed his eyes on his garnished rooms
To dream of meadows and clover-blooms.

And the proud man sighed, with a secret pain,
"Ah, that I were free again!

"Free as when I rode that day,
Where the barefoot maiden raked her hay."

She wedded a man unlearned and poor,
And many children played round her door.

But care and sorrow, and childbirth pain,
Left their traces on heart and brain.

And oft, when the summer sun shone hot
On the new-mown hay in the meadow lot,

And she heard the little spring brook fall
Over the roadside, through the wall,

In the shade of the apple-tree again
She saw a rider draw his rein.

And, gazing down with timid grace,
She felt his pleased eyes read her face.

Sometimes her narrow kitchen walls
Stretched away into stately halls;

The weary wheel to a spinnet turned,
The tallow candle an astral burned,

And for him who sat by the chimney lug,
Dozing and grumbling o'er pipe and mug,

A manly form at her side she saw,
And joy was duty and love was law.

Then she took up her burden of life again,
Saying only, "It might have been."

Alas for maiden, alas for Judge,
For rich repiner and household drudge.

God pity them both! and pity us all,
Who vainly the dreams of youth recall.

For of all sad words of tongue or pen,
The saddest are these: "It might have been!"

Ah, well! for us all some sweet hope lies
Deeply buried from human eyes;

And, in the hereafter, angels may
Roll the stone from its grave away!

CERELLE

Margaret Bell Houston

There was a score of likely girls
Around the prairieside,
But I went down to Galveston
And brought me home a bride.

A score or more of handsome girls,
Of proper age and size,
But the pale girls of Galveston
Have sea-shine in their eyes.

As pale as any orange flower,
Cerelle. The gold-white sands
Were like her hair, and drifting shells,
White fairy shells, her hands.

I think she liked my silver spurs,
A-clinking in the sun.
She'd never seen a cowboy till
I rode to Galveston.

She'd never known the chaparral,
Nor smell of saddle leather,
Nor seen a round-up or a ranch,
Till we rode back together.

Shall I forget my mother's eyes?
"Is this the wife you need?
Is this the way to bring me rest
From forty men to feed?"

chaparral: stiff, thorny shrubs growing in the desert.

Cerelle—I think she did her best
All year. She'd lots to learn.
Dishes would slip from out her hands
And break. The bread would burn.

And she would steal away at times
And wander off to me.
And when the wind was in the south
She'd say, "I smell the sea!"

She changed. The white and gold grew dull
As when a soft flame dies,
And yet she kept until the last
The sea-shine in her eyes.

.   .   .   .   .

There are (I make a husband's boast)
No stronger arms than Ann's.
She has a quip for all the boys,
And sings among the pans.

At last my mother takes her rest.
And that's how things should be.
But when the wind is in the south
There is no rest for me.

THE IMPULSE

Robert Frost

It was too lonely for her there,
    And too wild,
And since there were but two of them,
    And no child,

And work was little in the house,
    She was free,
And followed where he furrowed field,
    Or felled tree.

She rested on a log and tossed
    The fresh chips,
With a song only to herself
    On her lips.

And once she went to break a bough
    Of black alder.
She strayed so far she scarcely heard
    When he called her—

And didn't answer—didn't speak—
    Or return.
She stood, and then she ran and hid
    In the fern.

He never found her, though he looked
    Everywhere,
And he asked at her mother's house
    Was she there.

Sudden and swift and light as that
   The ties gave,
And he learned of finalities
   Besides the grave.

MY LAST DUCHESS

Robert Browning

That's my last Duchess painted on the wall,
Looking as if she were alive. I call
That piece a wonder, now: Frà Pandolf's hands
Worked busily a day, and there she stands.
Will 't please you sit and look at her? I said
"Frà Pandolf" by design, for never read
Strangers like you that pictured countenance,
The depth and passion of its earnest glance,
But to myself they turned (since none puts by
The curtain I have drawn for you, but I)
And seemed as they would ask me, if they durst,
How such a glance came there; so, not the first
Are you to turn and ask thus. Sir, 't was not
Her husband's presence only, called that spot
Of joy into the Duchess' cheek: perhaps
Frà Pandolf chanced to say, "Her mantle laps
Over my lady's wrist too much," or "Paint
Must never hope to reproduce the faint
Half-flush that dies along her throat:" such stuff
Was courtesy, she thought, and cause enough
For calling up that spot of joy. She had
A heart—how shall I say?—too soon made glad,

Too easily impressed; she liked whate'er
She looked on, and her looks went everywhere.
Sir, 't was all one! My favor at her breast,
The dropping of the daylight in the West,
The bough of cherries some officious fool
Broke in the orchard for her, the white mule
She rode with round the terrace—all and each
Would draw from her alike the approving speech,
Or blush, at least. She thanked men,—good! but thanked
Somehow—I know not how—as if she ranked
My gift of a nine-hundred-years-old name
With anybody's gift. Who'd stoop to blame
This sort of trifling? Even had you skill
In speech—(which I have not)—to make your will
Quite clear to such an one, and say, "Just this
Or that in you disgusts me; here you miss,
Or there exceed the mark"—and if she let
Herself be lessoned so, nor plainly set
Her wits to yours, forsooth, and made excuse,
—E'en then would be some stooping; and I choose
Never to stoop. Oh sir, she smiled, no doubt,
Whene'er I passed her; but who passed without
Much the same smile? This grew; I gave commands;
Then all smiles stopped together. There she stands
As if alive. Will 't please you rise? We'll meet
The company below, then. I repeat,
The Count your master's known munificence
Is ample warrant that no just pretence
Of mine for dowry will be disallowed;
Though his fair daughter's self, as I avowed
At starting, is my object. Nay, we'll go
Together down, sir. Notice Neptune, though,
Taming a sea-horse, thought a rarity,
Which Claus of Innsbruck cast in bronze for me!

ULYSSES

Alfred, Lord Tennyson

This famous poem has been included because the character and the narrative details referred to by Ulysses are familiar to many students who have read the *Iliad* or the *Odyssey*.

It little profits that an idle king,
By this still heart, among these barren crags,
Match'd with an agèd wife, I mete and dole
Unequal laws unto a savage race,
That hoard, and sleep, and feed, and know not me.
I cannot rest from travel: I will drink
Life to the lees all times I have enjoy'd
Greatly, have suffer'd greatly, both with those
That loved me, and alone; on shore, and when
Thro' scudding drifts the rainy Hyades
Vext the dim sea; I am become a name;
For always roaming with a hungry heart
Much have I seen and known; cities of men,
And manners, climates, councils, governments,
Myself not least, but honour'd of them all;
And drunk delight of battle with my peers,
Far on the ringing plains of windy Troy.
I am a part of all that I have met.
Yet all experience is an arch where-thro'
Gleams that untravell'd world, whose margin fades
Forever and forever when I move.
How dull it is to pause, to make an end,
To rust unburnish'd, not to shine in use!
As tho' to breathe were life. Life piled on life

Hyades: a constellation in the sky.
Troy: ancient city in Asia Minor, where the Trojan War was fought.

Were all too little, and of one to me
Little remains: but every hour is saved
From that eternal silence, something more,
A bringer of new things; and vile it were
For some three suns to store and hoard myself,
And this grey spirit yearning in desire
To follow knowledge like a sinking star,
Beyond the utmost bound of human thought.
 This is my son, mine own Telemachus,
To whom I leave the sceptre and the isle—
Well-loved of me, discerning to fulfil
This labour, by slow prudence to make mild
A rugged people, and thro' soft degrees
Subdue them to the useful and the good.
Most blameless is he, centred in the sphere .
Of common duties, decent not to fail
In offices of tenderness, and pay
Meet adoration to my household gods,
When I am gone. He works his work, I mine.
 There lies the port; the vessel puffs her sail:
There gloom the dark broad seas. My mariners,
Souls that have toil'd, and wrought, and thought with me—
That ever with a frolic welcome took
The thunder and the sunshine, and opposed
Free hearts, free foreheads—you and I are old;
Old age hath yet his honour and his toil;
Death closes all: but something ere the end,
Some work of noble note, may yet be done,
Not unbecoming men that strove with Gods.
The lights begin to twinkle from the rocks:
The long day wanes: the slow moon climbs: the deep
Moans round with many voices. Come, my friends,
'Tis not too late to seek a newer world.

Push off, and sitting well in order smite
The sounding furrows; for my purpose holds
To sail beyond the sunset, and the baths
Of all the western stars, until I die.
It may be that the gulfs will wash us down:
It may be we shall touch the Happy Isles,
And see the great Achilles, whom we knew.
Tho' much is taken, much abides; and tho'
We are not now that strength which in old days
Moved earth and heaven; that which we are, we are;
One equal temper of heroic hearts,
Made weak by time and fate, but strong in will
To strive, to seek, to find, and not to yield.

MINIVER CHEEVY

Edwin Arlington Robinson

Miniver Cheevy, child of scorn,
    Grew lean while he assailed the seasons;
He wept that he was ever born,
    And he had reasons.

Miniver loved the days of old
    When swords were bright and steeds were prancing;
The vision of a warrior bold
    Would set him dancing.

Miniver sighed for what was not,
    And dreamed, and rested from his labors;

He dreamed of Thebes and Camelot,
    And Priam's neighbors.

Miniver mourned the ripe renown
    That made so many a name so fragrant;
He mourned Romance, now on the town,
    And Art, a vagrant.

Miniver loved the Medici,
    Albeit he had never seen one;
He would have sinned incessantly
    Could he have been one.

Miniver cursed the commonplace
    And eyed a khaki suit with loathing;
He missed the medieval grace
    Of iron clothing.

Miniver scorned the gold he sought,
    But sore annoyed was he without it;
Miniver thought, and thought, and thought,
    And thought about it.

Miniver Cheevy, born too late,
    Scratched his head and kept on thinking;
Miniver coughed, and called it fate,
    And kept on drinking.

Thebes: city-state of ancient Greece.
Camelot: city where King Arthur had his Court.
Priam: king of ancient Troy.
Medici: powerful ruling family of Florence, Italy, in the 14th, 15th, and
    16th centuries.

RICHARD CORY

Edwin Arlington Robinson

Whenever Richard Cory went downtown,
    We people on the pavement looked at him:
He was a gentleman from sole to crown,
    Clean favored, and imperially slim.

And he was always quietly arrayed,
    And he was always human when he talked;
But still he fluttered pulses when he said,
    "Good morning," and he glittered when he walked.

And he was rich—yes, richer than a king,
    And admirably schooled in every grace:
In fine, we thought that he was everything
    To make us wish that we were in his place.

So on we worked, and waited for the light,
    And went without the meat, and cursed the bread;
And Richard Cory, one calm summer night,
    Went home and put a bullet through his head.

OLD GRAY SQUIRREL

Alfred Noyes

A great while ago, there was a schoolboy.
He lived in a cottage by the sea.
And the very first thing he could remember
Was the rigging of the schooners by the quay.

He could watch them, when he woke, from his window,
With the tall cranes hoisting out the freight.
And he used to think of shipping as a sea cook,
And sailing to the Golden Gate.

For he used to buy the yellow penny dreadfuls,
And read them where he fished for conger eels,
And listened to the lapping of the water,
The green and oily water round the keels.

There were trawlers with their shark-mouthed flatfish,
And red nets hanging out to dry,
And the skate the skipper kept because he liked 'em,
And landsmen never knew the fish to fry.

There were brigantines with timber out of Norroway,
Oozing with the syrups of the pine.
There were rusty dusty schooners out of Sunderland,
And the ships of the Blue Cross Line.

And to tumble down a hatch into the cabin
Was better than the best of broken rules;
For the smell of 'em was like a Christmas dinner,
And the feel of 'em was like a box of tools.

yellow penny dreadfuls: sensational stories in cheap editions.
Sunderland: northeast England.

And, before he went to sleep in the evening,
The very last thing that he could see
Was the sailormen a-dancing in the moonlight
By the capstan that stood upon the quay.

He is perched upon a high stool in London.
The Golden Gate is very far away.
They caught him, and they caged him, like a squirrel.
He is totting up accounts, and going gray.

He will never, never, never, sail to 'Frisco.
But the very last thing that he will see
Will be sailormen a-dancing in the sunrise
By the capstan that stands upon the quay. . . .

To the tune of an old concertina,
By the capstan that stands upon the quay.

THE BALLAD OF WILLIAM SYCAMORE

Stephen Vincent Benét

My father, he was a mountaineer,
His fist was a knotty hammer;
He was quick on his feet as a running deer,
And he spoke with a Yankee stammer.

My mother, she was merry and brave,
And so she came to her labor,
With a tall green fir for her doctor grave
And a stream for her comforting neighbor.

And some are wrapped in the linen fine,
And some like a godling's scion;
But I was cradled on twigs of pine
In the skin of a mountain lion.

And some remember a white, starched lap
And a ewer with silver handles;
But I remember a coonskin cap
And the smell of bayberry candles.

The cabin logs, with the bark still rough,
And my mother who laughed at trifles,
And the tall, lank visitors, brown as snuff,
With their long, straight squirrel-rifles.

I can hear them dance, like a foggy song,
Through the deepest one of my slumbers,
The fiddle squeaking the boots along
And my father calling the numbers.

The quick feet shaking the puncheon floor,
And the fiddle squealing and squealing,
Till the dried herbs rattled above the door
And the dust went up to the ceiling.

There are children lucky from dawn till dusk,
But never a child so lucky!
For I cut my teeth on "Money Musk"
In the Bloody Ground of Kentucky!

When I grew tall as the Indian corn,
My father had little to lend me,

puncheon: split logs, with the flat surface smoothed.
"Money Musk": A folk dance, or folk music for dancing.

But he gave me his great, old powder-horn
And his woodsman's skill to befriend me.

With a leather shirt to cover my back,
And a redskin nose to unravel
Each forest sign, I carried my pack
As far as a scout could travel.

Till I lost my boyhood and found my wife,
A girl like a Salem clipper!
A woman straight as a hunting knife
With eyes as bright as the Dipper!

We cleared our camp where the buffalo feed,
Unheard-of streams were our flagons;
And I sowed my sons like the apple seed
On the trail of the Western wagons.

They were right, tight boys, never sulky or slow,
A fruitful, a goodly muster.
The eldest died at the Alamo.
The youngest fell with Custer.

The letter that told it burned my hand.
Yet we smiled and said, "So be it!"
But I could not live when they fenced the land,
For it broke my heart to see it.

I saddled a red, unbroken colt
And rode him into the day there;
And he threw me down like a thunderbolt
And rolled on me as I lay there.

The hunter's whistle hummed in my ear
As the city-men tried to move me,
And I died in my boots like a pioneer
With the whole wide sky above me.

Now I lie in the heart of the fat, black soil,
Like the seed of a prairie-thistle;
It has washed my bones with honey and oil
And picked them clean as a whistle.

And my youth returns, like the rains of Spring,
And my sons, like the wild-geese flying;
And I lie and hear the meadow-lark sing
And have much content in my dying.

Go play with the towns you have built of blocks,
The towns where you would have bound me!
I sleep in my earth like a tired fox,
And my buffalo have found me.

A FARMER REMEMBERS LINCOLN

Witter Bynner

"Lincoln?—
Well, I was in the old Second Maine,
The first regiment in Washington from the Pine Tree State.
Of course I didn't get the butt of the clip;
We was there for guardin' Washington—
We was all green.

Second Maine: an army regiment from Maine, the Pine Tree State.
the butt of the clip: the full force of the war.

"I ain't never ben to but one theater in my life—
I didn't know how to behave.
I ain't never ben since.
I can see as plain as my hat the box where he sat in
When he was shot.
I can tell you, sir, that was a panic
When we found our President was in the shape he was in!
Never saw a soldier in the world but what liked him.

"Yes, sir. His looks was kind o' hard to forget.
He was a spare man,
An old farmer.
Everything was all right, you know,
But he wa'n't a smooth-appearin' man at all—
Not in no ways;
Thin-faced, long-necked,
And a swellin' kind of a thick lip like.

"And he was a jolly old fellow—always cheerful;
He wa'n't so high but the boys could talk to him their own
        ways.
While I was servin' at the hospital
He'd come in and say, 'You look nice in here,'
Praise us up, you know.
And he'd bend over and talk to the boys—
And he'd talk so good to 'em—so close—
That's why I call him a farmer.
I don't mean that everything about him wa'n't all right, you
        understand,
It's just—well, I was a farmer—
And he was my neighbor, anybody's neighbor.

"I guess even you young folks would 'a' liked him."

POCAHONTAS

William Makepeace Thackeray

Wearied arm and broken sword
　Wage in vain the desperate fight;
Round him press a countless horde,
　He is but a single knight.
Hark! a cry of triumph shrill
　Through the wilderness resounds,
　As, with twenty bleeding wounds,
Sinks the warrior, fighting still.

Now they heap the funeral pyre,
　And the torch of death they light;
Ah! 't is hard to die by fire!
　Who will shield the captive knight?
Round the stake with fiendish cry
　Wheel and dance the savage crowd,
　Cold the victim's mien and proud,
And his breast is bared to die.

Who will shield the fearless heart?
　Who avert the murderous blade?
From the throng with sudden start
　See, there springs an Indian maid.
Quick she stands before the knight:
　"Loose the chain, unbind the ring!
　I am daughter of the king,
And I claim the Indian right!"

Dauntlessly aside she flings
　Lifted axe and thirsty knife,

Fondly to his heart she clings,
    And her bosom guards his life!
In the woods of Powhatan,
    Still 't is told by Indian fires
    How a daughter of their sires
Saved a captive Englishman.

BARBARA FRIETCHIE

John Greenleaf Whittier

Up from the meadows rich with corn,
Clear in the cool September morn,

The clustered spires of Frederick stand
Green-walled by the hills of Maryland.

Round about them orchards sweep,
Apple and peach tree fruited deep,

Fair as the garden of the Lord
To the eyes of the famished rebel horde,

On that pleasant morn of the early fall
When Lee marched over the mountain-wall;

Over the mountains winding down,
Horse and foot, into Frederick town.

Forty flags with their silver stars,
Forty flags with their crimson bars,

Flapped in the morning wind: the sun
Of noon looked down, and saw not one.

Up rose old Barbara Frietchie then,
Bowed with her fourscore years and ten;

Bravest of all in Frederick town,
She took up the flag the men hauled down;

In her attic window the staff she set,
To show that one heart was loyal yet.

Up the street came the rebel tread,
Stonewall Jackson riding ahead.

Under his slouched hat left and right
He glanced; the old flag met his sight.

"Halt!"—the dust-brown ranks stood fast.
"Fire!"—out blazed the rifle-blast.

It shivered the window, pane and sash;
It rent the banner with seam and gash.

Quick, as it fell, from the broken staff
Dame Barbara snatched the silken scarf.

She leaned far out on the window-sill,
And shook it forth with a royal will.

"Shoot, if you must, this old gray head,
But spare your country's flag," she said.

A shade of sadness, a blush of shame,
Over the face of the leader came;

The nobler nature within him stirred
To life at that woman's deed and word;

"Who touches a hair of yon gray head
Dies like a dog! March on!" he said.

All day long through Frederick street
Sounded the tread of marching feet:

All day long that free flag tost
Over the heads of the rebel host.

Ever its torn folds rose and fell
On the loyal winds that loved it well;

And through the hill-gaps sunset light
Shone over it with a warm good-night.

Barbara Frietchie's work is o'er,
And the Rebel rides on his raids no more.

Honor to her! and let a tear
Fall, for her sake, on Stonewall's bier.

Over Barbara Frietchie's grave,
Flag of Freedom and Union, wave!

Peace and order and beauty draw
Round thy symbol of light and law;

And ever the stars above look down
On thy stars below in Frederick town!

THE LEGEND OF THE BRONX

Arthur Guiterman

Legends have sometimes a basis of truth. Surely it is true that up to very recent times the frogs of the Bronx, loving that fair and peaceful borough, have lifted up their hearts—and throats—in grateful song.

With sword and Bible, brood and dame,
Across the seas from Denmark came
Stout Jonas Bronck. He roved among
The wooded vales of Ah-qua-hung.
"Good sooth! on every hand," quoth he,
"Are pleasant lands and fair to see;
But which were best to plow and till
And meetest both for manse and mill?"

"Bronck! Bronck! Bronck!"
Called the frogs from the reeds of the river;
"Bronck! Bronck! Bronck!"
From the marshes and pools of the stream.
"Here let your journeyings cease;
Blest of the Bounteous Giver,
Yours is the Valley of Peace,
Here is the home of your dream."

"Oho!" laughed Jonas Bronck; "I ween
These pop-eyed elves in bottle-green
Do call my name to show the spot
Predestined!—Here I cast my lot!"
So there he reared his dwelling-place
And built a mill, with wheel and race.
And even now, beneath the hill
When summer nights are fair and still:

"Bronck! Bronck! Bronck!"
Rise the cadenced batrachian numbers;
"Bronck! Bronck! Bronck!"
Chant a myriad chorister gnomes;
"High on the shadowy crest
Under the hemlock he slumbers.
Here in the region of rest;
Come to our Valley of Homes!"

COLUMBUS

Joaquin Miller

Behind him lay the gray Azores,
   Behind the Gates of Hercules;
Before him not the ghost of shores,
   Before him only shoreless seas.
The good mate said: "Now must we pray,
   For lo! the very stars are gone.
Brave Adm'r'l, speak, what shall I say?"
   "Why, say: 'Sail on! sail on! and on!'"

"My men grow mutinous day by day;
   My men grow ghastly wan and weak."
The stout mate thought of home; a spray
   Of salt wave washed his swarthy cheek.
"What shall I say, brave Adm'r'l, say,
   If we sight naught but seas at dawn?"
"Why, you shall say at break of day:
   'Sail on! sail on! sail on! and on!'"

Gates of Hercules: Strait of Gibraltar.

They sailed and sailed, as winds might blow,
    Until at last the blanched mate said:
"Why, now not even God would know
    Should I and all my men fall dead.
These very winds forget their way,
    For God from these dread seas is gone.
Now speak, brave Adm'r'l, speak and say"—
    He said: "Sail on! sail on! and on!"

They sailed. They sailed. Then spake the mate:
    "This mad sea shows his teeth tonight.
He curls his lip, he lies in wait,
    With lifted teeth, as if to bite!
Brave Adm'r'l, say but one good word:
    What shall we do when hope is gone?"
The words leapt like a leaping sword:
    "Sail on! sail on! sail on! and on!"

Then, pale and worn, he kept his deck,
    And peered through darkness. Ah, that night
Of all dark nights! And then a speck—
    A light! A light! A light! A light!
It grew, a starlit flag unfurled!
    It grew to be Time's burst of dawn.
He gained a world; he gave that world
    Its grandest lesson: "On! sail on!"

KITTYHAWK

William Rose Benét

On December 17, 1903, Orville and Wilbur Wright made successful airplane flights from Kill-Devil Hill, four miles south of Kittyhawk, North Carolina. The poem is a tribute to the character and accomplishments of these pioneers of the air.

Where are the winds most strong and steady?
Kill-Devil Hill. And the Wrights are ready.

Lonely sandhills of Kittyhawk
Where a white shaft raises its marble stalk

Whisper into a wind that sings
Now that all skies are adrone with wings!

The century's turn, and the sons of a preacher,
Each to become an era's teacher

Of wings that lift and drift and glide
On the yet uncharted airy tide—

Ball-bearings, sprockets, bicycle-chains—
First it was wheels, but next it was 'planes.

Though those that peeped at their work in the shed
Jeeringly gestured, "Wheels in the head!"

But their veins and brains were quick with fevers
For surfaces lifted and warped by levers

To give them the balance of birds in flight:
The sky had challenged the Brothers Wright.

They forced the air through the first wind tunnel
And marked its effect on wings in a funnel.

In a thousand trials one summer through
They lay on their glider's wing and flew

Grasshopper flights, and hardly that;
Skimming a dune, then falling flat,

But learning, learning resistance, drift,
Curve and surface and weight and lift.

And next for an engine they laid their plans—
Like a soap-box topped with tomato-cans!

But now it is easy enough to mock its
Opposed propellers cross-chained on sprockets

Or to say, "How clumsy, and bound to fail!"
As a car ran their plane down a mono-rail

And Wilbur crashed from pointing too high
At the gray seductive height of sky;

For Kittyhawk in that cold December
Is the place all men of the air remember.

Eight days before Christmas, Nineteen Three,
The impossible marvel came to be

In spite of all visions that seemed insane,
A gas-engine-driven aeroplane!

Orville Wright, with mechanic knack,
Lifted the queer bird off the track

And for forty yards it climbed and dipped,
Struck on a sandhill, shuddered and tipped,

But later that day, with Wilbur in it,
Stayed in the air for nearly a minute

And proved it was clearly on the cards
To fly two hundred and sixty yards!

Then the paw of the wind, in a sudden spite,
Obliterated the thing from sight,

Or almost that, for a catlike gust
Rolled it to ruin in the dust . . .

But the Dayton men were inured to chance . . .
Five years later their plane, in France,

Steered through the blue by Wilbur Wright,
Bore off all laurels for distance flight . . .

Medals and honors and trophies fade,
But the pioneers and the thing they made,
The faith and patience often betrayed,

The careful work and the cheerful will,
The sleepless dream and unwearied skill,
Heighten the sky over Kill-Devil Hill!

ALABAMA EARTH

(At Booker Washington's Grave)

Langston Hughes

Deep in Alabama earth
His buried body lies—
But higher than the singing pines
And taller than the skies
And out of Alabama earth
To all the world there goes
The truth a simple heart has held
And the strength a strong hand knows,
While over Alabama earth
These words are gently spoken:
Serve—and hate will die unborn.
Love—and chains are broken.

THE MICROSCOPE

Maxine W. Kumin

Anton Leeuwenhoek was Dutch.
He sold pincushions, cloth, and such.
The waiting townsfolk fumed and fussed
As Anton's dry goods gathered dust.

He worked, instead of tending store,
At grinding special lenses for
A microscope. Some of the things
He looked at were:
                mosquitoes' wings,
the hairs of sheep, the legs of lice,
the skin of people, dogs, and mice;
ox eyes, spiders' spinning gear,
fishes' scales, a little smear
of his own blood,
             and best of all,
the unknown, busy, very small
bugs that swim and bump and hop
inside a simple water drop.

Impossible! Most Dutchmen said.
This Anton's crazy in the head.
We ought to ship him off to Spain.
He says he's seen a housefly's brain.
He says the water that we drink
Is full of bugs. He's mad, we think!

They called him *domkop*, which means dope.
That's how we got the microscope.

QUESTIONS FOR UNDERSTANDING AND APPRECIATION

MAUD MULLER

1. What were the Judge's reasons for deciding against marriage to Maud? Do you think he and Maud would have been happier if they had married? Do you sympathize with them?
2. Why do you think this simple poem has survived through the years? Quote a stanza which expresses an observation about life. Do you agree with this statement? Can you apply it to an experience in your own life?
3. The Judge's mother and sister are briefly, but effectively, characterized in one short stanza. Find the stanza and tell what you learn from it.

CERELLE

1. Can you picture Cerelle from the poet's description? What qualities had attracted her husband? Why was his mother disappointed with his choice of wife? Why was Cerelle unsuited to her duties as a cowboy's wife? Do you sympathize with her?
2. Explain the last two stanzas. Cite examples of figures of speech.

THE IMPULSE

1. Are you sympathetic toward this lonely woman? If you would like to know more about her life, obtain a copy of Robert Frost's poems and read "The Hill Wife," which is a series of five short poems about her, including "The Impulse."

MY LAST DUCHESS

1. This poem is one of Robert Browning's famous dramatic monologues. The setting is in Italy during the Renaissance,

and the speaker, a Duke who, through his monologue, presents two portraits—one of his last Duchess, and the other of himself. To whom is the Duke speaking? What characteristics are portrayed in the Duke's description of his wife? What qualities does he reveal in himself? Why was he displeased with the Duchess?

2. What happened to the Duchess? At what point in the poem is this revealed to you?

3. What is the Duke's attitude toward art? Is he typical of other Renaissance gentlemen in this respect? In what arrangement is he interested at the moment? What significance do you find in the mention of the bronze statue in the last lines of the poem?

4. In what verse form is the poem written? Note that the end words usually run over into the next lines. Does this make the poem seem more like natural conversation?

ULYSSES

1. How would you characterize Ulysses? Proud? Ruthless? Vain? Ambitious? Sad? Could any of these characteristics be combined? Which ones? Explain.

2. What fears does Ulysses express? What is his final consolation?

3. Explain the meaning of:

I am part of all that I have met.
Yet all experience is an arch where-thro'
Gleams that untravelled world, whose margin fades
Forever and forever when I move.

4. In what metrical form is this poem written?

MINIVER CHEEVY

1. What kind of wishful thinking does Miniver pursue? Is his discontent his own fault? Do you pity him?

2. Are there Miniver Cheevys living today? Why are they not likely to make a great contribution to the world?

3. Explain lines 11–12, 15–16, 23–26.

RICHARD CORY

1. Name all the possible reasons why Richard Cory should have been content with life. Consider all the specific things his riches could buy for him.
2. What possible reasons could Richard Cory have had for committing suicide? How could his tragedy have been prevented?
3. Why do we ordinary people, who possess few of Richard Cory's advantages, nevertheless cling to life? What is meant by "meat" and "bread" in the last stanza?
4. Compare Richard Cory with Miniver Cheevy and with any other similar character about whom you may have read.

OLD GRAY SQUIRREL

1. What influenced the boy's dreaming about distant places? Describe the interesting sights and experiences he visualizes. Why is San Francisco a city which excites the imagination?
2. Compare the boy's adult life with his daydreams. Explain the title.
3. In what way is this man's life typical of the lives of so many people?

THE BALLAD OF WILLIAM SYCAMORE

1. Pick out all the details in this poem that appeal to your senses of sight, hearing, smell, touch.
2. Find examples of similes, metaphors. Are the pictures they call forth in your mind vivid? Do they stir you in any way?
3. *Hyperbole* is a poetic device that uses exaggeration to produce a dramatic or comic effect. Point out the instances where this device is used in the poem. Do you find it effective?
4. What physical qualities was it necessary for our pioneers to possess in order to survive? What traits of character made it possible for them to be contented in the face of great hardship?
5. What hardships in the life of the pioneers does this poem reveal? Name all the comforts and conveniences you enjoy

in life that the pioneers had to do without. What pleasures
and accomplishments made the pioneer's life worth living?
6. Quote lines from the poem that reveal the following qualities
of William Sycamore: bravery, love of the outdoors, courage
in the face of personal sorrow, restlessness, contentment, self-
reliance, love of freedom.

A FARMER REMEMBERS LINCOLN

1. This poem is an example of a *dramatic monologue,* a poem
   in which one character speaks and gives an insight into a
   situation or into another person's character and also into his
   own. What qualities of Lincoln's character and appearance
   are portrayed? Which particular trait impresses the farmer?
2. What was the farmer's assignment in the war, and which
   tragic incident does he recall?
3. What effect has the language of the poem in projecting the
   character of Lincoln to the reader? Do you agree with the
   farmer that "You young folks would 'a' liked him"?

POCAHONTAS

1. Do you recall any information you may have read about
   Pocahontas, John Rolfe, or Captain John Smith? If you do
   not, consult a reference book for further understanding of the
   background of the poem. John Smith, whose life Pocahontas
   saved, described her bravery as follows: Pocahontas . . . got
   his head in her arms, and laid her own upon his to save him
   from death." How does the English poet depict this incident?

BARBARA FRIETCHIE

1. Where did Barbara Frietchie live? What was Barbara
   Frietchie's heroic deed and oft-repeated quotation? What
   quality does Stonewall Jackson demonstrate?
2. Do you think this is a great poem? Why has it remained a
   popular one?

THE LEGEND OF THE BRONX

1. Does this poem exhibit a nice sense of fanciful humor, or is it
   merely silly?

2. What is it that the frogs are telling Jonas Bronck? Why does he decide to settle where he does?
3. What well-known "cheer" does the poet allude to? Who are the "myriad chorister gnomes"? Of whom are they speaking in the last stanza?

COLUMBUS

1. How does the character of Columbus as depicted in this poem present a lesson for our country in any kind of crisis?
2. Cite examples of alliteration, simile, metaphor, personification, and of effective repetition.

KITTYHAWK

1. Identify the setting—time and place.
2. How did the interests of the Wright brothers as boys prepare them for success in later life? What quality of character was responsible? Enumerate the difficulties the Wrights encountered.
3. Explain the last six lines. What other air pioneers would you like to have honored in literature?

ALABAMA EARTH

1. What is the message that goes from the grave of Booker T. Washington to all the world? Why is this a very timely message? What were Washington's contributions to his country and the world?
2. What is the subject of the verb *goes* in line 6? What is compared with *higher* and *taller*? Is the figure of speech a simile or a metaphor?

THE MICROSCOPE

1. What is the central thought of the poem? Does the light tone add to or detract from the message?
2. Name other persons with whom Anton Leeuwenhoek can be compared in his contribution to the world.
3. Does this poem reveal at least one quality that a poet and a scientist or inventor must have in common? Why is this quality essential in both?

COMPARATIVE STUDY

1. Apply these words of the English poet, Shelley, to Maud Muller, Cerelle, Ulysses, and the woman in the "Impulse":

   "We look before and after
   And pine for what is not."

2. Explain how wishful thinking affects the lives of Miniver Cheevy and the Old Gray Squirrel.

3. How does "My Last Duchess" differ from the other poems in this section in regard to the characters portrayed? the poetic form? dramatic development and climax?

4. Do "My Last Duchess" and "The Impulse" reveal keen psychological insight into two different kinds of character? If so, in what ways?

5. Both "My Last Duchess" and "Ulysses" employ the same type of metrical line. Name the metrical line, and illustrate the different ways in which the two poets handled it.

6. Name the character trait exemplified in the poems about Pocahontas and Barbara Frietchie. Which poem do you prefer? Which is more effective in its narration of the story?

7. Apply Shakespeare's quotation from *Macbeth* to the characters in "Kittyhawk," "Columbus" and "Ulysses."

   "But screw your courage to the sticking place
   And you'll not fail."

8. In what way does "The Legend of the Bronx" differ from the other character portraits which you have read? How, for example, might Guiterman have written "Columbus"?

9. Compare the characters of Miniver Cheevy and William Sycamore. Why is one unhappy while the other is contented?

10. Reexamine all the character portraits in this group of poems. Which ones do you think give you a deep understanding of the characters portrayed? Which do you think are too broad, too sweeping to be effective analyses of character?

11. Although "Miniver Cheevy" seems to be a more popular and better known poem than "Richard Cory," you may have

other ideas about their relative effectiveness. Which of the two poems do you think is the better character portrait?

12. Why do you think Richard Cory commits suicide while the old gray squirrel goes on plodding through life?

SUGGESTED THEME TOPICS:

Read Robert Frost's "The Road Not Taken" and relate it to one of the characters.

Compare or contrast two of the characters.

Humor and pathos

■ HUMOR AND PATHOS

■ In this section you will read poems which illustrate two contrasting qualities—humor and pathos, both of which are part of daily life. Literature is the expression of man's thoughts, feeling, and actions; and it reflects the sad as well as the happy aspects of life.

Humor in literature is the expression of amusing, comical, or ridiculous incidents or situations; it aims to make the reader laugh, or at least chuckle inwardly. Obviously humor is a vital ingredient of daily life, as is evident from the popularity of comic strips and of humorous television programs and motion pictures. Humor often deals with the inconsistencies and weaknesses of human nature; and in a good-natured way it presents these to the reader. Sometimes humor may be sharp when it aims to ridicule the customs, abuses, and vices of human beings or groups. Such humor is referred to as *satire*.

Pathos in literature is that quality which arouses feelings of pity, sympathy, or tenderness. It appeals to the emotions of the reader in making him share an experience with a character in the story. In "The Wreck of the *Hesperus*" and "Lord

Ullin's Daughter," for example, the reader can experience the tragedies and sympathize with both the fathers and the daughters.

Very often both qualities are found in the same story, especially in the longer works of literature. The poems in this section, however, represent either humor or pathos.

GET UP AND BAR THE DOOR

Anonymous

It fell about the Martinmas time,
    And a gay time it was then,
When our goodwife got puddings to make,
    And she's boiled them in the pan.

The wind so cold blew south and north,
    And blew into the floor;
Quoth our goodman to our goodwife,
    "Get up and bar the door."

"My hand is in my household work,
    Goodman, as ye may see;
And it will not be barred for a hundred years,
    If it's to be barred by me!"

They made a pact between them both,
    They made it firm and sure,
That whosoe'er should speak the first,
    Should rise and bar the door.

Martinmas: St. Martin's Day, November 11.   *quoth:* said, spoke.

Then by there came two gentlemen,
   At twelve o'clock at night,
And they could see neither house nor hall,
   Nor coal nor candlelight.

"Now whether is this a rich man's house,
   Or whether is it a poor?"
But never a word would one of them speak,
   For barring of the door.

The guests they ate the white puddings,
   And then they ate the black;
Tho' much the goodwife thought to herself,
   Yet never a word she spake.

Then said one stranger to the other,
   "Here, man, take ye my knife;
Do ye take off the old man's beard,
   And I'll kiss the goodwife."

"There's no hot water to scrape it off,
   And what shall we do then?"
"Then why not use the pudding broth,
   That boils into the pan?"

O up then started our goodman,
   An angry man was he;
"Will ye kiss my wife before my eyes!
   And with pudding broth scald me!"

Then up and started our goodwife,
   Gave three skips on the floor:
"Goodman, you've spoken the foremost word.
   Get up and bar the door!"

THE WELL OF ST. KEYNE

Robert Southey

A well there is in the West country,
  And a clearer one never was seen;
There is not a wife in the West country
  But has heard of the well of St. Keyne.

An oak and an elm tree stand beside,
  And behind does an ash-tree grow,
And a willow from the bank above
  Droops to the water below.

A traveler came to the well of St. Keyne;
  Pleasant it was to his eye,
For from cock-crow he had been traveling,
  And there was not a cloud in the sky.

He drank of the water so cool and clear,
  For thirsty and hot was he,
And he sat down upon the bank,
  Under the willow tree.

There came a man from the neighboring town
  At the well to fill his pail,
On the well-side he rested it,
  And bade the stranger hail.

"Now art thou a bachelor, stranger?" quoth he,
  "For an if thou hast a wife,
The happiest draught thou hast drank this day
  That ever thou didst in thy life.

"Or has your good woman, if one you have,
    In Cornwall ever been?
For an if she have, I'll venture my life
    She has drank of the well of St. Keyne."

"I have left a good woman who never was here,"
    The stranger he made reply;
"But that my draught should be better for that,
    I pray you answer me why."

"St. Keyne," quoth the countryman, "many a time
    Drank of this crystal well,
And before the angel summoned her
    She laid on the water a spell.

"If the husband of this gifted well
    Shall drink before his wife,
A happy man thenceforth is he,
    For he shall be master for life.

"But if the wife should drink of it first,
    Heaven help the husband then!"
The stranger stooped to the well of St. Keyne,
    And drank of the waters again.

"You drank of the well I warrant, betimes?"
    He to the countryman said.
But the countryman smiled as the stranger spake,
    And sheepishly shook his head.

"I hastened, as soon as the wedding was done,
    And left my wife in the porch.
But i' faith, she had been wiser than me,
    For she took a bottle to church."

THE BALLAD OF THE OYSTERMAN

Oliver Wendell Holmes

It was a tall young oysterman lived by the riverside,
His shop was just upon the bank, his boat was on the tide;
The daughter of a fisherman, that was so straight and slim,
Lived over on the other bank, right opposite to him.

It was the pensive oysterman that saw a lovely maid,
Upon a moonlight evening, a-sitting in the shade;
He saw her wave a handkerchief, as much as if to say,
"I'm wide awake, young oysterman, and all the folks away."

Then up arose the oysterman, and to himself said he,
"I guess I'll leave the skiff at home, for fear that folks should
      see;
I read it in the story book, that, for to kiss his dear,
Leander swam the Hellespont—and I will swim this here."

And he has leaped into the waves, and crossed the shining
      stream,
And he has clambered up the bank, all in the moonlight
      gleam;
Oh, there are kisses sweet as dew, and words as soft as rain—
But they have heard her father's steps, and in he leaps again!

Out spoke the ancient fisherman: "Oh, what was that, my
      daughter?"
" 'Twas nothing but a pebble, sir, I threw into the water."

Leander swam the Hellespont: The legend is that Leander loved Hero
   so deeply that he swam across the Hellespont (the Dardanelles) every
   night to see her. When he drowned in a stormy sea one night, Hero,
   too, drowned herself.

"And what is that, pray tell me, love, that paddles off so
  fast?"
"It's nothing but a porpoise, sir, that's been a-swimming
  past."

Out spoke the ancient fisherman: "Now bring me my
  harpoon!
I'll get into my fishing boat, and fix the fellow soon."
Down fell the pretty innocent, as falls a snow-white lamb;
Her hair drooped round her pallid cheeks, like seaweed on
  a clam.

Alas for those two loving ones! she waked not from her
  swound,
And he was taken with the cramp, and in the waves was
  drowned;
But Fate has metamorphosed them, in pity of their woe,
And now they keep an oyster shop for mermaids down below.

THE DEACON'S MASTERPIECE

Or, The Wonderful "One-Hoss Shay"

Oliver Wendell Holmes

A Logical Story

Have you heard of the wonderful one-hoss shay,
That was built in such a logical way
It ran a hundred years to a day,
And then, of a sudden, it—ah, but stay,
I'll tell you what happened without delay,

metamorphosed: transformed.

Scaring the parson into fits,
Frightening people out of their wits,—
Have you ever heard of that, I say?

Seventeen hundred and fifty-five,
Georgius Secundus was then alive,—
Snuffy old drone from the German hive;
That was the year when Lisbon-town
Saw the earth open and gulp her down,
And Braddock's army was done so brown,
Left without a scalp to its crown.
It was on the terrible Earthquake-day
That the Deacon finished the one-hoss shay.

Now in building of chaises, I tell you what,
There is always *somewhere* a weakest spot,—
In hub, tire, felloe, in spring or thill,
In panel, or crossbar, or floor, or sill,
In screw, bolt, thoroughbrace,—lurking still,
Find it somewhere you must and will,—
Above or below, within or without,—
And that's the reason, beyond a doubt,
That a chaise *breaks down*, but doesn't *wear out.*

But the Deacon swore, (as Deacons do,
With an "I dew vum," or an "I tell *yeou,*")
He would build one shay to beat the taown
'N' the keounty 'n' all the kentry raoun';
It should be so built that it couldn't break daown;
"Fur," said the Deacon, "t's mighty plain

felloe: the outer rim of a wheel.
thill: the thills are the two shafts between which the horse is hitched.

That the weakes' place mus' stan' the strain;
'N' the way t' fix it, uz I maintain,
   Is only jist
T' make that place uz strong uz the rest."

So the Deacon inquired of the village folk
Where he could find the strongest oak,
That couldn't be split nor bent nor broke,—
That was for spokes and floor and sills;
He sent for lancewood to make the thills;
The crossbars were ash, from the straightest trees,
The panels of white-wood, that cuts like cheese,
But lasts like iron for things like these;
The hubs of logs from the "Settler's ellum,"—
Last of its timber,—they couldn't sell 'em,
Never an axe had seen their chips
And the wedges flew from between their lips,
Their blunt ends frizzled like celery-tips;
Step and prop-iron, bolt and screw,
Spring, tire, axle, and linchpin too,
Steel of the finest, bright and blue;
Throughbrace bison-skin, thick and wide;
Boot, top, dasher, from tough old hide
Found in the pit when the tanner died.
That was the way he "put her through."—
"There!" said the Deacon, "naow she'll dew!"
Do! I tell you, I rather guess
She was a wonder, and nothing less!
Colts grew horses, beards turned gray,
Deacon and deaconess dropped away,
Children and grandchildren—where were they?
But there stood the stout old one-hoss shay
As fresh as on Lisbon-earthquake-day!

EIGHTEEN HUNDRED;—it came and found
The Deacon's masterpiece strong and sound.
Eighteen hundred increased by ten;—
"Hahnsum kerridge" they called it then.
Eighteen hundred and twenty came;—
Running as usual, much the same.
Thirty and forty at last arrive,
And then came fifty, and FIFTY-FIVE.

Little of all we value here
Wakes on the morn of its hundredth year
Without both feeling and looking queer
In fact, there's nothing that keeps its youth,
So far as I know, but a tree and truth.
(This is a moral that runs at large;
Take it.—You're welcome.—No extra charge.)

FIRST OF NOVEMBER,—the Earthquake-day
There are traces of age in the one-hoss shay,
A general flavor of mild decay,
But nothing local, as one may say.
There couldn't be,—for the Deacon's art
Had made it so like in every part
That there wasn't a chance for one to start.
For the wheels were just as strong as the thills.
And the floor was just as strong as the sills
And the panels just as strong as the floor,
And the whipple-tree neither less nor more,
And the back-crossbar as strong as the fore,
And spring and axle and hub *encore.*
And yet, *as a whole,* it is past a doubt,
In another hour it will be *worn out!*

First of November, 'Fifty-five!
This morning the parson takes a drive.

Now, small boys, get out of the way!
Here comes the wonderful one-hoss shay,
Drawn by a rat-tailed, ewe-necked bay.
"Huddup!" said the parson.—Off went they.
The parson was working his Sunday's text,—
Had got to *fifthly*, and stopped perplexed
At what the—Moses—was coming next.
All at once the horse stood still,
Close by the meet'n'-house on the hill.
—First a shiver, and then a thrill,
Then something decidedly like a spill,—
And the parson was sitting upon a rock,
At half past nine by the meet'n'-house clock,—
Just the hour of the Earthquake shock!
—What do you think the parson found,
When he got up and stared around?
The poor old chaise in a heap or mound,
As if it had been to the mill and ground!
How it went to pieces all at once,—
All at once, and nothing first,—
Just as bubbles do when they burst.

End of the wonderful one-hoss shay.
Logic is logic. That's all I say.

THE WALRUS AND THE CARPENTER

Lewis Carroll

The sun was shining on the sea,
    Shining with all his might:
He did his very best to make
    The billows smooth and bright—

And this was odd, because it was
   The middle of the night.

The moon was shining sulkily,
   Because she thought the sun
Had got no business to be there
   After the day was done—
"It's very rude of him," she said,
   "To come and spoil the fun!"

The sea was wet as wet could be,
   The sands were dry as dry.
You could not see a cloud, because
   No cloud was in the sky:
No birds were flying overhead—
   There were no birds to fly.

The Walrus and the Carpenter
   Were walking close at hand:
They wept like anything to see
   Such quantities of sand.
"If this were only cleared away,"
   They said, "it *would* be grand!"

"If seven maids with seven mops
   Swept it for half a year,
Do you suppose," the Walrus said,
   "That they could get it clear?"
"I doubt it," said the Carpenter,
   And shed a bitter tear.

"O Oysters, come and walk with us!"
   The Walrus did beseech.
"A pleasant talk, a pleasant walk,

Along the briny beach:
We cannot do with more than four,
  To give a hand to each."

The eldest Oyster looked at him,
  But never a word he said:
The eldest Oyster winked his eye,
  And shook his heavy head—
Meaning to say he did not choose
  To leave the oyster-bed.

But four young Oysters hurried up,
  All eager for the treat:
Their coats were brushed, their faces washed,
  Their shoes were clean and neat—
And this was odd, because, you know,
  They hadn't any feet.

Four other Oysters followed them,
  And yet another four;
And thick and fast they came at last,
  And more, and more, and more—
All hopping through the frothy waves,
  And scrambling to the shore.

The Walrus and the Carpenter
  Walked on a mile or so,
And then they rested on a rock
  Conveniently low:
And all the little Oysters stood
  And waited in a row.

"The time has come," the Walrus said,
  "To talk of many things:

Of shoes and ships and sealing-wax,
  Of cabbages and kings;
And why the sea is boiling hot—
  And whether pigs have wings."

"But wait a bit," the Oysters cried,
  "Before we have our chat;
For some of us are out of breath,
  And all of us are fat!"
"No hurry!" said the Carpenter.
  They thanked him much for that.

"A loaf of bread," the Walrus said,
  "Is what we chiefly need:
Pepper and vinegar besides
  Are very good indeed—
Now, if you're ready, Oysters dear,
  We can begin to feed."

"But not on us!" the Oysters cried,
  Turning a little blue.
"After such kindness, that would be
  A dismal thing to do!"
"The night is fine," the Walrus said
  "Do you admire the view?

"It was so kind of you to come!
  And you are very nice!"
The Carpenter said nothing but
  "Cut us another slice.
I wish you were not quite so deaf—
  I've had to ask you twice!"

"It seems a shame," the Walrus said,
  "To play them such a trick,
After we've brought them out so far,
  And made them trot so quick!'
The Carpenter said nothing but
  "The butter's spread too thick!"

"I weep for you," the Walrus said:
  "I deeply sympathize."
With sobs and tears he sorted out
  Those of the largest size,
Holding his pocket-handkerchief
  Before his streaming eyes.

"O Oysters," said the Carpenter,
  "You've had a pleasant run!
Shall we be trotting home again?"
  But answer came there none—
And this was scarcely odd, because
  They'd eaten every one.

ON THE DEATH OF A FAVORITE CAT, DROWNED IN A TUB OF GOLD FISHES

Thomas Gray

'Twas on a lofty vase's side,
Where China's gayest art had dyed
  The azure flowers that blow;

Demurest of the tabby kind,
The pensive Selima, reclined,
   Gaz'd on the lake below.

Her conscious tail her joy declared;
The fair round face, the snowy beard,
   The velvet of her paws,
Her coat, that with the tortoise vies,
Her ears of jet, and emerald eyes,
   She saw, and purred applause.

Still had she gazed, but 'midst the tide
Two angel forms were seen to glide,
   The Genii of the stream;
Their scaly armor's Tyrian hue
Through richest purple to the view
   Betrayed a golden gleam.

The hapless Nymph with wonder saw;
A whisker first and then a claw,
   With many an ardent wish,
She stretched, in vain, to reach the prize.
What female heart can gold despise?
   What Cat's averse to fish?

Presumptuous Maid! with looks intent
Again she stretched, again she bent,
   Nor knew the gulf between.
(Malignant Fate sat by, and smiled.)
The slippery verge her feet beguiled,
   She tumbled headlong in.

Genii: presiding spirits.
Tyrian hue: a bluish-red dye made originally in ancient Tyre.

Eight times emerging from the flood
She mewed to every watery god,
   Some speedy aid to send.
No Dolphin came, no Nereid stirred:
Nor cruel Tom nor Susan heard,—
   A Favorite has no friend!

From hence, ye Beauties, undeceived,
Know, one false step is ne'er retrieved,
   And be with caution bold,
Not all that tempts your wandering eyes
And heedless hearts, is lawful prize;
   Nor all that glisters, gold.

MATILDA

Who Told Lies, and Was Burned to Death

Hilaire Belloc

Matilda told such Dreadful Lies,
It made one Gasp and Stretch one's Eyes;
Her Aunt, who, from her Earliest Youth,
Had kept a Strict Regard for Truth,
Attempted to believe Matilda:
The effort very nearly killed her,
And would have done so, had not She
Discovered this Infirmity.
For once, towards the Close of Day,
Matilda, growing tired of play,
And finding she was left alone,

Nereid: a sea nymph.

Went tiptoe to the Telephone
And summoned the Immediate Aid
Of London's Noble Fire-Brigade.
Within an hour the Gallant Band
Were pouring in on every hand,
From Putney, Hackney Downs, and Bow
With Courage high and Hearts a-glow
They galloped, roaring through the Town,
"Matilda's House is Burning Down!"
Inspired by British Cheers and Loud
Proceeding from the Frenzied Crowd,
They ran their Ladders through a Score
Of windows on the Ball Room Floor;
And took Peculiar Pains to Souse
The Pictures up and down the House,
Until Matilda's Aunt succeeded
In showing them they were not needed;
And even then she had to Pay
To get the Men to go Away!

It happened that a few Weeks later
Her Aunt was off to the Theatre
To see that Interesting Play
The Second Mrs. Tanqueray.
She had refused to take her Niece
To hear this Entertaining Piece:
(A Deprivation Just and Wise
To punish her for Telling Lies.)
That Night a Fire *did* break out—
You should have heard Matilda Shout!
You should have heard her Scream and Bawl,
And throw the window up and call
To People passing in the Street—
(The rapidly increasing Heat

Encouraging her to obtain
Their confidence)—but all In Vain!
For every time She shouted, "Fire!"
They only answered, "Little Liar!"
And therefore when her Aunt returned,
Matilda, and the House, were Burned.

MACAVITY: THE MYSTERY CAT

T. S. Eliot

Macavity's a Mystery Cat: he's called the Hidden Paw—
For he's the master criminal who can defy the Law.
He's the bafflement of Scotland Yard, the Flying Squad's
    despair:
For when they reach the scene of crime—*Macavity's not
    there!*

Macavity, Macavity, there's no one like Macavity,
He's broken every human law, he breaks the law of gravity.
His powers of levitation would make a fakir stare,
And when you reach the scene of crime—*Macavity's not
    there!*
You may seek him in the basement, you may look up in the
    air—
But I tell you once again, *Macavity's not there!*

Macavity's a ginger cat, he's very tall and thin;
You would know him if you saw him, for his eyes **are**
    sunken in.
His brow is deeply lined with thought, his head is highly
    domed;

His coat is dusty from neglect, his whiskers are uncombed.
He sways his head from side to side, with movements like a
    snake;
And when you think he's half asleep, he's always wide awake.

Macavity, Macavity, there's no one like Macavity,
For he's a fiend in feline shape, a monster of depravity.
You may meet him in a by-street, you may see him in the
    square—
But when a crime's discovered, then *Macavity's not there!*

He's outwardly respectable. (They say he cheats at cards.)
And his footprints are not found in any file of Scotland
    Yard's.
And when the larder's looted, or the jewel-case is rifled,
And when the milk is missing, or another Peke's been stifled,
Or when the greenhouse glass is broken, and the trellis past
    repair—
Ay, there's the wonder of the thing! *Macavity's not there!*

And when the Foreign Office find a Treaty's gone astray,
Or the Admiralty lose some plans and drawings by the way,
There may be a scrap of paper in the hall or on the stair—
But it's useless to investigate—*Macavity's not there!*
And when the loss has been disclosed, the Secret Service say:
"It *must* have been Macavity!"—but he's a mile away.
You'll be sure to find him resting, or a-licking of his thumbs,
Or engaged in doing complicated long division sums.

Macavity, Macavity, there's no one like Macavity,
There never was a Cat of such deceitfulness and suavity.
He always has an alibi, and one or two to spare:
At whatever time the deed took place—*MACAVITY
WASN'T THERE!*

And they say that all the Cats whose wicked deeds are
    widely known
(I might mention Mungojerrie, I might mention Griddle-
    bone)
Are nothing more than agents for the Cat who all the time
Just controls the operations: the Napoleon of Crime!

THE DIVERTING HISTORY
OF JOHN GILPIN

William Cowper

John Gilpin was a citizen
    Of credit and renown,
A trainband captain eke was he
    Of famous London town.

John Gilpin's spouse said to her dear,
    "Though wedded we have been
These twice ten tedious years, yet we
    No holiday have seen.

"Tomorrow is our wedding-day,
    And we will then repair
Unto the Bell at Edmonton,
    All in a chaise and pair.

"My sister, and my sister's child,
    Myself, and children three,
Will fill the chaise; so you must ride
    On horseback after we."

He soon replied—"I do admire
  Of womankind but one,
And you are she, my dearest dear,
  Therefore it shall be done.

"I am a linen draper bold,
  As all the world doth know,
And my good friend the calender
  Will lend his horse to go."

Quoth Mrs. Gilpin,—"That's well said;
  And for that wine is dear,
We will be furnished with our own,
  Which is both bright and clear."

John Gilpin kissed his loving wife;
  O'erjoyed was he to find,
That, though on pleasure she was bent,
  She had a frugal mind.

The morning came, the chaise was brought,
  But yet was not allowed
To drive up to the door, lest all
  Should say that she was proud.

So three doors off the chaise was stayed,
  Where they did all get in;
Six precious souls, and all agog
  To dash through thick and thin.

Smack went the whip, round went the wheels,
  Were never folk so glad,
The stones did rattle underneath,
  As if Cheapside were mad.

John Gilpin at his horse's side
    Seized fast the flowing mane,
And he got up, in haste to ride,
    But soon came down again;

For saddletree scarce reached had he,
    His journey to begin,
When, turning round his head, he saw
    Three customers come in.

So down he came; for loss of time,
    Although it grieved him sore,
Yet loss of pence, full well he knew,
    Would trouble him much more.

'T was long before the customers
    Were suited to their mind,
When Betty screaming came down stairs,
    "The wine is left behind!"

"Good lack!" quoth he, "yet bring it me
    My leathern belt likewise,
In which I bear my trusty sword
    When I do exercise."

Now Mistress Gilpin (careful soul!)
    Had two stone bottles found,
To hold the liquor that she loved,
    And keep it safe and sound.

Each bottle had a curling ear,
    Through which the belt he drew,
And hung a bottle on each side
    To make his balance true.

Then over all, that he might be
   Equipped from top to toe,
His long red cloak, well brushed and neat,
   He manfully did throw.

Now see him mounted once again
   Upon his nimble steed,
Full slowly pacing o'er the stones,
   With caution and good heed.

But finding soon a smoother road
   Beneath his well-shod feet,
The snorting beast began to trot,
   Which galled him in his seat.

So "Fair and softly," John he cried,
   But John he cried in vain;
That trot became a gallop soon,
   In spite of curb and rein.

So stooping down, as needs he must
   Who cannot sit upright,
He grasped the mane with both his hands
   And eke with all his might.

His horse, who never in that sort
   Had handled been before,
What thing upon his back had got
   Did wonder more and more.

Away went Gilpin, neck or nought;
   Away went hat and wig;
He little dreamt, when he set out,
   Of running such a rig.

The wind did blow, the cloak did fly,
 Like streamer long and gay,
Till, loop and button failing both,
 At last it flew away.

Then might all people well discern
 The bottles he had slung;
A bottle swinging at each side,
 As hath been said or sung.

The dogs did bark, the children screamed,
 Up flew the windows all;
And every soul cried out, "Well done!"
 As loud as he could bawl.

Away went Gilpin—who but he?
 His fame soon spread around;
"He carries weight!" "He rides a race!"
 " 'T is for a thousand pound!"

And still as fast as he drew near,
 'T was wonderful to view,
How in a trice the turnpike men
 Their gates wide open threw.

And now, as he went bowing down
 His reeking head full low,
The bottles twain behind his back
 Were shattered at a blow.

Down ran the wine into the road,
 Most piteous to be seen,
Which made his horse's flanks to smoke
 As they had basted been.

But still he seemed to carry weight,
  With leathern girdle braced;
For all might see the bottle necks
  Still dangling at his waist.

Thus all through merry Islington,
  These gambols he did play,
Until he came unto the Wash
  Of Edmonton so gay;

And there he threw the Wash about,
  On both sides of the way,
Just like unto a trundling mop,
  Of a wild goose at play.

At Edmonton, his loving wife
  From the balcony spied
Her tender husband, wondering much
  To see how he did ride.

"Stop, stop, John Gilpin!—Here's the house!"
  They all at once did cry;
"The dinner waits, and we are tired."—
  Said Gilpin—"So am I!"

But yet his horse was not a whit
  Inclined to tarry there;
For why?—his owner had a house
  Full ten miles off, at Ware.

So like an arrow swift he flew
  Shot by an archer strong;
So did he fly—which brings me to
  The middle of my song.

Away went Gilpin, out of breath,
    And sore against his will,
Till, at his friend the calender's,
    His horse at last stood still.

The calender, amazed to see
    His neighbor in such trim,
Laid down his pipe, flew to the gate,
    And thus accosted him:—

"What news? what news? your tidings tell;
    Tell me you must and shall—
Say why bareheaded you are come,
    Or why you come at all?"

Now Gilpin had a pleasant wit,
    And loved a timely joke;
And thus unto the calender,
    In merry guise, he spoke:—

"I came because your horse would come;
    And, if I well forbode,
My hat and wig will soon be here,—
    They are upon the road."

The calender, right glad to find
    His friend in merry pin,
Returned him not a single word,
    But to the house went in;

When straight he came with hat and wig;
    A wig that flowed behind,
A hat not much the worse for wear,
    Each comely in its kind.

He held them up, and in his turn,
    Thus showed his ready wit:
"My head is twice as big as yours,
    They therefore needs must fit.

"But let me scrape the dirt away
    That hangs upon your face;
And stop and eat, for well you may
    Be in a hungry case."

Said John,—"It is my wedding day,
    And all the world would stare,
If wife should dine at Edmonton,
    And I should dine at Ware."

So turning to his horse, he said,
    "I am in haste to dine;
'T was for your pleasure you came here,
    You shall go back for mine."

Ah! luckless speech, and bootless boast,
    For which he paid full dear;
For while he spake, a braying ass
    Did sing most loud and clear;

Whereat his horse did snort, as he
    Had heard a lion roar,
And galloped off with all his might,
    As he had done before.

Away went Gilpin, and away
    Went Gilpin's hat and wig;
He lost them sooner than at first,
    For why?—they were too big.

Now Mistress Gilpin, when she saw
　　Her husband posting down
Into the country far away,
　　She pulled out half-a-crown;

And thus unto the youth she said,
　　That drove them to the Bell,
"This shall be yours, when you bring back
　　My husband safe and well."

The youth did ride, and soon did meet
　　John coming back amain;
Whom in a trice he tried to stop
　　By catching at his rein;

But not performing what he meant,
　　And gladly would have done,
The frighted steed he frighted more
　　And made him faster run.

Away went Gilpin, and away
　　Went postboy at his heels,
The postboy's horse right glad to miss
　　The lumbering of the wheels.

Six gentlemen upon the road,
　　Thus seeing Gilpin fly,
With postboy scampering in the rear,
　　They raised the hue and cry:—

"Stop thief! stop thief!—a highwayman!"
　　Not one of them was mute;
And all and each that passed that way
　　Did join in the pursuit.

And now the turnpike-gates again
   Flew open in short space;
The toll-men thinking as before,
   That Gilpin rode a race.

And so he did, and won it too,
   For he got first to town,
Nor stopped till where he had got up
   He did again get down.

Now let us sing, Long live the King,
   And Gilpin, long live he;
And when he next doth ride abroad,
   May I be there to see!

LAZYBONES

Robert P. Tristram Coffin

Of all the Tipsham lazybones
   The Yanceys took the cake,
Only in blueberry time
   Did Mother Yancey bake.

And then it was but six or so
   Pies that had the pip,
And the soggy bottom crust
   Would sink an iron ship.

The Yancey boys went bare of foot
   Till the snowflakes flew,

And you could put in your right eye
   The corn Dan Yancey grew.

They were folks for whom the skies
   Were always low and murky.
They were always on hard-pan
   And poor as old Job's turkey.

One winter when the bay froze up
   From Whaleboat out to Ram,
The Yanceys did not have so much
   As a knuckle-bone of ham.

They sat around their dying stove
   And worried at the weather,
The neighbors went and got a cord
   Of seasoned birch together.

"Here you are, Dan Yancey, this
   Will keep you for a spell."
They left the wood and went back **home**
   Feeling pretty well.

But there was not a sign of smoke
   From the Yancey flue
Going up that afternoon
   On the Winter blue.

And when the dusk was coming on,
   Dan came to Abel Leigh,
"Can't you send one of your boys
   To saw my birch for me?"

BROWN'S DESCENT
OR
THE WILLY-NILLY SLIDE

Robert Frost

Brown lived at such a lofty farm
   That everyone for miles could see
His lantern when he did his chores
   In winter after half-past three.

And many must have seen him make
   His wild descent from there one night,
'Cross lots, 'cross walls, 'cross everything,
   Describing rings of lantern light.

Between the house and barn the gale
   Got him by something he had on
And blew him out on the icy crust
   That cased the world, and he was gone!

Walls were all buried, trees were few;
   He saw no stay unless he stove
A hole in somewhere with his heel.
   But though repeatedly he strove

And stamped and said things to himself,
   And sometimes something seemed to yield,
He gained no foothold, but pursued
   His journey down from field to field.

Sometimes he came with arms outspread
   Like wings revolving in the scene
Upon his longer axis, and
   With no small dignity of mien.

Faster or slower as he chanced,
    Sitting or standing as he chose,
According as he feared to risk
    His neck, or thought to spare his clothes.

He never let the lantern drop.
    And some exclaimed who saw afar
The figures he described with it,
    "I wonder what those signals are

Brown makes at such an hour of night!
    He's celebrating something strange.
I wonder if he's sold his farm,
    Or been made Master of the Grange."

He reeled, he lurched, be bobbed, he checked;
    He fell and made the lantern rattle
(But saved the light from going out.)
    So half-way down he fought the battle,

Incredulous of his own bad luck.
    And then becoming reconciled
To everything, he gave it up
    And came down like a coasting child.

"Well-I-be-" that was all he said,
    As standing in the river road,
He looked back up the slippery slope
    (Two miles it was) to his abode.

Sometimes as an authority
    On motor-cars, I'm asked if I
Should say our stock was petered out,
    And this is my sincere reply:

Yankees are what they always were.
  Don't think Brown ever gave up hope
Of getting home again because
  He couldn't climb that slippery slope;

Or ever thought of standing there
  Until the January thaw
Should take the polish off the crust.
  He bowed with grace to natural law,

And then went round it on his feet,
  After the manner of our stock;
Not much concerned for those to whom,
  At that particular time o'clock,

It must have looked as if the course
  He steered was really straight away
From that which he was headed for—
  Not much concerned for them, I say;

No more so than became a man—
  And politician at odd seasons.
I've kept Brown standing in the cold
  While I invested him with reasons;

But now he snapped his eyes three times;
  Then shook his lantern, saying, "Ile's
'Bout out!" and took the long way home
  By road, a matter of several miles.

LUCY GRAY

William Wordsworth

Oft I had heard of Lucy Gray:
And when I cross'd the wild,
I chanced to see at break of day
The solitary child.

No mate, no comrade Lucy knew;
She dwelt on a wide moor,
The sweetest thing that ever grew
Beside a human door!

You yet may spy the fawn at play,
The hare upon the green;
But the sweet face of Lucy Gray
Will never more be seen.

"Tonight will be a stormy night—
You to the town must go;
And take a lantern, Child, to light
Your mother through the snow."

"That, Father! will I gladly do:
'Tis scarcely afternoon—
The minster-clock has just struck two,
And yonder is the moon!"

At this the father raised his hook,
And snapp'd a faggot-band;
He plied his work;—and Luck took
The lantern in her hand.

Not blither is the mountain roe:
With many a wanton stroke
Her feet disperse the powdery snow,
That rises up like smoke.

The storm came on before its time:
She wander'd up and down;
And many a hill did Lucy climb:
But never reach'd the town.

The wretched parents all that night
Went shouting far and wide;
But there was neither sound nor sight
To serve them for a guide.

At day-break on a hill they stood
That overlook'd the moor;
And thence they saw the bridge of wood
A furlong from their door.

They wept—and, turning homeward, cried
"In heaven we all shall meet!"
—When in the snow the mother spied
The print of Lucy's feet.

Then downwards from the steep hill's edge
They track'd the footmarks small;
And through the broken hawthorn hedge,
And by the long stone-wall:

And then an open field they cross'd:
The marks were still the same;
They track'd them on, nor ever lost;
And to the bridge they came:

They follow'd from the snowy bank
Those footmarks, one by one,
Into the middle of the plank;
And further there were none!

—Yet some maintain that to this day
She is a living child;
That you may see sweet Lucy Gray
Upon the lonesome wild.

O'er rough and smooth she trips along,
And never looks behind;
And sings a solitary song
That whistles in the wind.

BONNIE GEORGE CAMPBELL

Anonymous

High upon Highlands,
   And low upon Tay,
Bonnie George Campbell
   Rode out on a day;
Saddled and bridled,
   And gallant to see:
Home came his good horse,
   But home came not he.

Out ran his old mother,
   Wild with despair;

Tay: a river in Scotland.

Out ran his bonnie bride,
  Tearing her hair.
He rode saddled and bridled,
  With boots to the knee:
Home came his good horse,
  But never came he.

"My meadow lies green,
  And my corn is unshorn,
My barn is unbuilt,
  And my babe is unborn."
He rode saddled and bridled,
  Careless and free:
Safe home came the saddle,
  But never came he.

WE ARE SEVEN

William Wordsworth

—A simple child,
That lightly draws its breath,
And feels its life in every limb,
What should it know of death?

I met a little cottage girl:
She was eight years old, she said;
Her hair was thick with many a curl
That clustered round her head.

She had a rustic, woodland air,
And she was wildly clad:

Her eyes were fair, and very fair;
—Her beauty made me glad.

"Sisters and brothers, little maid,
How many may you be?"
"How many? Seven in all," she said,
And wondering looked at me.

"And where are they? I pray you tell."
She answered, "Seven are we;
And two of us at Conway dwell,
And two are gone to sea.

"Two of us in the church-yard lie,
My sister and my brother;
And, in the church-yard cottage, I
Dwell near them with my mother."

"You say that two at Conway dwell,
And two are gone to sea,
Yet ye are seven!—I pray you tell,
Sweet maid, how this may be."

Then did the little maid reply,
"Seven boys and girls are we;
Two of us in the church-yard lie,
Beneath the church-yard tree."

"You run about, my little maid,
Your limbs they are alive;
If two are in the church-yard laid,
Then ye are only five."

"Their graves are green, they may be seen,"
The little maid replied,

"Twelve steps or more from my mother's door,
And they are side by side.

"My stockings there I often knit,
My kerchief there I hem;
And there upon the ground I sit,
And sing a song to them.

"And often after sunset, sir,
When it is light and fair,
I take my little porringer,
And eat my supper there.

"The first that died was sister Jane;
In bed she moaning lay,
Till God released her of her pain;
And then she went away.

"So in the church-yard she was laid;
And, when the grass was dry,
Together round her grave we played,
My brother John and I.

"And when the ground was white with snow,
And I could run and slide
My brother John was forced to go,
And he lies by her side."

"How many are you, then," said I,
"If they two are in heaven?"
Quick was the little maid's reply,
"O master! we are seven."

"But they are dead; those two are dead!
Their spirits are in heaven!"

'Twas throwing words away; for still
The little maid would have her will,
And said, "Nay, we are seven!"

THE STONE

Wilfrid Wilson Gibson

"And will you cut a stone for him,
To set above his head?
And will you cut a stone for him—
A stone for him?" she said.

Three days before, a splintered rock
Had struck her lover dead—
Had struck him in the quarry dead,
Where, careless of the warning call,
He loitered, while the shot was fired—
A lively stripling, brave and tall,
And sure of all his heart desired . . .
A flash, a shock,
A rumbling fall . . .
And, broken 'neath the broken rock,
A lifeless heap, with face of clay,
And still as any stone he lay,
With eyes that saw the end of all.

I went to break the news to her:
And I could hear my own heart beat
With dread of what my lips might say;
But some poor fool had sped before;
And, flinging wide her father's door,
Had blurted out the news to her,

Had struck her lover dead for her,
Had struck the girl's heart dead in her,
Had struck life, lifeless, at a word,
And dropped it at her feet:
Then hurried on his witless way,
Scarce knowing she had heard.

And when I came, she stood alone—
A woman, turned to stone:
And, though no word at all she said,
I knew that all was known.

Because her heart was dead,
She did not sigh nor moan.
His mother wept:
She could not weep.
Her lover slept:
She could not sleep.
Three days, three nights,
She did not stir:
Three days, three nights,
Were one to her,
Who never closed her eyes
From sunset to sunrise,
From dawn to evenfall—
Her tearless, staring eyes,
That, seeing naught, saw all.

The fourth night when I came from work,
I found her at my door.
"And will you cut a stone for him?"
She said: and spoke no more:
But followed me, as I went in,
And sank upon a chair;
And fixed her grey eyes on my face,

With still, unseeing stare.
And, as she waited patiently,
I could not bear to feel
Those still, grey eyes that followed me,
Those eyes that plucked the heart from me,
Those eyes that sucked the breath from me
And curdled the warm blood in me,
Those eyes that cut me to the bone,
And pierced my marrow like cold steel.

And so I rose, and sought a stone;
And cut it, smooth and square:
And, as I worked, she sat and watched,
Beside me, in her chair.
Night after night, by candlelight,
I cut her lover's name:
Night after night, so still and white,
And like a ghost she came;
And sat beside me, in her chair,
And watched with eyes aflame.
She eyed each stroke,
And hardly stirred:
She never spoke
A single word:
And not a sound or murmur broke
The quiet, save the mallet-stroke.

With still eyes ever on my hands,
With eyes that seemed to burn my hands,
My wincing, overwearied hands,
She watched, with bloodless lips apart,
And silent, indrawn breath:
And every stroke my chisel cut,
Death cut still deeper in her heart:

The two of us were chiseling,
Together, I and death.

And when at length the job was done,
And I had laid the mallet by,
As if, at last, her peace were won,
She breathed his name; and, with a sigh,
Passed slowly through the open door:
And never crossed my threshold more.

Next night I labored late, alone,
To cut her name upon the stone.

COME UP FROM THE FIELDS FATHER

Walt Whitman

Come up from the fields father, here's a letter from our
  Pete,
And come to the front door mother, here's a letter from thy
  dear son.

Lo, 'tis autumn,
Lo, where the trees, deeper green, yellower and redder,
Cool and sweeten Ohio's villages with leaves fluttering in
  the moderate wind,
Where apples ripe in the orchards hang and grapes on the
  trellis'd vines,
(Smell you the smell of the grapes on the vines?
Smell you the buckwheat where the bees were lately buzz-
  ing?)

Above all, lo, the sky so calm, so transparent after the rain,
and with wondrous clouds,
Below too, all calm, all vital and beautiful, and the farm
prospers well.

Down in the fields all prospers well,
But now from the fields come father, come at the daugh-
ter's call,
And come to the entry mother, to the front door come
right away.
Fast as she can she hurries, something ominous, her steps
trembling,
She does not tarry to smooth her hair nor adjust her cap.

Open the envelope quickly,
O this is not our son's writing, yet his name is sign'd,
O a strange hand writes for our dear son, O stricken
mother's soul!

All swims before her eyes, flashes with black, she catches
the main words only,
Sentences broken, *gunshot wound in the breast, cavalry
skirmish, taken to hospital,*
At present low, but will soon be better.

Ah now the single figure to me,
Amid all teeming and wealthy Ohio with all its cities and
farms,
Sickly white in the face and dull in the head, very faint,
By the jamb of a door leans.

Grieve not so, dear mother, (the just-grown daughter speaks
through her sobs,

The little sisters huddle around speechless and dismay'd,)
See, dearest mother, the letter says Pete will soon be better.

Alas poor boy, he will never be better, (nor may-be needs to
    be better that brave and simple soul,)
While they stand at home at the door he is dead already,
The only son is dead.

But the mother needs to be better,
She with thin form presently drest in black,
By day her meals untouch'd, then at night fitfully sleeping,
    often waking,
In the midnight waking, weeping, longing with one deep
    longing,
O that she might withdraw unnoticed, silent from life es-
    cape and withdraw,
To follow, to seek, to be with her dear dead son.

QUESTIONS FOR UNDERSTANDING AND APPRECIATION

Humor

GET UP AND BAR THE DOOR

1. Cite descriptive details which help you to visualize the situation in the home. What is the humor in this domestic incident? Can the cause of the conflict be applied to modern situations? Give an example.
2. Why is the poem classified as an old ballad?

THE WELL OF ST. KEYNE

1. What is the legend of St. Keyne, and how is it interpreted humorously in the poem?

THE BALLAD OF THE OYSTERMAN

1. What is the legend of Hero and Leander, and how is it related to the story in this poem? What humorous twist turns the tragedy into a comedy? Explain the meaning of *metamorphosed* as applied to the characters.
2. Give the meter and rhyme scheme of the poem.

VOCABULARY: pensive, skiff, clamber, pallid, metamorphose.

THE DEACON'S MASTERPIECE

1. What is the meaning of the word "logic"? In what sense is this a "logical tale"?
2. What details of the building of the "masterpiece" are given? Could an antique car be the subject of a similar poem?
3. Explain the last line of the poem.

THE WALRUS AND THE CARPENTER

1. Is this poem an example of pure nonsense? Do you think the author intended a deeper meaning than the surface one?
2. The eleventh stanza is often quoted. Which line was used as the title of a book? Who is the author?
3. Discuss some of the ways by which the poet achieves his comic effects.
4. Refer to the biographical notes to find other facts about the author, and decide whether there are any indications in this poem of his other achievements.

ON THE DEATH OF A FAVORITE CAT
DROWNED IN A TUB OF GOLD FISHES

1. This poem is an example of *mock heroic*; that is, it treats a trivial subject in a grand, serious manner for humorous effect. How does the poet give the impression of a solemn theme? What is the humorous conclusion?
2. What is the expressed moral of the poem? Give another example to illustrate this moral. Discuss the line of the poem: "A favorite has no friends." Do you agree with the statement?
3. In this poem Gray's powers of observation and description are evident. Note the description of the cat and of the vase; also the exact use of adjectives in these expressions: *hapless* nymph, *conscious* tail, *presumptuous* maid, *malignant* fate. Give the meanings of these adjectives.

MATILDA

1. This is a humorous poem which states a moral lesson. Do you feel that the poet means to be taken seriously?
2. What famous Aesop fable does this poem remind you of?
3. The capital letters which the poet uses stress the words to be emphasized. Does the rhythm contribute to the comic effect?

MACAVITY: THE MYSTERY CAT

1. Why is Macavity called the "bafflement of Scotland Yard" and "the Napoleon of Crime"? How does the poet succeed in giving Macavity a distinct personality? Describe the cat's appearance.

2. Explain the meanings of these expressions: *powers of levitation, a friend in feline shape, monster of depravity, deceitfulness and depravity.*

THE DIVERTING HISTORY OF JOHN GILPIN

1. Do you think the humor in the poem is dated, or does it have an appeal which will continue to amuse readers?
2. Why may the poem be called an imitation ballad?

LAZYBONES

1. Why would the Yanceys be an interesting family to write a story about? Is their laziness exaggerated?
2. What is the meaning of the last two lines? Do they form a satisfying climax to the poem?

BROWN'S DESCENT

OR

THE WILLY-NILLY SLIDE

1. Follow the details of Brown's descent. How far did he slide? Note the verbs the poet uses to describe the scenes. What typical qualities of the New England Yankee are mentioned or exemplified in the poem?
2. Explain the meaning of these lines:

"He bowed with grace to natural law"

"Not much concerned for them, I say;
No more so than becomes a man—
And politician at all seasons."

Pathos

LUCY GRAY

1. What kind of child is Lucy? Can you visualize her? Quote examples of pathos. Do the last two stanzas lessen the effect of the tragedy?
2. The author, Wordsworth, believed that poetry could be written in simple language about humble people in everyday life.

How does this poem illustrate his theory? In what ways is "Lucy Gray" like the old ballads?

BONNIE GEORGE CAMPBELL

1. How does this simple story of the Scottish Highlands arouse your sympathy? Do you think it would be more effective if you knew the details of the tragedy?
2. In what ways is this old ballad different from and like the traditional ballad form?

WE ARE SEVEN

1. State briefly what you feel to be the central idea of the poem.
2. How is the child's attitude toward death different from the adult's?
3. How does the poem escape being sentimental? Explain.
4. Has the poet achieved the right tone, the right style for what he has to say?
5. Does childhood hold a certain kind of wisdom which we are apt to lose on growing older? Is this one of the things that the poet is saying?

THE STONE

1. Why is the title very appropriate? What effect is achieved by the short lines? Who is telling the story? State the plot briefly.
2. As in the old ballads, this poem omits many details. What questions would you like to have answered? Would more details have added to the force of the poem or weakened it?
3. Explain the meaning of these lines:

"The two of us were chiseling
Together, I and death."

Quote other effective examples of pathos.
4. Gibson's writings are often realistic, representing life as it is in its more difficult circumstances. In what respect is this poem realistic and also romantic? Are the books and plays of our day generally more realistic or romantic?

COME UP FROM THE FIELDS FATHER

1. How could this Civil War poem apply to any war? Select lines which have universal appeal; others which express very deep feeling.
2. Point out examples of contrast and of very vivid descriptions. What verse form is used? Why does it seem appropriate for the poem?

COMPARATIVE STUDY

1. What characteristic of human nature is the basis of "Get Up and Bar the Door" and "The Well of St. Keyne"? What details date "Get Up and Bar the Door" as an old ballad? What ballad characteristics has "The Well of St. Keyne"?

2. Which poem in this section seems closest in tone to "The Walrus and the Carpenter"? Why? Can you name any other poem in this book with which it may be compared?

3. Which cat, Macavity or Selima, is given the more human qualities? Which poem offers a moral at the end? In what different ways do Gray and Eliot approach their subject?

4. "In Brown's headlong descent there is something madcap and ridiculous and yet determined: a tart New England version of 'John Gilpin's Ride.' " * Compare "Brown's Descent" and "John Gilpin's Ride" as follows: the forms of the poems, plot, character traits, humor. Compare these two poems with "Lazybones." Which of the poems depends primarily upon its conclusion for comic effect?

5. Which poem is for you a more vivid portrayal of grief, "Come Up from the Fields Father" or "Lucy Gray"? Does the simple language in each poem contribute to the dramatic effect?

6. Are there similarities between "The Stone" and "Bonnie George Campbell"? How do they differ? Quote a line from the old ballad which expresses tragedy comparable with that in "The Stone."

7. Did you prefer the poems of humor or of pathos? Why?

8. What contrasts do you find between "We Are Seven" and "The Stone"?

---

* Commentary by Louis Untermeyer in Robert Frost, *The Road Not Taken* (New York: Henry Holt, 1951).

Courage and conflict in war

■ COURAGE AND CONFLICT IN WAR

■ The poems in this section present various aspects of war—the bravery and initiative of individuals in wartime, the response of young people to the call of duty, the love of country which prompts courageous action, and the needless suffering and horror which any war produces. A touch of humor during times of strife and a questioning attitude about the causes and effects of war are other aspects considered by the poets.

These war poems illustrate the power of literature to keep alive the deeds and heroes of the past—an attribute of literature you have already seen in "Paul Revere's Ride," which has preserved the memory of a Revolutionary War patriot, and in Tennyson's poem, which has immortalized the Light Brigade. Simple poems such as these can be more lasting than a statue or a monument. A poem can reach people in distant places, and the characters and deeds it depicts are no longer the possession of only one nation; they become the heritage of the whole world.

DUNKIRK

Robert Nathan

The dramatic rescue at Dunkirk is the scene of this poem. In May, 1940, a large number of British and French troops were stranded on the beaches of Dunkirk, France, with no apparent hope of escape. The English people, cooperating with the Allied forces, procured and manned every kind of small boat; and, under cover of fog, they sailed across the channel to Dunkirk, rescued the men, and ferried them to the big ships off shore. In the poem you will participate in the rescue through the courage of two children.

Will came back from school that day
And he had little to say.
But he stood a long time looking down
To where the gray-green Channel water
Slapped at the foot of the little town,
And to where his boat, the *Sarah P*,
Bobbed at the tide on an even keel,
With her one old sail, patched at the leech,
Furled like a slattern down at heel.

He stood for a while above the beach;
He saw how the wind and current caught her.
He looked a long time out to sea.
There was steady wind and the sky was pale,
And a haze in the east that looked like smoke.

Will went back to the house to dress.
He was half way through when his sister Bess,
Who was near fourteen and younger than he
By just two years, came home from play.
She asked him, "Where are you going, Will?"
He said, "For a good long sail."
"Can I come along?"

"No, Bess," he spoke.
"I may be gone for a night and a day."

Bess looked at him. She kept very still.
She had heard the news of the Flanders rout,
How the English were trapped above Dunkirk,
And the fleet had gone to get them out—
But everyone thought that it wouldn't work.
There was too much fear, there was too much doubt.

She looked at him and he looked at her.
They were English children, born and bred.
He frowned her down, but she wouldn't stir.
She shook her proud young head.
"You'll need a crew," she said.
They raised the sail on the *Sarah P*,
Like a penoncel on a young knight's lance,
And headed *Sarah* out to sea,
To bring their soldiers home from France.

There was no command, there was no set plan,
But six hundred boats went out with them
On the gray-green waters, sailing fast,
River excursion and fisherman,
Tug and schooner and racing M,
And the little boats came following last.

From every harbor and town they went
Who had sailed their craft in the sun and rain,
From the South Downs, from the cliffs of Kent,
From the village street, from the country lane.
There are twenty miles of rolling sea

penoncel: a small, narrow flag or streamer.

From coast to coast, by the seagull's flight,
But the tides were fair and the wind was free,
And they raised Dunkirk by the fall of night.

They raised Dunkirk with its harbor torn
By the blasted stern and the sunken prow;
They had raced for fun on an English tide,
They were English children bred and born,
And whether they lived or whether they died,
They raced for England now.

Bess was as white as the *Sarah's* sail,
She set her teeth and smiled at Will.
He held his course for the smoky veil
Where the harbor narrowed thin and long.
The British ships were firing strong.

He took the *Sarah* into his hands,
He drove her in through fire and death
To the wet men waiting on the sands.
He got his load and he got his breath,
And she came about, and the wind fought her.

He shut his eyes and he tried to pray.
He saw his England where she lay,
The wind's green home, the sea's proud daughter,
Still in the moonlight, dreaming deep,
The English cliffs and the English loam—
He had fourteen men to get away,
And the moon was clear and the night like day
For planes to see where the white sails creep
Over the black water.

He closed his eyes and he prayed for her;
He prayed to the men who had made her great,
Who had built her land of forest and park,
Who had made the seas an English lake;
He prayed for a fog to bring the dark;
He prayed to get home for England's sake.
And the fog came down on the rolling sea,
And covered the ships with English mist.
The diving planes were baffled and blind.

For Nelson was there in the *Victory*,
With his one good eye, and his sullen twist,
And guns were out on *The Golden Hind*,
Their shot flashed over the *Sarah P*.
He could hear them cheer as he came about.

By burning wharves, by battered slips,
Galleon, frigate, and brigantine,
The old dead Captains fought their ships,
And the great dead Admirals led the line.
It was England's night, it was England's sea.

The fog rolled over the harbor key.
Bess held to the stays and conned him out.
And all through the dark, while the *Sarah's* wake
Hissed behind him, and vanished in foam,
There at his side sat Francis Drake,
And held him true and steered him home.

Nelson: great English naval hero.
The Golden Hind: flagship of Sir Francis Drake, first Englishman to sail
    around the world, from 1577 to 1580.

HERVÉ RIEL

Robert Browning

An incident in the Franco-British clash of 1692 is the basis of this poem, which relates the skill of Hervé Riel, a Breton sailor, in piloting many French vessels through the shallows of the Rance River in St. Malo.

On the sea and at the Hogue, sixteen hundred ninety-two,
    Did the English fight the French,—woe to France!
And, the thirty-first of May, helter-skelter through the blue,
Like a crowd of frightened porpoises a shoal of sharks pursue,
    Came crowding ship on ship to St. Malo on the Rance,
With the English fleet in view.

'Twas the squadron that escaped, with the victor in full
    chase;
    First and foremost of the drove, in his great ship, Dam-
      freville;
      Close on him fled, great and small,
      Twenty-two good ships in all;
And they signalled to the place
"Help the winners of a race!
    Give us guidance, give us harbor, take us quick—or, quicker
      still,
    Here's the English can and will!"

Then the pilots of the place put out brisk and leapt on
    board;
    "Why, what hope or chance have ships like these to pass?"
      laughed they:
"Rocks to starboard, rocks to port, all the passage scarred and
    scored,
Shall the *Formidable* here with her twelve and eighty guns
    Think to make the river-mouth by the single narrow way,
Trust to enter where 'tis ticklish for a craft of twenty tons,

And with flow at full beside?
   Now, 'tis slackest ebb of tide.
 Reach the mooring? Rather say,
While rock stands or water runs,
   Not a ship will leave the bay!"

Then was called a council straight.
Brief and bitter the debate:
"Here's the English at our heels; would you have them take
      in tow
All that's left us of the fleet, linked together stern and bow,
For a prize to Plymouth Sound?
Better run the ships aground!"
   (Ended Damfreville his speech.)
"Not a minute more to wait!
   Let the Captains all and each
   Shove ashore, then blow up, burn the vessels on the beach!
France must undergo her fate.

"Give the word!" But no such word
Was ever spoke or heard;
   For up stood, for out stepped, for in struck amid all these
—A Captain? A Lieutenant? A Mate—first, second, third?
      No such man of mark, and meet
      With his betters to compete!
      But a simple Breton sailor pressed by Tourville for the
      fleet,
A poor coasting-pilot he, Hervé Riel the Croisickese.

And, "What mockery or malice have we here?" cries Hervé
      Riel:
   "Are you mad, you Malouins? Are you cowards, fools, or
      rogues?
Talk to me of rocks and shoals, me who took the soundings,
      tell

On my fingers every bank, every shallow, every swell
    'Twixt the offing here and Grève where the river disem-
        bogues?
Are you bought by English gold? Is it love the lying's for?
      Morn and eve, night and day,
      Have I piloted your bay,
Entered free and anchored fast at foot of Solidor.
    Burn the fleet and ruin France? That were worse than fifty
        Hogues!
    Sirs, they know I speak the truth! Sirs, believe me there's
      a way!
Only let me lead the line,
    Have the biggest ship to steer,
    Get this *Formidable* clear,
Make the others follow mine,
And I lead them, most and least, by a passage I know well,
    Right to Solidor past Grève,
      And there lay them safe and sound;
    And if one ship misbehave,
      —Keel so much as grate the ground,
Why, I've nothing but my life,—here's my head!" cries Hervé
    Riel.

Not a minute more to wait.
"Steer us in, then, small and great!
    Take the helm, lead the line, save the squadron!" cried its
      chief.
Captains, give the sailor place!
    He is Admiral, in brief.
Still the north-wind, by God's grace!
See the noble fellow's face
As the big ship, with a bound,
Clears the entry like a hound,
Keeps the passage as its inch of way were the wide seas pro-
    found!

See, safe through shoal and rock,
    How they follow in a flock,
Not a ship that misbehaves, not a keel that grates the ground,
    Not a spar that comes to grief!
The peril, see, is past,
All are harbored to the last,
And just as Hervé Riel hollas "Anchor!"—sure as fate
Up the English come—too late!

So, the storm subsides to calm:
    They see the green trees wave
    On the heights o'erlooking Grève.
Hearts that bled are stanched with balm.
"Just our rapture to enhance,
    Let the English rake the bay,
Gnash their teeth and glare askance
    As they cannonade away!
'Neath rampired Solidor pleasant riding on the Rance!"
How hope succeeds despair on each Captain's countenance!
Out burst all with one accord,
    "This is Paradise for Hell!
      Let France, let France's King
      Thank the man that did the thing!"
What a shout, and all one word,
    "Hervé Riel!"
As he stepped in front once more,
    Not a symptom of surprise
    In the frank blue Breton eyes,
Just the same man as before.

Then said Damfreville, "My friend,
I must speak out at the end,
    Though I find the speaking hard.
Praise is deeper than the lips:
You have saved the King his ships,

You must name your own reward.
'Faith, our sun was near eclipse!
Demand whate'er you will,
France remains your debtor still.
Ask to heart's content and have! or my name's not Dam-
    freville."

Then a beam of fun outbroke
On the bearded mouth that spoke,
As the honest heart laughed through
Those frank eyes of Breton blue:
"Since I needs must say my say,
  Since on board the duty's done,
    And from Malo Roads to Croisic Point, what is it but a
    run?—
Since 'tis ask and have, I may—
  Since the others go ashore—
Come! A good whole holiday!
  Leave to go and see my wife, whom I call the Belle
    Aurore!"
  That he asked and that he got,—nothing more.

Name and deed alike are lost:
Not a pillar nor a post
  In his Croisic keeps alive the feat as it befell;
Not a head in white and black
On a single fishing smack,
In memory of the man but for whom had gone to wrack
  All that France saved from the fight whence England bore
    the bell.
Go to Paris: rank on rank
  Search the heroes flung pell-mell
On the Louvre, face and flank!
  You shall look long enough ere you come to Hervé Riel.

So, for better and for worse,
Hervé Riel, accept my verse!
In my verse, Hervé Riel, do thou once more
Save the squadron, honor France, love thy wife the Belle
    Aurore!

ARNOLD VON WINKELRIED

James Montgomery

This is a poem based on one of the national heroes of Switzerland, who, during the Battle of Sempach (1386), was supposed to have been responsible for driving Austria from his country.

"Make way for Liberty!"—he cried:
Made way for Liberty, and died!

In arms the Austrian phalanx stood,
A living wall, a human wood!
A wall, where every conscious stone
Seemed to its kindred thousands grown;
A rampart all assaults to bear,
Till time to dust their frame should wear;
A wood, like that enchanted grove
In which with fiends Rinaldo strove,
Where every silent tree possessed
A spirit prisoned in its breast,
Which the first stroke of coming strife
Would startle into hideous life;
So dense, so still, the Austrians stood,
A living wall, a human wood!
Impregnable their front appears,
All horrent with projected spears,

Whose polished points before them shine,
From flank to flank, one brilliant line,
Bright as the breakers' splendors run
Along the billows to the sun.

Opposed to these, a hovering band
Contended for their native land:
Peasants, whose new-found strength had broke
From manly necks the ignoble yoke,
And forged their fetters into swords,
On equal terms to fight their lords,
And what insurgent rage had gained
In many a mortal fray maintained;
Marshalled once more at Freedom's call,
They came to conquer or to fall,
Where he who conquered, he who fell,
Was deemed a dead, or living Tell!
Such virtue had that patriot breathed,
So to the soil his soul bequeathed,
That wheresoe'er his arrows flew,
Heroes in his own likeness grew,
And warriors sprang from every sod
Which his awakening footsteps trod.

And now the work of life and death
Hung on the passing of a breath;
The fire of conflict burnt within,
The battle trembled to begin;
Yet, while the Austrians held their ground,
Point for attack was nowhere found,
Where'er the impatient Switzers gazed,
The unbroken line of lances blazed;
That line 't were suicide to meet,
And perish at their tyrants' feet,—

How could they rest within their graves,
And leave their homes the homes of slaves?
Would they not feel their children tread
With clanging chains above their head?

It must not be: this day, this hour,
Annihilates the oppressor's power;
All Switzerland is in the field,
She will not fly, she cannot yield,—
She must not fall; her better fate
Here gives her an immortal date.
Few were the number she could boast;
But every freeman was a host,
And felt as though himself were he
On whose sole arm hung victory.

It did depend on *one* indeed;
Behold him,—Arnold Winkelried!
There sounds not to the trump of fame
The echo of a nobler name.
Unmarked he stood amid the throng,
In rumination deep and long,
Till you might see, with sudden grace,
The very thought come o'er his face,
And by the motion of his form
Anticipate the bursting storm,
And by the uplifting of his brow
Tell where the bolt would strike, and how.

But 't was no sooner thought than done,
The field was in a moment won:—

"Make way for Liberty!" he cried,
Then ran, with arms extended wide,

As if his dearest friend to clasp;
Ten spears he swept within his grasp.

"Make way for Liberty!" he cried;
Their keen points met from side to side;
He bowed amongst them like a tree,
And thus made way for Liberty.

Swift to the breach his comrades fly;
"Make way for Liberty!" they cry,
And through the Austrian phalanx dart,
As rushed the spears through Arnold's heart;
While, instantaneous as his fall,
Rout, ruin, panic, scattered all;
An earthquake could not overthrow
A city with a surer blow,

Thus Switzerland again was free;
Thus death made way for Liberty!

LITTLE GIFFEN

Francis Orray Ticknor

This story of Little Giffen is based upon a true Civil War experience.
Dr. Ticknor, the author of the poem, was the physician who cared for
the wounded boy.

Out of the focal and foremost fire,
Out of the hospital walls as dire;
Smitten of grape-shot and gangrene,
(Eighteenth battle, and *he* sixteen!)

Specter! such as you seldom see,
Little Giffen, of Tennessee!

"Take him and welcome!" the surgeons said;
Little the doctor can help the dead!
So we took him; and brought him where
The balm was sweet in the summer air;
And we laid him down on a wholesome bed,—
Utter Lazarus heel to head!

And we watched the war with abated breath,—
Skeleton Boy against skeleton Death.
Months of torture, how many such?
Weary weeks of the stick and crutch;
And still a glint of the steel-blue eye
Told of a spirit that wouldn't die,

And didn't. Nay, more! in death's despite
The crippled skeleton "learned to write."
"Dear mother," at first, of course; and then
"Dear captain," inquiring about the men.
Captain's answer: "Of eighty-and-five,
Giffen and I are left alive."

Word of gloom from the war, one day;
Johnston pressed at the front, they say.
Little Giffen was up and away;
A tear—his first—as he bade good-bye,
Dimmed the glint of his steel-blue eye.
"I'll write, if spared!" There was news of the fight;
But none of Giffen.—He did not write.

Lazarus: a Biblical character who suffered from a loathsome **disease.**
Johnston: General Johnston, a Confederate commander.

I sometimes fancy that, were I king
Of the princely Knights of the Golden Ring,
With the song of the minstrel in mine ear,
And the tender legend that trembles here,
I'd give the best on his bended knee,
The whitest soul of my chivalry,
For "Little Giffen," of Tennessee.

VITAÏ LAMPADA

Henry Newbolt

There's a breathless hush in the Close tonight—
  Ten to make and the match to win—
A bumping pitch and a blinding light,
  An hour to play and the last man in.
And it's not for the sake of a ribboned coat,
  Or the selfish hope of a season's fame,
But his Captain's hand on his shoulder smote,
  "Play up! play up! and play the game!"

The sand of the desert is sodden red,—
  Red with the wreck of a square that broke;—
The Gatling's jammed and the colonel dead
  And the regiment blind with dust and smoke.
The river of death has brimmed his banks,
  And England's far, and Honor a name,

Vitaï Lampada: the torch of life.
Close: an enclosed athletic field.
bumping pitch: an expression used in the game of cricket. It refers to a
  throw to the batter. Because the ground is uneven, the ball does not
  bounce true.

But the voice of a schoolboy rallies the ranks,
   "Play up! play up! and play the game!"

This is the word that year by year
   While in her place the School is set
Every one of her sons must hear,
   And none that hears it dare forget.
This they all with a joyful mind
   Bear through life like a torch in flame,
And falling fling to the host behind—
   "Play up! play up! and play the game!"

ACHILLES DEATHERIDGE

Edgar Lee Masters

"Your name is Achilles Deatheridge?
How old are you, my boy?"
"I'm sixteen past and I went to the war
From Athens, Illinois."

"Achilles Deatheridge, you have done
A deed of dreadful note."
"It comes of his wearing a battered hat,
And a rusty, wrinkled coat."

"Why, didn't you know how plain he is?
And didn't you ever hear,
He goes through the lines by day or night
Like a sooty cannoneer?

"You must have been half dead for sleep,
For the dawn was growing bright."

"Well, Captain, I had stood right there
Since six o'clock last night.

"I cocked my gun at the swish of the grass,
And how am I at fault
When a dangerous-looking man won't stop
When a sentry hollers halt?

"I cried out halt and he only smiled,
And waved his hand like that.
Why, any Johnnie could wear the coat,
And any fellow the hat.

"I hollered halt again and he stopped,
And lighted a fresh cigar.
I never noticed his shoulder badge,
And I never noticed a star."

"So you arrested him? Well, Achilles,
When you hear the swish of the grass,
If it's General Grant inspecting the lines
Hereafter let him pass."

MARCO BOZZARIS

Fitz-Greene Halleck

At midnight, in his guarded tent,
   The Turk was dreaming of the hour

Marco Bozzaris: a Greek patriot (1790–1823) killed in the War of Independence against Turkey.

When Greece, her knee in suppliance bent,
  Should tremble at his power:
In dreams, through camp and court, he bore
The trophies of a conqueror;
  In dreams his song of triumph heard;
Then wore his monarch's signet ring:
Then pressed that monarch's throne—a king;
As wild his thoughts, and gay of wing,
  As Eden's garden bird.

At midnight, in the forest shades,
  Bozzaris ranged his Suliote band,
True as the steel of their tried blades,
  Heroes in heart and hand.
There had the Persian's thousands stood,
There had the glad earth drunk their blood
  On old Platæa's day;
And now there breathed that haunted air
The sons of sires who conquered there,
With arm to strike and soul to dare,
  As quick, as far as they.

An hour passed on—the Turk awoke;
  That bright dream was his last;
He woke—to hear his sentries shriek,
  "To arms! they come! the Greek! the Greek!"
He woke—to die midst flames and smoke,
And shout, and groan, and sabre-stroke,
  And death-shots falling thick and fast
As lightnings from the mountain cloud;
And heard, with voice as trumpet loud,
  Bozzaris cheer his band:

Suliote: Greek troops from Souli.

"Strike—till the last armed foe expires;
Strike—for your altars and your fires;
Strike—for the green graves of your sires;
    God—and your native land!"

They fought—like brave men, long and well;
    They piled that ground with Moslem slain,
They conquered—but Bozzaris fell,
    Bleeding at every vein.
His few surviving comrades saw
His smile when rang their proud hurrah,
    And the red field was won;
Then saw in death his eyelids close
Calmly, as to a night's repose,
    Like flowers at set of sun.

Come to the bridal-chamber, Death!
    Come to the mother's, when she feels,
For the first time, her first-born's breath;
    Come when the blessed seals
That close the pestilence are broke,
And crowded cities wail its stroke;
Come in consumption's ghastly form,
The earthquake shock, the ocean storm;
Come when the heart beats high and warm
    With banquet song, and dance, and wine;
And thou art terrible—the tear,
The groan, the knell, the pall, the bier,
And all we know, or dream, or fear
    Of agony, are thine.

But to the hero, when his sword
    Has won the battle for the free,
Thy voice sounds like a prophet's word;

And in its hollow tones are heard
   The thanks of millions yet to be.
Come, when his task of fame is wrought—
Come, with her laurel leaf, blood-bought—
   Come in her crowning hour—and then
Thy sunken eye's unearthly light
To him is welcome as the sight
   Of sky and stars to prisoned men;
Thy grasp is welcome as the hand
Of brother in a foreign land;
Thy summons welcome as the cry
That told the Indian isles were nigh
   To the world-seeking Genoese,
When the land wind, from woods of palm,
And orange groves, and fields of balm,
   Blew o'er the Haytian seas.

Bozzaris! with the storied brave
   Greece nurtured in her glory's time,
Rest thee—there is no prouder grave,
   Even in her own proud clime.
She wore no funeral weeds for thee,
   Nor bade the dark hearse wave its plume
Like torn branch from death's leafless tree
In sorrow's pomp and pageantry,
   The heartless luxury of the tomb;
But she remembers thee as one
Long loved and for a season gone;
For thee her poet's lyre is wreathed,
Her marble wrought, her music breathed;
For thee she rings the birthday bells;
Of thee her babe's first lisping tells;

world-seeking Genoese: Columbus.

For thine her evening prayer is said
At palace couch and cottage bed;
Her soldier, closing with the foe,
Gives for thy sake a deadlier blow;
His plighted maiden, when she fears
For him the joy of her young years,
Thinks of thy fate, and checks her tears;

    And she, the mother of thy boys,
Though in her eye and faded cheek
Is read the grief she will not speak,

    The memory of her buried joys,
And even she who gave thee birth,
Will, by their pilgrim-circled hearth,

    Talk of thy doom without a sigh;
For thou art Freedom's now, and Fame's:
One of the few, the immortal names,

    That were not born to die.

FLEURETTE

(The Wounded Canadian Speaks)

1916

Robert W. Service

My leg? It's off at the knee.
Do I miss it? Well, some. You see
I've had it since I was born;
And lately a devilish corn.
(I rather chuckle with glee
To think how I've fooled that corn.)

But I'll hobble around all right.
It isn't that, it's my face.
Oh, I know I'm a hideous sight,
Hardly a thing in place.
Sort of gargoyle, you'd say.
Nurse won't give me a glass,
But I see the folks as they pass
Shudder and turn away;
Turn away in distress . . .
Mirror enough, I guess.
I'm gay! You bet I *am* gay;
But I wasn't a while ago.
If you'd seen me even today,
The darndest picture of woe,
With this Caliban mug of mine,
So ravaged and raw and red,
Turned to the wall—in fine
Wishing that I was dead . . .
What has happened since then,
Since I lay with my face to the wall,
The most despairing of men?
Listen! I'll tell you all.

That *poilu* across the way,
With the shrapnel wound on his head,
Has a sister: she came today
To sit a while by his bed.
All morning I heard him fret:
"Oh, when will she come, Fleurette?"

gargoyle: an ugly or fantastic carved head used as an architectural decoration.
Caliban: a deformed, savage creature in Shakespeare's *Tempest*.
poilu: a French soldier in the ranks.

Then sudden, a joyous cry;
The tripping of little feet;
The softest, tenderest sigh;
A voice so fresh and sweet;

Clear as a silver bell,
Fresh as the morning dews:
"C'est toi, c'est toi, Marcel!
Mon frère, comme je suis heureuse!"

So over the blanket's rim
I raised my terrible face,
And I saw—how I envied him!
A girl of such delicate grace;
Sixteen, all laughter and love;
As gay as a linnet, and yet
As tenderly sweet as a dove;
Half woman, half child—Fleurette.

Then I turned to the wall again.
(I was awfully blue, you see),
And I thought with a bitter pain:
"Such visions are not for me."
So there like a log I lay,
All hidden, I thought, from view,
When sudden I heard her say:
"Ah! Who is that *malheureux?*"
Then briefly I heard him tell
(However he came to know)
How I'd smothered a bomb that fell

"C'est toi, c'est toi, Marcel!: "It's you, it's you. Marcel!"
"Mon frère, comme je suis heureuse!": "My brother, how happy I am!"
malheureux: unhappy man.

Into the trench, and so
None of my men were hit,
Though it busted me up a bit.

Well, I didn't quiver an eye,
And he chattered and there she sat;
And I fancied I heard her sigh—
But I wouldn't just swear to that.
And maybe she wasn't so bright,
Though she talked in a merry strain,
And I closed my eyes ever so tight,
Yet I saw her ever so plain:
Her dear little tilted nose,
Her delicate, dimpled chin,
Her mouth like a budding rose,
And the glistening pearls within;
Her eyes like the violet:
Such a rare little queen—Fleurette.

And at last when she rose to go,
The light was a little dim,
And I ventured to peep, and so
I saw her graceful and slim,
And she kissed him and kissed him, and oh
How I envied and envied him!

So when she was gone I said
In rather a dreary voice
To him of the opposite bed:
"Ah, friend, how you must rejoice!
But me, I'm a thing of dread.
For me nevermore the bliss,
The thrill of a woman's kiss."

Then I stopped, for lo! she was there,
And a great light shone in her eyes.
And me! I could only stare,
I was taken so by surprise,
When gently she bent her head:
"May I kiss you, sergeant?" she said.
Then she kissed my burning lips,
With her mouth like a scented flower,
And I thrilled to the finger-tips,
And I hadn't even the power
To say: "God bless you, dear!
And I felt such a precious tear
Fall on my withered cheek,
And darn it! I couldn't speak.

And so she went sadly away,
And I know that my eyes were wet.
Ah, not to my dying day
Will I forget, forget!
Can you wonder now I am gay?
God bless her, that little Fleurette!

AN INCIDENT OF THE FRENCH CAMP

Robert Browning

You know, we French stormed Ratisbon:
    A mile or so away,
On a little mound, Napoleon
    Stood on our storming-day;
With neck out-thrust, you fancy how,

Legs wide, arms locked behind,
As if to balance the prone brow
   Oppressive with its mind.

Just as perhaps he mused, "My plans
   That soar, to earth may fall,
Let once my army-leader Lannes
   Waver at yonder wall,"—
Out 'twixt the battery-smokes there flew
   A rider, bound on bound
Full-galloping; nor bridle drew
   Until he reached the mound.

Then off there flung in smiling joy,
   And held himself erect
By just his horse's mane, a boy:
   You hardly could suspect—
(So tight he kept his lips compressed,
   Scarce any blood came through)
You looked twice e'er you saw his breast
   Was all but shot in two.

"Well," cried he, "Emperor, by God's grace
   We've got you Ratisbon!
The Marshal's in the market-place,
   And you'll be there anon
To see your flag-bird flap his vans
   Where I, to heart's desire,
Perched him!" The chief's eye flashed; his plans
   Soared up again like fire.

The chief's eye flashed; but presently
   Softened itself, as sheathes
A film the mother eagle's eye

When her bruised eaglet breathes;
"You're wounded!" "Nay," his soldier's pride
   Touched to the quick, he said:
"I'm killed, Sire!" And his chief beside,
   Smiling, the boy fell dead.

THE BATTLE OF BLENHEIM

Robert Southey

The Battle of Blenheim was fought in 1704 during the War of the
Spanish Succession, in which the English and their allies defeated the
French and Bavarian armies at Blenheim, in Bavaria. As you read the
poem, observe the attitudes of the grandfather and the two children
toward the war.

It was a summer evening,
   Old Kaspar's work was done,
And he before his cottage door
   Was sitting in the sun,
And by him sported on the green
His little grandchild Wilhelmine.

She saw her brother Peterkin
   Roll something large and round,
Which he beside the rivulet
   In playing there had found;
He came to ask what he had found,
That was so large, and smooth, and round.

Old Kaspar took it from the boy,
   Who stood expectant by;
And then the old man shook his head,

And with a natural sigh,
" 'Tis some poor fellow's skull," said he,
"Who fell in the great victory.

"I find them in the garden,
    For there's many hereabout;
And often when I go to plow,
    The plowshare turns them out!
For many thousand men," said he,
"Were slain in that great victory."

"Now tell us what 't was all about,"
    Young Peterkin, he cries;
And little Wilhelmine looks up
    With wonder-waiting eyes;
"Now tell us all about the war,
And what they fought each other for."

"It was the English," Kaspar cried,
    "Who put the French to rout;
But what they fought each other for,
    I could not well make out;
But everybody said," quoth he,
"That 'twas a famous victory.

"My father lived at Blenheim then,
    Yon little stream hard by;
They burnt his dwelling to the ground,
    And he was forced to fly;
So with his wife and child he fled,
Nor had he where to rest his head.

"With fire and sword the country round
    Was wasted far and wide,

And many a childing mother then
   And new-born baby died;
But things like that, you know, must be
At every famous victory.

"They say it was a shocking sight
   After the field was won;
For many thousand bodies here
   Lay rotting in the sun;
But things like that, you know, must be
After a famous victory.

"Great praise the Duke of Marlboro' won,
   And our good Prince Eugene."
"Why, 'twas a very wicked thing!"
   Said little Wilhelmine.
"Nay . . . nay . . . my little girl," quoth he,
"It was a famous victory.

"And everybody praised the Duke
   Who this great fight did win."
"But what good came of it at last?"
   Quoth little Peterkin.
"Why, that I cannot tell," said he,
"But 'twas a famous victory."

THE SONG OF THE CAMP

Bayard Taylor

The background of this poem is the Crimean War between England
and her allies, and Russia (1853–56).

"Give us a song!" the soldiers cried,
   The outer trenches guarding,
When the heated guns of the camps allied
   Grew weary of bombarding.

The dark Redan, in silent scoff,
   Lay grim and threatening, under;
And the tawny mound of the Malakoff
   No longer belched its thunder.

There was a pause. A guardsman said:
   "We storm the forts tomorrow;
Sing while we may, another day
   Will bring enough of sorrow."

They lay along the battery's side,
   Below the smoking cannon:
Brave hearts, from Severn and from Clyde,
   And from the banks of Shannon.

They sang of love, and not of fame;
   Forgot was Britain's glory:
Each heart recalled a different name,
   But all sang "Annie Lawrie."

Voice after voice caught up the song,
   Until its tender passion

Rose like an anthem, rich and strong,—
    Their battle-eve confession.

Dear girl, her name he dared not speak,
    But, as the song grew louder,
Something upon the soldier's cheek
    Washed off the stains of powder.

Beyond the darkening ocean burned
    The bloody sunset's embers,
While the Crimean valleys learned
    How English love remembers.

And once again a fire of hell
    Rained on the Russian quarters,
With scream of shot, and burst of shell,
    And bellowing of the mortars!

And Irish Nora's eyes are dim
    For a singer, dumb and gory;
And English Mary mourns for him
    Who sang of "Annie Lawrie."

Sleep, soldiers! still in honored rest
    Your truth and valor wearing:
The bravest are the tenderest,—
    The loving are the daring.

THE BURIAL OF SIR JOHN MOORE AT CORUNNA

Charles Wolfe

The British under Sir John Moore held back the French at Corunna, Spain, in 1809, until the British army were able to embark safely; but their leader was killed.

Not a drum was heard, not a funeral note,
    As his corpse to the rampart we hurried;
Not a soldier discharged his farewell shot
    O'er the grave where our hero we buried.

We buried him darkly at dead of night,
    The sods with our bayonets turning;
By the struggling moonbeam's misty light
    And the lantern dimly burning.

No useless coffin enclosed his breast,
    Not in sheet or in shroud we wound him;
But he lay like a warrior taking his rest,
    With his martial cloak around him.

Few and short were the prayers we said,
    And we spoke not a word of sorrow;
But we steadfastly gazed on the face that was dead,
    And we bitterly thought of the morrow.

We thought, as we hollow'd his narrow bed
    And smoothed down his lonely pillow,
That the foe and the stranger would tread o'er his head,
    And we far away on the billow!

Lightly they'll talk of the spirit that's gone
   And o'er his cold ashes upbraid him,—
But little he'll reck, if they let him sleep on
   In the grave where a Briton has laid him.

But half of our heavy task was done
   When the clock struck the hour for retiring:
And we heard the distant and random gun
   That the foe was sullenly firing.

Slowly and sadly we laid him down,
   From the field of his fame fresh and gory;
We carved not a line, and we raised not a stone,
   But we left him alone with his glory.

THE MAN HE KILLED

Thomas Hardy

  "Had he and I but met
    By some old ancient inn,
We should have sat us down to wet
    Right many a nipperkin!

  "But ranged as infantry,
    And staring face to face,
I shot at him as he at me,
    And killed him in his place.

  "I shot him dead because—
    Because he was my foe,

Just so: my foe of course he was;
  That's clear enough; although

  "He thought he'd 'list, perhaps
  Off-hand like—just as I—
Was out of work—had sold his traps—
  No other reason why.

  "Yes; quaint and curious war is!
  You shoot a fellow down
You'd treat if met where any bar is,
  Or help to half-a-crown."

THE MESSAGES

Wilfrid Wilson Gibson

"I cannot quite remember. . . . There were five
Dropped dead beside me in the trench—and three
Whispered their dying messages to me. . . ."

Back from the trenches, more dead than alive,
Stone-deaf and dazed, and with a broken knee,
He hobbled slowly, muttering vacantly:

"I cannot quite remember. . . . There were five
Dropped dead beside me in the trench, and three
Whispered their dying messages to me. . . .

"Their friends are waiting, wondering how they thrive—
Waiting a word in silence patiently. . . .
But what they said, or who their friends may be

"I cannot quite remember. . . . There were five
Dropped dead beside me in the trench—and three
Whispered their dying messages to me. . . ."

QUESTIONS FOR UNDERSTANDING AND APPRECIATION

DUNKIRK

1. What effect is gained by having a girl and a boy, rather than adults, represent the bravery of the rescue at Dunkirk? How do Bess and Will illustrate the indomitable spirit of their country?
2. In what sense are the great sea fighters of England present at this dramatic event? Name them.
3. Do you find this is an inspirational poem? Why?

HERVÉ RIEL

1. How and why is the feat described in the poem accomplished? Why is Hervé Riel able to accept the challenge offered him? What does he ask for, and what does he receive?
2. Quote lines giving Browning's reason for writing the poem.
3. Compare the achievement of Hervé Riel with an example in everyday life in which a person acquires courage to accomplish a great task through doing his simple daily duties.

ARNOLD VON WINKELRIED

1. In what way does the hero of this poem save his country from the enemy? Can you cite other examples of personal self-sacrifice in battle?
2. Are the events described dramatically convincing or oversimplified?

LITTLE GIFFEN

1. How old is Little Giffen, and in how many battles has he fought? How does he demonstrate that he is a valiant patriot?
2. How does the Doctor help Little Giffen, and what tribute does he pay the boy?

347

VITAÏ LAMPADA

1. What is the subject of this poem? To what is this subject being compared?
2. Does the central thought of the poem have a universal, patriotic, or only sentimental appeal? Does it combine all three?

ACHILLES DEATHERIDGE

1. How old is Achilles? What is his "deed of dreadful note"? Why does he make this mistake?
2. What quality of General Grant's is indicated in the poem?

MARCO BOZZARIS

1. Who were the opponents in the struggle described in this poem?
2. Why was the death of Bozzaris peaceful? Discuss this question in regard to the poem's last three stanzas.
3. Do you find this poem dramatically convincing, or too single-minded in its praise and condemnation? Explain.

FLEURETTE

1. How does the poet express both humor and pathos in the poem? Cite details which present realistic pictures of war, and others which depict tenderness and heroism.
2. Can you visualize Fleurette? Select descriptive similes.

INCIDENT OF THE FRENCH CAMP

1. Does this poem present a glorified portrait of Napoleon or a critical one? Discuss the poem in relation to your previous knowledge of Napoleon.
2. How would you characterize the young soldier?
3. Do you find the poem dramatically effective? Explain.

THE BATTLE OF BLENHEIM

1. Who are the speakers in the poem? What questions do the children ask? How does the grandfather reply? Do you think the differences in attitude toward the war are based on the characters' respective ages? Would ideas of the older and younger generations today follow a similar pattern? Why?

2. This poem may be classed as a *satire*. Which lines are particularly satiric? What criticism of war do you find ironically expressed in the grandfather's final words? Could this apply to all wars?

THE SONG OF THE CAMP

1. Identify two of the countries engaged in this conflict.
2. What quality of human nature is illustrated in the poem?
3. Do you agree completely with the thought expressed in the last stanza? Why would the poem have been more effective without this stanza? Explain.

THE BURIAL OF SIR JOHN MOORE AT CORUNNA

1. What is the attitude of the soldiers toward Sir John? Do they feel sorrow at his death? How would you explain their behavior, and would you describe them as callous or compassionate?
2. Explain the last line in relation to the rest of the poem.

THE MAN HE KILLED

1. What thought troubles the speaker? What is his reflected opinion about his deed in wartime? Why did he feel differently during the war?
2. Do you think that the poem expresses an idea common to soldiers in all wars? What is that idea?

THE MESSAGES

1. Describe the soldier's physical and mental condition. Why is he more concerned about his failing memory than about his physical health?
2. What attitude about war is expressed in the poem?

COMPARATIVE STUDY

1. War is the background of the poems in this section, and in five poems the central characters are young people. What nations are represented by the characters in "Hervé Riel," "Little Giffen," "Dunkirk," "Fleurette," and "Achilles Deatheridge"? Based upon these poems, what general statement about national patriotism in wartime may logically be made?

2. What common quality is portrayed by Will and Bess, Little Giffen, and Hervé Riel? What trait of character does Fleurette portray? Is there any characteristic of Achilles Deatheridge implied or expressed in the poem about him? Which of the five poems about young patriots do you like best? Why?

3. Name two poems based upon historical events. How do poems such as these illustrate the value of literature in relation to history?

4. What similarities of tone or attitude seem to underlie such poems as "Arnold von Winkelried," "Vitaï Lampada," "Marco Bozzaris," "Incident of the French Camp," "The Song of the Camp," and "The Burial of Sir John Moore at Corunna"? What striking contrast do these poems have with "The Battle of Blenheim," "The Man He Killed," and "The Messages"?

5. In what way is dramatic irony a part of "The Man He Killed," "The Messages," and "The Battle of Blenheim"? If you do not know the meaning of the word *irony*, look it up in your dictionary.

Quest for the good

■ QUEST FOR THE GOOD

■ In reading the poems in this book, you have learned that poetry is written on a wide variety of subjects and that it offers pleasure and meaning for you. Poetry can make you aware of the beauty of language and of the world about you. It can enlarge your experience and bring the past to life for you. It can give you a knowledge of human nature and express thoughts and feelings which you yourself have experienced.

Another important area in which poetry can communicate with you is its portrayal of man's quest for the good. Ideals as well as ideas are subjects for poetry. Ideas are what a person thinks; ideals are what he strives to achieve. The emphasis in the poems and songs in this section of the book is on the ideals reflected in the lives of characters who have been successful in their search for the good and on the close personal relationship between human beings and the supernatural.

ELDORADO

Edgar Allan Poe

The literal meaning of *Eldorado* is the *gilded*, a place of riches. At one time the name was applied to an imaginary country, supposedly rich in gold and jewels, a place eagerly sought by early Spanish explorers. In Poe's poem, the search is not for gold, but for an ideal existence.

Gaily bedight,
A gallant knight,
In sunshine and in shadow,
Had journeyed long,
Singing a song,
In search of Eldorado.

But he grew old,
This knight so bold,
And o'er his heart a shadow
Fell as he found
No spot of ground
That looked like Eldorado.

And, as his strength
Failed him at length,
He met a pilgrim shadow.
"Shadow," said he,
"Where can it be—
This land of Eldorado?"

"Over the Mountains
Of the Moon,

bedight: dressed.

Down the Valley of the Shadow,
   Ride, boldly ride,"
   The shade replied,
"If you seek for Eldorado!"

ABOU BEN ADHEM

Leigh Hunt

Abou Ben Adhem (may his tribe increase!)
Awoke one night from a deep dream of peace,
And saw within the moonlight in his room,
Making it rich and like a lily in bloom,
An angel writing in a book of gold:—
Exceeding peace had made Ben Adhem bold,
And to the presence in the room he said,
"What writest thou?" The vision raised its head,
And, with a look made of all sweet accord,
Answered, "The names of those who love the Lord."
"And is mine one?" said Abou. "Nay, not so,"
Replied the angel. Abou spoke more low,
But cheerly still; and said, "I pray thee, then,
Write me as one that loves his fellow-men."

The angel wrote, and vanished. The next night
It came again, with a great wakening light,
And showed the names whom love of God had blessed,—
And, lo! Ben Adhem's name led all the rest!

THE FOOL'S PRAYER

Edward Rowland Sill

The royal feast was done; the King
    Sought some new sport to banish care,
And to his jester cried: "Sir Fool,
    Kneel now, and make for us a prayer!"

The jester doffed his cap and bells,
    And stood the mocking court before;
They could not see the bitter smile
    Behind the painted grin he wore.

He bowed his head, and bent his knee
    Upon the monarch's silken stool;
His pleading voice arose: "O Lord,
    Be merciful to me, a fool!

"No pity, Lord, could change the heart
    From red with wrong to white as wool:
The rod must heal the sin; but, Lord,
    Be merciful to me, a fool!

" 'Tis not by guilt the onward sweep
    Of truth and right, O Lord, we stay;
'Tis by our follies that so long
    We hold the earth from heaven away.

"These clumsy feet, still in the mire,
    Go crushing blossoms without end;
These hard, well-meaning hands we thrust
    Among the heartstrings of a friend.

"The ill-timed truth we might have kept—
  Who knows how sharp it pierced and stung!
The word we had not sense to say—
  Who knows how grandly it had rung!

"Our faults no tenderness should ask,
  The chastening stripes must cleanse them all;
But for our blunders—Oh, in shame
  Before the eyes of heaven we fall.

"Earth bears no balsam for mistakes;
  Men crown the knave, and scourge the tool
That did his will; but Thou, O Lord,
  Be merciful to me, a fool!"

The room was hushed; in silence rose
  The King, and sought his gardens cool,
And walked apart, and murmured low,
  "Be merciful to me, a fool!"

HOW THE GREAT GUEST CAME

Edwin Markham

Before the Cathedral in grandeur rose,
At Ingelburg where the Danube goes;
Before its forest of silver spires
Went airily up to the clouds and fires;
Before the oak had ready a beam,
While yet the arch was stone and dream—

There where the altar was later laid,
Conrad the cobbler plied his trade.

Doubled all day on his busy bench,
Hard at his cobbling for master and hench,
He pounded away at a brisk rat-tat,
Shearing and shaping with pull and pat,
Hide well hammered and pegs sent home,
Till the shoe was fit for the Prince of Rome.
And he sang as the threads went to and fro:
"Whether 'tis hidden or whether it show,
Let the work be sound, for the Lord will know."

Tall was the cobbler, and gray and thin,
And a full moon shone where the hair had been.
His eyes peered out, intent and afar,
As looking beyond the things that are.
He walked as one who is done with fear,
Knowing at last that God is near.
Only the half of him cobbled the shoes:
The rest was away for the heavenly news.
Indeed, so thin was the mystic screen
That parted the Unseen from the Seen,
You could not tell, from the cobbler's theme
If his dream were truth or his truth were dream.

It happened one day at the year's white end,
Two neighbors called on their old-time friend;
And they found the shop, so meager and mean,
Made gay with a hundred boughs of green.
Conrad was stitching with face ashine,
But suddenly stopped as he twitched a twine:
"Old friends, good news! At dawn today,
As the cocks were scaring the night away,

The Lord appeared in a dream to me,
And said, 'I am coming your guest to be!'
So I've been busy with feet astir,
Strewing the floor with branches of fir.
The wall is washed and the shelf is shined,
And over the rafter the holly twined.
He comes today, and the table is spread
With milk and honey and wheaten bread."

His friends went home; and his face grew still
As he watched for the shadow across the sill.
He lived all the moments o'er and o'er,
When the Lord should enter the lowly door—
The knock, the call, the latch pulled up,
The lighted face, the offered cup.
He would wash the feet where the spikes had been;
He would kiss the hands where the nails went in;
And then at last he would sit with Him
And break the bread as the day grew dim.

While the cobbler mused, there passed his pane
A beggar drenched by the driving rain.
He called him in from the stony street
And gave him shoes for his bruiséd feet.
The beggar went and there came a crone,
Her face with wrinkles of sorrow sown.
A bundle of fagots bowed her back,
And she was spent with the wrench and rack.
He gave her his loaf and steadied her load
As she took her way on the weary road.
Then came to his door a little child,
Lost and afraid in the world so wild,
In the big, dark world. Catching it up,
He gave it the milk in the waiting cup,

And led it home to its mother's arms,
Out of the reach of the world's alarms.

The day went down in the crimson west
And with it the hope of the blessèd Guest,
And Conrad sighed as the world turned gray:
"Why is it, Lord, that your feet delay?
Did You forget that this was the day?"
Then soft in the silence a Voice he heard:
"Lift up your heart, for I kept my word.
Three times I came to your friendly door;
Three times my shadow was on your floor.
I was the beggar with bruisèd feet;
I was the woman you gave to eat;
I was the child on the homeless street!"

THE PRISONER OF CHILLON

George Gordon, Lord Byron

My hair is gray, but not with years,
    Nor grew it white
    In a single night,
As men's have grown from sudden fears;
My limbs are bowed, though not with toil,
   But rusted with a vile repose,
For they have been a dungeon's spoil,
   And mine has been the fate of those
To whom the goodly earth and air
Are banned, and barred—forbidden fare;
But this was for my father's faith
I suffered chains and courted death;

That father perished at the stake
For tenets he would not forsake;
And for the same his lineal race
In darkness found a dwelling place;
We were seven—who now are one,
   Six in youth, and one in age,
Finished as they had begun,
   Proud of Persecution's rage;
One in fire, and two in field,
Their belief with blood have sealed:
Dying as their father died,
For the God their foes denied;—
Three were in a dungeon cast,
Of whom this wreck is left the last.

There are seven pillars of Gothic mold
In Chillon's dungeons deep and old,
There are seven columns massy and gray,
Dim with a dull imprisoned ray,
A sunbeam which hath lost its way,
And through the crevice and the cleft
Of the thick wall is fallen and left:
Creeping o'er the floor so damp,
Like a marsh's meteor lamp:
And in each pillar there is a ring,
   And in each ring there is a chain;
That iron is a cankering thing,
   For in these limbs its teeth remain,
With marks that will not wear away
Till I have done with this new day,
Which now is painful to these eyes,
Which have not seen the sun so rise

tenets: principles.

For years—I cannot count them o'er,
I lost their long and heavy score
When my last brother drooped and died,
And I lay living by his side.

They chained us each to a column stone,
And we were three—yet, each alone;
We could not move a single pace,
We could not see each other's face.
But with that pale and livid light
That made us strangers in our sight:
And thus together—yet apart,
Fettered in hand, but joined in heart,
'T was still some solace, in the dearth
Of the pure elements of earth,
To hearken to each other's speech,
And each turn comforter to each
With some new hope or legend old,
Or song heroically bold;
But even these at length grew cold.
Our voices took a dreary tone,
An echo of the dungeon stone,
    A grating sound—not full and free
    As they of yore were wont to be;
    It might be fancy—but to me
They never sounded like our own.

I was the eldest of the three,
    And to uphold and cheer the rest
    I ought to do—and did my best—
And each did well in his degree.
    The youngest, whom my father loved,
Because our mother's brow was given
To him—with eyes as blue as heaven,
    For him my soul was sorely moved:

And truly might it be distressed
To see such bird in such a nest;
For he was beautiful as day—
    (When day was beautiful to me
    As to young eagles being free)—
    A polar day, which will not see
A sunset till its summer's gone,
    Its sleepless summer of long light,
The snow-clad offspring of the sun:
    And thus he was as pure and bright,
And in his natural spirit gay,
    With tears for naught but others' ills,
    And then they flowed like mountain rills,
Unless he could assuage the woe
Which he abhorred to view below.

The other was as pure of mind,
But formed to combat with his kind;
Strong in his frame, and of a mood
Which 'gainst the world in war had stood,
And perished in the foremost rank
    With joy:—but not in chains to pine:
His spirit withered with their clank,
    I saw it silently decline—
    And so perchance in sooth did mine:
But yet I forced it on to cheer
Those relics of a home so dear.
He was a hunter of the hills,
    Had followed there the deer and wolf;
    To him this dungeon was a gulf,
And fettered feet the worst of ills.

    Lake Leman lies by Chillon's walls:
A thousand feet in depth below

Its massy waters meet and flow;
Thus much the fathom-line was sent
From Chillon's snow-white battlement,
   Which round about the wave inthrals:
A double dungeon wall and wave
Have made—and like a living grave.
Below the surface of the lake
The dark vault lies wherein we lay:
We heard it ripple night and day;
   Sounding o'er our heads it knocked;
And I have felt the winter's spray
Wash through the bars when winds were high
And wanton in the happy sky;
   And then the very rock hath rocked,
   And I have felt it shake, unshocked,
Because I could have smiled to see
The death that would have set me free.

I said my nearer brother pined,
I said his mighty heart declined,
He loathed and put away his food;
It was not that 't was coarse and rude,
For we were used to hunter's fare,
And for the like had little care:
The milk drawn from the mountain goat
Was changed for water from the moat,
Our bread was such as captive's tears
Have moistened many a thousand years,
Since man first pent his fellow men
Like brutes within an iron den;
But what were these to us or him?
These wasted not his heart or limb;
My brother's soul was of that mold

Which in a palace had grown cold,
Had his free breathing been denied
The range of the steep mountain's side.
But why delay the truth?—he died.
I saw, and could not hold his head,
Nor reach his dying hand—nor dead,—
Though hard I strove, but strove in vain,
To rend and gnash my bonds in twain.
He died, and they unlocked his chain,
And scooped for him a shallow grave
Even from the cold earth of our cave.
I begged them, as a boon, to lay
His corse in dust whereon the day
Might shine—it was a foolish thought,
But then within my brain it wrought,
That even in death his freeborn breast
In such a dungeon could not rest.
I might have spared my idle prayer—
They coldly laughed, and laid him there:
The flat and turfless earth above
The being we so much did love;
His empty chain above it leant,
Such murder's fitting monument!

But he, the favorite and the flower,
Most cherished since his natal hour,
His mother's image in fair face,
The infant love of all his race,
His martyred father's dearest thought,
My latest care, for whom I sought
To hoard my life, that his might be
Less wretched now, and one day free;
He, too, who yet had held untired

A spirit natural or inspired—
He, too, was struck, and day by day
Was withered on the stalk away.

Oh, God! it is a fearful thing
To see the human soul take wing
In any shape, in any mood:—
I've seen it rushing forth in blood,
I've seen it on the breaking ocean
Strive with a swol'n convulsive motion,
I've seen the sick and ghastly bed
Of Sin delirious with its dread:
But these were horrors—this was woe
Unmixed with such—but sure and slow;
He faded, and so calm and meek,
So softly worn, so sweetly weak,
So tearless, yet so tender—kind,
And grieved for those he left behind;
Withal the while a cheek whose bloom
Was as a mockery of the tomb,
Whose tints as gently sunk away
As a departing rainbow's ray—
An eye of most transparent light,
That almost made the dungeon bright,
And not a word of murmur, not
A groan o'er his untimely lot,—
A little talk of better days,
A little hope my own to raise,
For I was sunk in silence—lost
In this last loss, of all the most;
And then the sighs he would suppress
Of fainting nature's feebleness,
More slowly drawn, grew less and less:
I listened, but I could not hear—

I called, for I was wild with fear;
I knew 't was hopeless, but my dread
Would not be thus admonishéd;
I called, and thought I heard a sound—
I burst my chain with one strong bound,
And rushed to him:—I found him not,
I only stirred in this black spot,
I only lived—*I* only drew
The accursed breath of dungeon-dew;
The last, the sole, the dearest link
Between me and the eternal brink,
Which bound me to my failing race,
Was broken in this fatal place.
One on the earth, and one beneath—
My brothers—both had ceased to breathe.
I took that hand which lay so still,
Alas! my own was full as chill;
I had not strength to stir, or strive,
But felt that I was still alive—
A frantic feeling, when we know
That what we love shall ne'er be so.
    I know not why
    I could not die,
I had no earthly hope—but faith,
And that forbade a selfish death.

What next befell me then and there
   I know not well—I never knew—
First came the loss of light, and air,
   And then of darkness too:
I had no thought, no feeling—none—
Among the stones I stood a stone,
And was, scarce conscious what I wist,

selfish death: suicide.   *wist:* knew.

As shrubless crags within the mist;
For all was blank, and bleak, and gray;
It was not night—it was not day,
It was not even the dungeon-light,
So hateful to my heavy sight,
But vacancy absorbing space,
And fixedness, without a place;
There were no stars, no earth, no time,
No check, no change, no good, no crime,
But silence, and a stirless breath
Which neither was of life nor death;
A sea of stagnant idleness,
Blind, boundless mute, and motionless!

A light broke in upon my brain,—
    It was the carol of a bird;
It ceased, and then it came again,
    The sweetest song ear ever heard,
And mine was thankful till my eyes
Ran over with the glad surprise,
And they that moment could not see
I was the mate of misery;
But then by dull degrees came back
My senses to their wonted track;
I saw the dungeon walls and floor
Close slowly round me as before,
I saw the glimmer of the sun
Creeping as it before had done,
But through the crevice where it came
That bird was perched, as fond and tame,
    And tamer than upon the tree;
A lovely bird, with azure wings,
And song that said a thousand things,
    And seemed to say them all for me!

I never saw its like before,
I ne'er shall see its likeness more:
It seemed like me to want a mate,
But was not half so desolate,
And it was come to love me when
None lived to love me so again,
And cheering from my dungeon's brink,
Had brought me back to feel and think.
I know not if it late were free,
    Or broke its cage to perch on mine,
But knowing well captivity,
    Sweet bird! I could not wish for thine!
Or if it were, in wingéd guise,
A visitant from Paradise;
For—Heaven forgive that thought! the while
Which made me both to weep and smile;
I sometimes deemed that it might be
My brother's soul come down to me;
But then at last away it flew,
And then 't was mortal well I knew,
For he would never thus have flown,
And left me twice so doubly lone,—
Lone as the corse within its shroud,
Lone as a solitary cloud,
    A single cloud on a sunny day,
While all the rest of heaven is clear,
A frown upon the atmosphere,
That hath no business to appear
    When skies are blue, and earth is gay.

A kind of change came in my fate,
My keepers grew compassionate;
I know not what had made them so,
They were inured to sights of woe,

But so it was:—my broken chain
With links unfastened did remain,
And it was liberty to stride
Along my cell from side to side,
And up and down, and then athwart,
And tread it over every part;
And round the pillars one by one,
Returning where my walk begun,
Avoiding only, as I trod,
My brothers' graves without a sod;
For if I thought with heedless tread
My step profaned their lowly bed,
My breath came gaspingly and thick,
And my crushed heart fell blind and sick.

I made a footing in the wall,
    It was not therefrom to escape,
For I had buried one and all
    Who loved me in a human shape;
And the whole earth would henceforth be
A wider prison unto me:
No child, no sire, no kin had I,
No partner in my misery;
I thought of this, and I was glad,
For thought of them had made me mad;
But I was curious to ascend
To my barred windows, and to bend
Once more, upon the mountains high,
The quiet of a loving eye.

I saw them—and they were the same,
They were not changed like me in frame;
I saw their thousand years of snow
On high—their wide long lake below,

And the blue Rhone in fullest flow;
I heard the torrents leap and gush
O'er channelled rock and broken bush;
I saw the white-walled distant town,
And whiter sails go skimming down;
And then there was a little isle,
Which in my very face did smile,
   The only one in view;
A small green isle, it seemed no more,
Scarce broader than my dungeon floor,
But in it there were three tall trees,
And o'er it blew the mountain breeze,
And by it there were waters flowing,
And on it there were young flowers growing,
   Of gentle breath and hue.
The fish swam by the castle wall,
And they seemed joyous each and all;
The eagle rode the rising blast,
Methought he never flew so fast
As then to me he seemed to fly,
And then new tears came in my eye,
And I felt troubled—and would fain
I had not left my recent chain;
And when I did descend again,
The darkness of my dim abode
Fell on me as a heavy load;
It was as is a new-dug grave,
Closing o'er one we sought to save,—
And yet my glance, too much oppressed,
Had almost need of such a rest.

It might be months, or years or days,
   I kept no count—I took no note,
I had no hope my eyes to raise,

And clear them of their dreary mote:
At last men came to set me free,
    I asked not why, and recked not where;
It was at length the same to me,
Fettered or fetterless to be,
    I learned to love despair.
And thus when they appeared at last,
And all my bonds aside were cast,
These heavy walls to me had grown
A hermitage—and all my own!
And half I felt as they were come
To tear me from a second home:
With spiders I had friendship made,
And watched them in their sullen trade,
Had seen the mice by moonlight play,
And why should I feel less than they?
We were all inmates of one place,
And I, the monarch of each race,
Had power to kill—yet, strange to tell!
In quiet we had learned to dwell—
My very chains and I grew friends,
So much a long communion tends
To make us what we are:—even I
Regained my freedom with a sigh.

THE BALLAD OF FATHER GILLIGAN

William Butler Yeats

The old priest Peter Gilligan
Was weary night and day;
For half his flock were in their beds,
Or under green sods lay.

Once, while he nodded on a chair,
At the moth-hour of eve,
Another poor man sent for him,
And he began to grieve.

"I have no rest, nor joy, nor peace,
For people die and die";
And after cried he, "God forgive!
My body spake, not I!"

He knelt, and leaning on the chair
He prayed and fell asleep;
And the moth-hour went from the fields,
And stars began to peep.

They slowly into millions grew;
And leaves shook in the wind;
And God covered the world with shade,
And whispered to mankind.

Upon the time of sparrow-chirp,
When moths came once more,
The old priest Peter Gilligan
Stood upright on the floor.

"Mavrone, mavrone! the man has died
While I slept on the chair";
He roused his horse out of its sleep,
And rode with little care.

He rode now as he never rode,
By rocky lane and fen;
The sick man's wife opened the door:
"Father! you come again!"

"And is the poor man dead?" he cried.
"He died an hour ago."
The old priest Peter Gilligan
In grief swayed to and fro.

"When you were gone, he turned and died
As merry as a bird."
The old priest Peter Gilligan
He knelt him at that word.

"He who hath made the night of stars
For souls who tire and bleed,
Sent one of His great angels down
To help me in my need.

"He who is wrapped in purple robes,
With planets in His care,
Had pity on the least of things
Asleep upon a chair."

THE CREATION

James Weldon Johnson

This poetic interpretation of the Creation is one of a series of sermons
in verse written by the very gifted Negro poet, James Weldon Johnson.
After you have read this poem, you may wish to read others in the
collection of sermons, *God's Trombones.*

And God stepped out on space,
And He looked around and said:

I'm lonely—
I'll make me a world.

And far as the eye of God could see
Darkness covered everything,
Blacker than a hundred midnights
Down in a cypress swamp.

Then God smiled,
And the light broke,
And the darkness rolled up on one side,
And the light stood shining on the other,
And God said: That's good!

Then God reached out and took the light in His hands,
And God rolled the light around in His hands
Until He made the sun;
And He set that sun a-blazing in the heavens.
And the light that was left from making the sun
God gathered it up in a shining ball
And flung it against the darkness,
Spangling the night with the moon and stars.
Then down between
The darkness and the light
He hurled the world;
And God said: That's good!

Then God himself stepped down—
And the sun was on His right hand,
And the moon was on His left;
The stars were clustered about His head,
And the earth was under His feet.

And God walked, and where He trod
His footsteps hollowed the valleys out
And bulged the mountains up.

Then He stopped and looked and saw
That the earth was hot and barren.
So God stepped over to the edge of the world
And He spat out the seven seas—
He batted His eyes, and the lightnings flashed—
He clapped His hands, and the thunders rolled—
And the waters above the earth came down,
The cooling waters came down.

Then the green grass sprouted,
And the little red flowers blossomed,
The pine tree pointed his finger to the sky,
And the oak spread out his arms,
The lakes cuddled down in the hollows of the ground,
And the rivers ran down to the sea;
And God smiled again,
And the rainbow appeared,
And curled itself around His shoulder.

Then God raised His arm and He waved His hand
Over the sea and over the land,
And He said: Bring forth! Bring forth!
And quicker than God could drop His hand,
Fishes and fowls
And beasts and birds
Swam the rivers and the seas,
Roamed the forests and the woods,
And split the air with their wings.
And God said: That's good!

Then God walked around,
And God looked around
On all that He had made.
He looked at His sun,
And He looked at His moon,
And He looked at His little stars;
He looked on His world
With all its living things,
And God said: I'm lonely still.

Then God sat down—
On the side of a hill where He could think;
By a deep, wide river He sat down;
With His head in His hands,
God thought and thought,
Till He thought: I'll make me a man!

Up from the bed of the river
God scooped the clay;
And by the bank of the river
He kneeled Him down;
And there the great God Almighty
Who lit the sun and fixed it in the sky,
Who flung the stars to the most far corner of the night,
Who rounded the earth in the middle of His hand;
This Great God,
Like a mammy bending over her baby,
Kneeled down in the dust
Toiling over a lump of clay
Till He shaped it in His own image;

Then into it He blew the breath of life,
And man became a living soul.
Amen. Amen.

QUESTIONS FOR UNDERSTANDING AND APPRECIATION

ELDORADO

1. The name, Eldorado, now generally means an ideal life or place. Originally the name was applied to an unknown country, fabled to have great riches and eagerly sought for by Spanish explorers. How may this poem be interpreted to refer to man's quest for the good?
2. What does the knight seek, and what quality must he have to find it?
3. What poetic devices does Poe use to create an effective poem?

ABOU BEN ADHEM

1. What is the moral of the poem? How is Abou Ben Adhem assured that his quest for good has been achieved? Explain the meaning of the words, "May his tribe increase."

THE FOOL'S PRAYER

1. What was the function of the fool in the king's court? In this instance, how does the king hope to find diversion? Why is he so affected by the fool's prayer?
2. "The Fool's Prayer" is more sermon than prayer. Try to state clearly the fool's principle of good conduct.

HOW THE GREAT GUEST CAME

1. Whom was the cobbler expecting? Who really came?
2. Cite the details which indicate the cobbler's regard for his expected guest.
3. Explain the meaning of the last six lines. Would you call these lines the underlying message of the poem?

THE PRISONER OF CHILLON

1. The author, Lord Byron, had an intense interest in the cause of liberty. He fought and died in the Greek War of Independence in 1824. Select lines in "The Prisoner of Chillon" which express Byron's sympathy for oppressed people and his bitterness against tyrants. What is the central idea of the poem?

2. According to historical fact, the prisoner, François Bonnivard, was imprisoned alone in the Castle of Chillon for political reasons. Why do you think the author pictures the prisoner as the victim of religious, rather than political, persecution? What effect is gained in the poem through his being imprisoned with brothers?

3. Why and how were the members of the family punished? How do the three brothers' characteristics differ? How is the prisoner affected by the deaths of his two brothers? In what way is the bird used as a symbol? How does the bird affect his mental state? How does he accept his release? Is his reaction understandable?

4. Explain the last four lines of stanza VIII and also the following phrases: "Their belief with blood have sealed"; "inured to sights of woe"; "fettered feet the worst of ills."

5. In what respects has this poem the quality of universality in its theme and plot? To which more recent wars and persecutions could it apply?

For comparative study, read *The Diary of Anne Frank* and compare it with "The Prisoner of Chillon."

THE BALLAD OF FATHER GILLIGAN

1. In what ways is this poem like the old ballads? Point out examples of imagery.

2. Why does the old priest pray for forgiveness, and how is he assured of having received it?

THE CREATION

1. Give specific quotations from the poem to illustrate the human qualities attributed to God; lines to illustrate His power.

2. According to this poem, why did God make man? What prominence is given to man compared with the other creations of God?

3. Read aloud the description of the creation of the universe and of the living creatures. Point out lines in the poem which are very vivid examples of imagery.

4. Does "The Creation" give you a new idea of God? Did you ever think of loneliness as a characteristic of God? What references to loneliness can you find in other poems or stories you have read?

5. Has man, in your opinion, made this the kind of world God had in mind when He created it? In what ways do you think man could do better than he has done?

COMPARATIVE STUDY

1. Which of the poems in this section portray most effectively man's quest for the good? Which is most dramatic in presenting its message? Which poem has the most artistic imagery? Which poems show direct supernatural intervention in the lives of human beings? Which do you like best?
2. What is the similarity between "Abou Ben Adhem" and "How the Great Guest Came"? How do the poems differ in the presentation of their message? Which character is drawn in greater detail?
3. Compare the characters of Abou Ben Adhem, Father Gilligan, the prisoner of Chillon, and the king's jester. What guidelines do these characters follow for attaining contentment in their lives? Which of them display humility? love of neighbor? courage?
4. What attribute of God is shown in "The Creation" and in "Father Gilligan?"
5. Compare the effectiveness of the long poem, "The Prisoner of Chillon," with that of the shorter poem, "How the Great Guest Came." Which affects you more deeply as a religious experience?
6. Compare the imagery in "The Creation" with that in "The Prisoner of Chillon." Which is more elaborate? Which is more likely to stir the emotions of a reader?

COMPARATIVE STUDY

1.

2.

3.

4.

5.

6.

7.

More poems for enrichment

■ MORE POEMS FOR ENRICHMENT

■ The poems in this section are all by poets of this century; they represent, in their different ways, what is sometimes loosely referred to as "modern poetry." Although some of the poets whom you will be reading here have appeared in previous sections of this anthology, these particular poems were chosen for the extra challenge they offer an adventuresome reader and also because it is interesting to see modern poetry in a unit by itself.

The contrast between modern poetry and the poetry of other ages is no different from that which exists between the literature of any one given period of time and another. It is simply a question of changes in poetic technique and explorations of new subject matter. The poems that follow are extremely varied in both form and content, and they are not what could strictly be called narrative. What unites them is the high quality of verse that they exhibit, and the new, exciting experience they extend to the reader who is willing to enter into the poet's unique and shifting world.

FERN HILL

Dylan Thomas

Now as I was young and easy under the apple boughs
About the lilting house and happy as the grass was green,
   The night above the dingle starry,
     Time let me hail and climb
   Golden in the heydays of his eyes,
And honored among wagons I was prince of the apple towns
And once below a time I lordly had the trees and leaves
    Trail with daisies and barley
   Down the rivers of the windfall light.

And as I was green and carefree, famous among the barns
About the happy yard and singing as the farm was home.
   In the sun that is young once only,
     Time let me play and be
   Golden in the mercy of his means,
And green and golden I was huntsman and herdsman, the
      calves
Sang to my horn, the foxes on the hills barked clear and cold,
    And the sabbath rang slowly
   In the pebbles of the holy streams.

All the sun long it was running, it was lovely, the hay-
Fields high as the house, the tunes from the chimneys, it was
     air
   And playing, lovely and watery
    And fire green as grass.
   And highly under the simple stars
As I rode to sleep the owls were bearing the farm away,
All the moon long I heard, blessed among stables, the night-
     jars

Flying with the ricks, and horses
   Flashing into the dark

And then to awake, and the farm, like a wanderer white
With the dew, come back, the cock on his shoulder: it was all
   Shining, it was Adam and maiden,
      The sky gathered again
   And the sun grew round that very day.
So it must have been after the birth of the simple light
In the first, spinning place, the spellbound horses walking
      warm
   Out of the whinnying green stable
     On to the fields of praise.

And honored among foxes and pheasants by the gay house
Under the new-made clouds and happy as the heart was long
   In the sun born over and over,
     I ran my heedless ways,
    My wishes raced through the house-high hay
And nothing I cared, at my sky blue trades, that time allows
In all his tuneful turning so few and such morning songs
   Before the children green and golden
     Follow him out of grace.

Nothing I cared, in the lamb white days, that time would
      take me
Up to the swallow-thronged loft by the shadow of my hand,
   In the moon that is always rising,
     Nor that riding to sleep
   I should hear him fly with the high fields
And wake to the farm forever fled from the childless land.
Oh as I was young and easy in the mercy of his means,
    Time held me green and dying
   Though I sang in my chains like the sea.

ALL IN GREEN WENT MY LOVE RIDING

E. E. Cummings

All in green went my love riding
on a great horse of gold
into the silver dawn.

four lean hounds crouched low and smiling
the merry deer ran before.

Fleeter be they than dappled dreams
the swift sweet deer
the red rare deer.

Four red roebuck at a white water
the cruel bugle sang before.

Horn at hip went my love riding
riding the echo down
into the silver dawn.

four lean hounds crouched low and smiling
the level meadows ran before.

Softer be they than slippered sleep
the lean lithe deer
the fleet flown deer

Four fleet does at a gold valley
the famished arrow sang before.

Bow at belt went my love riding
riding the mountain down
into the silver dawn.

four lean hounds crouched low and smiling
the sheer peaks ran before.

Paler be they than daunting death
the sleek slim deer
the tall tense deer.

Four tall stags at a green mountain
the lucky hunter sang before.

All in green went my love riding
on a great horse of gold
into the silver dawn.

four lean hounds crouched low and smiling
my heart fell dead before.

THE TELEPHONE

Robert Frost

"When I was just as far as I could walk
From here today,
There was an hour
All still
When leaning with my head against a flower

I heard you talk.
Don't say I didn't, for I heard you say—
You spoke from that flower on the window sill—
Do you remember what it was you said?"

"First tell me what it was you thought you heard."

"Having found the flower and driven a bee away,
I leaned my head,
And holding by the stalk,
I listened and I thought I caught the word—
What was it? Did you call me by my name?
Or did you say—
Someone said 'Come'—I heard it as I bowed."

"I may have thought as much, but not aloud."

"Well, so I came."

AUTO WRECK

Karl Shapiro

Its quick soft silver bell beating, beating,
And down the dark one ruby flare
Pulsing out red light like an artery,
The ambulance at top speed floating down
Past beacons and illuminated clocks
Wings in a heavy curve, dips down,
And brakes speed, entering the crowd.
The doors leap open, emptying light;

Stretchers are laid out, the mangled lifted
And stowed into the little hospital.
Then the bell, breaking the hush, tolls once,
And the ambulance with its terrible cargo
Rocking, slightly rocking, moves away,
As the doors, an afterthought, are closed.

We are deranged, walking among the cops
Who sweep glass and are large and composed.
One is still making notes under the light.
One with a bucket douches ponds of blood
Into the street and gutter.
One hangs lanterns on the wrecks that cling,
Empty husks of locusts, to iron poles.

Our throats were tight as tourniquets,
Our feet were bound with splints, but now
Like convalescents intimate and gauche,
We speak through sickly smiles and warn
With the stubborn saw of common sense,
The grim joke and the banal resolution.
The traffic moves around with care,
But we remain, touching a wound
That opens to our richest horror.

Already old, the question Who shall die?
Becomes unspoken Who is innocent?
For death in war is done by hands;
Suicide has cause and stillbirth, logic.
But this invites the occult mind,
Cancels our physics with a sneer,
And spatters all we knew of dénouement
Across the expedient and wicked stones.

STRANGE MEETING

Wilfred Owen

It seemed that out of the battle I escaped
Down some profound dull tunnel, long since scooped
Through granites which Titanic wars had groined.
Yet also there encumbered sleepers groaned,
Too fast in thought or death to be bestirred.
Then, as I probed them, one sprang up, and stared
With piteous recognition in fixed eyes,
Lifting distressful hands as if to bless.
And by his smile, I knew that sullen hall;
By his dead smile I knew I stood in Hell.
With a thousand pains that vision's face was grained;
Yet no blood reached there from the upper ground,
And no guns thumped, or down the flues made moan.
"Strange, friend," I said, "here is no cause to mourn."
"None," said the other, "save the undone years,
The hopelessness. Whatever hope is yours,
Was my life also; I went hunting wild
After the wildest beauty in the world,
Which lies not calm in eyes, or braided hair,
But mocks the steady running of the hour,
And if it grieves, grieves richlier than here.
For by my glee might many men have laughed,
And of my weeping something has been left,
Which must die now. I mean the truth untold.
The pity of war, the pity war distilled.
Now men will go content with what we spoiled,
Or, discontent, boil bloody, and be spilled.
They will be swift with swiftness of the tigress,
None will break ranks, though nations trek from progress.
Courage was mine, and I had mystery,

Wisdom was mine, and I had mastery;
To miss the march of this retreating world
Into vain citadels that are not walled.
Then when much blood had clogged their chariot-wheels
I would go up and wash them from sweet wells,
Even with truths that lie too deep for taint.
I would have poured my spirit without stint
But not through wounds; not on the cess of war.
Foreheads of men have bled where no wounds were.
I am the enemy you killed, my friend.
I knew you in this death; for so you frowned
Yesterday through me as you jabbed and killed.
I parried; but my hands were loath and cold.
Let us sleep now. . . ."

O WHERE ARE YOU GOING?

W. H. Auden

"O where are you going?" said reader to rider,
"That valley is fatal when furnaces burn,
Yonder's the midden whose odours will madden,
That gap is the grave where the tall return."

"O do you imagine," said fearer to farer,
"That dusk will delay on your path to the pass,
Your diligent looking discover the lacking
Your footsteps feel from granite to grass?"

"O what was that bird," said horror to hearer,
"Did you see that shape in the twisted trees?

Behind you swiftly the figure comes softly,
The spot on your skin is a shocking disease?"

"Out of this house"—said rider to reader,
"Yours never will"—said farer to fearer,
"They're looking for you"—said hearer to horror,
As he left them there, as he left them there.

EROS TURANNOS

Edwin Arlington Robinson

She fears him, and will always ask
    What fated her to choose him;
She meets in his engaging mask
    All reasons to refuse him;
But what she meets and what she fears
Are less than are the downward years,
Drawn slowly to the foamless weirs
    Of age, were she to lose him.

Between a blurred sagacity
    That once had power to sound him,
And Love, that will not let him be
    The Judas that she found him,
Her pride assuages her almost,
As if it were alone the cost.
He sees that he will not be lost,
    And waits and looks around him.

A sense of ocean and old trees
    Envelops and allures him;

Tradition, touching all he sees,
   Beguiles and reassures him;
And all her doubts of what he says
Are dimmed with what she knows of days—
Till even prejudice delays
   And fades, and she secures him.

The falling leaf inaugurates
   The reign of her confusion;
The pounding wave reverberates
   The dirge of her illusion;
And home, where passion lived and died,
Becomes a place where she can hide,
While all the town and harbor-side
   Vibrate with her seclusion.

We tell you, tapping on our brows,
   The story as it should be,
As if the story of a house
   Were told, or ever could be;
We'll have no kindly veil between
Her visions and those we have seen,—
As if we guessed what hers have been,
   Or what they are or would be.

Meanwhile we do no harm; for they
   That with a god have striven,
Not hearing much of what we say,
   Take what the god has given;
Though like waves breaking it may be,
Or like a changed familiar tree,
Or like a stairway to the sea
   Where down the blind are driven.

EVE

Ralph Hodgson

Eve, with her basket, was
Deep in the bells and grass,
Wading in bells and grass
Up to her knees.

Picking a dish of sweet
Berries and plums to eat,
Down in the bells and grass
Under the trees.

Mute as a mouse in a
Corner the cobra lay,
Curled round a bough of the
Cinnamon tall. . . .
Now to get even and
Humble proud heaven and
Now was the moment or
Never at all.

"Eva!" Each syllable
Light as a flower fell,
"Eva!" he whispered the
Wondering maid,
Soft as a bubble sung
Out of a linnet's lung,
Soft and most silvery
"Eva!" he said.

Picture that orchard sprite;
Eve, with her body white,

Supple and smooth to her
Slim finger tips;
Wondering, listening,
Listening, wondering,
Eve with a berry
Half-way to her lips.

Oh, had our simple Eve
Seen through the make-believe!
Had she but known the
Pretender he was!
Out of the boughs he came,
Whispering still her name,
Tumbling in twenty rings
Into the grass.

Here was the strangest pair
In the world anywhere,
Eve in the bells and grass
Kneeling, and he
Telling his story low. . . .
Singing birds saw them go
Down the dark path to
The Blasphemous Tree.

Oh, what a clatter when
Titmouse and Jenny Wren
Saw him successful and
Taking his leave!
How the birds rated him,
How they all hated him!
How they all pitied
Poor motherless Eve!

Picture her crying
Outside in the lane,
Eve, with no dish of sweet
Berries and plums to eat,
Haunting the gate of the
Orchard in vain. . . .
Picture the lewd delight
Under the hill tonight—
"Eva!" the toast goes round,
"Eva!" again.

LAMENT

David Lougée

Her iron-chested gentleman (soft-eyed and harsh of tongue),
One moonless night, plucked out the flower of my life,
Took her away,
And left me sitting, reading in a book
How caution, prudence pay.
I have had word since then
He went to sea. Returns once, twice a year.
They have a tidy bungalow somewhere,
Off shore. That's all I know.

And wish for nothing more.
I shall not grieve her body's fancy
Nor how the wind would stray her hair
On summer nights. Over the gin and tonic
Nothing matters really.
And there are books to read.
My job looks good, am seldom sick.

And then, strange bliss,
I have my picture still:

A bungalow, an oak tree, a sandy road perhaps
And her there on the porch, rocking,
Marking how the winds talk,
How the widowing seas cry out
That time shall claim its iron-chested gentlemen
(Soft-eyed and harsh of tongue);
And not till that old oak lifts up its boughs to walk
Shall she, my lady, my lost and only quite forever one,
Change this.

QUESTIONS FOR UNDERSTANDING AND APPRECIATION

FERN HILL

1. This is a poem which is both about childhood and the loss of childhood. What is the poet's attitude toward growing up?
2. What images does the poet use to describe falling asleep and awakening from sleep? What extended comparison does the poet make to awakening?
3. Cite the unusual examples of epithet and simile. Does the poet establish any relationship between falling asleep and growing older? Between growing older and dying?
4. Quote the references to time, and explain why these are examples of personification.
5. Write a short paragraph of what you feel to be the meaning of the final two lines. Does the entire poem build up to this dramatic conclusion?
6. Dylan Thomas is famous for the music and original imagery of his verse. Do you think that this praise is justified?

ALL IN GREEN WENT MY LOVE RIDING

1. Does the unusual form of this poem add to or detract from its effectiveness? Do you feel that the poem's progression is dramatic or merely repetitious?
2. Can the plot of the poem be summarized in one sentence? Is the last line effective or would you prefer further elaboration?
3. Cite lines which present effective pictures; others which are examples of alliteration. What figure of speech is illustrated by *famished arrow* and *cruel bugle*?

THE TELEPHONE

1. You know what the term *metaphor* means. Could this entire poem be considered one extended metaphor? Explain. Discuss what is meant by the first two lines.

2. Why do you think that the poet chose the title which he did? Consult your dictionary for the meaning of the prefix *tele*?

3. Notice that this poem, which expresses emotions tenderly and quietly, builds to a very dramatic climax. Do the short words, and conversational style, contribute to this effect?

4. Could this be called a love poem? Why?

AUTO WRECK

1. How does this poem differ from a newspaper account of an accident? In the first stanza, what does the poet mean by *hospital* and *terrible cargo*?

2. Describe the activity following the departure of the ambulance. What effect does the accident have on the spectators? Explain the question which comes to their minds. Do they find an answer?

3. How does the kind of death described in this poem differ from that in other circumstances?

4. Give examples of vivid imagery and figures of speech and show how they are in harmony with the mood and story of the poem.
   VOCABULARY: deranged, tourniquet, gauche, banal, occult, dénouement, expedient.

STRANGE MEETING

1. What is the setting of this poem? Could the poem possibly be the account of a soldier's dream?

2. Select lines which express the vain hope of the dead soldier and the futility of war. What do you think that the two soldiers finally felt about each other?

3. Examine the rhyme scheme. Owen is using here what is sometimes called *slant* or *partial* rhyme. Slant rhyme occurs where the words do not completely rhyme but have certain sounds in common. In this poem you will notice that it is only the

stressed consonants that are repeated. It is a form of rhyme which allows a poet a wide variety of effects. Does it appeal to you?

O WHERE ARE YOU GOING?

1. The first three stanzas contain questions and warnings; in the last stanza these questions and warnings are answered. Do you think that each stanza revolves about the same two persons? Why?

2. What dramatic consistencies can you locate in the final stanza?

3. There is a poetic device used throughout this poem. Can you name it?

EROS TURANNOS

1. The title of this poem is in Greek, and its literal translation would be "tyrant love." We would, however, be more likely to say "the tyranny of love." What meaning does this title have in regard to Robinson's poem? Who was Eros in Greek mythology?

2. Why does the woman of the poem hesitate before marrying the man she loves? What is meant by the first three words of the fourth stanza?

3. Who is narrating this poem? In which stanza do we find this out?

4. The poet's rhyme scheme is an intricate one. In what way do the rhymes at the end of the second, fourth, and eighth lines differ from the other rhymes? What changes in the rhyme pattern occur in the last three stanzas?

5. Do you feel that the poet has prepared us for the climax of the poem? Why?

VOCABULARY: sagacity, Judas, assuages, inaugurates.

EVE

1. In what ways is this account similar to and different from the Biblical story of Eve? How do the birds react to what occurs?

2. How is the poem applicable to other situations and times?

3. Do you find the rhyme scheme more unusual than others you have encountered. Why? Where are some instances of slant rhyme (see question 3, *Strange Meeting*, p. 401)?

4. What effect is gained by the use of short lines? Select several examples of vivid imagery.

L A M E N T

1. This poem is in the form of a dramatic monologue. How would you characterize the speaker's tone?

2. Is the title to be taken literally, ironically, or both?

3. What particular rhyme scheme does the poem have?

4. Pick out the word pictures in the poem that you find most striking.

5. What is it that the winds and seas are saying in the last stanza?

6. What is the meaning of the last three lines?

Memorable Quotations
Biographical Notes

■ MEMORABLE QUOTATIONS

■ The following quotations selected from the poems in this book can be applied to circumstances other than those referred to by the poet. Some of these quotations can serve as a springboard for theme writing or for interesting class discussions. Can you identify the source of the lines?

"Life, an adventure, perilous and gay."

"It takes life to love Life."

"He lives to learn, in life's hard school,
How few who pass above him
Lament their triumph and his loss."

"If we've promised them aught, let us keep our promise."

"Of all sad words of tongue or pen
The saddest are these: 'It might have been!' "

"Not all that tempts your wandering eyes

407

And heedless hearts is lawful prize;
Nor all that glisters, gold."

"The fate of a nation was riding that night."

"But there is neither East nor West, Border nor Breed nor
  Birth,
When two strong men come face to face tho' they come from
  the ends of the earth."

"The ill-timed truth we might have kept,
Who knows how sharp it pierced and stung."

"Name and deed alike are lost;
Not a pillar nor a post
. . . keeps alive the deed as it befell."

"An old man's past's a strange one, for it never leaves his
  mind."

"I liked all learning
And wished to share it
Abroad like pollen
For all who merit."

"Serve—and hate will die unborn.
Love—and chains are broken."

"I had no earthly hope but faith,
And that forbade a selfish death."

■ BIOGRAPHICAL NOTES
ABOUT THE POETS

W. H. (Wystan Hugh) Auden (1907——), one of the most influential poets of his generation, was born in York, England, and educated at Oxford. In 1939 he became an American citizen. In addition to being a poet (his poetry has won numerous awards, including the Pulitzer prize), Auden is a prolific essayist and lecturer. In 1956, he was named Professor of Poetry at Oxford University. It was the first time an American citizen had received this honor.

Hilaire Belloc (1870–1953), was born near Paris, the son of a French father and an English mother. He became a naturalized British citizen and was a member of Parliament for four years. He wrote essays, history, biography, travel sketches, and poetry.

Stephen Vincent Benét (1898–1943), poet, novelist, and short-story writer, was born in Pennsylvania and graduated from Yale. With his wife, Rosemary Benét, he shared authorship in A Book of Americans, a collection of poems about a variety of interesting personalities. Among Benét's works are John Brown's Body, a narrative poem about the Civil War, which won the

Pulitzer prize in 1921; and "The Devil and Daniel Webster," a short story first published in the *Saturday Evening Post* and later made into a one-act opera and a motion picture.

WILLIAM ROSE BENÉT (1886–1950), older brother of Stephen Vincent, also graduated from Yale and pursued a career of writing and editing. He was a co-founder and first editor of the *Saturday Review*. In 1942 he was awarded the Pulitzer prize for his poetry. His wife, Elinor Wylie, was also an accomplished poet.

ROBERT BROWNING (1812–1889), one of England's great poets, was the son of wealthy, cultured parents. His marriage to the poet, Elizabeth Barrett, became the subject of a play and a motion picture, *The Barretts of Wimpole Street*. Browning's poetry often presents an optimistic, vital outlook on life. He was, however, in no way blind to evil and suffering, as can be seen in his book-length narrative poem, *The Ring and the Book*. He is very successful in portraying character in his poems, often in a form which we call the dramatic monologue. "My Last Duchess" is one of the most famous dramatic monologues in our literature.

WITTER BYNNER (1881———) was born in Brooklyn and educated at Harvard. He studied the art of the American Indian and has given a poetic interpretation of the Indian dances of the Southwest in his *Indian Earth*.

GEORGE GORDON, LORD BYRON (1788–1824), a famous English poet, lived a rebellious, tempestuous life. He inherited his title at the age of ten when his father died. Despite his royal ancestry, handsome appearance, and literary fame, he was not accepted in English society because of his unconventional conduct. Though he was lame, he became a superb swimmer and swam the Hellespont. His zeal for freedom dominated his life. He became interested in the Greek struggle for independence and died of fever on his way to join the Greeks in a military expedition against the Turks. Byron's most famous work is his long poem, *Don Juan*, an exuberant satire on the manners and society of his time.

THOMAS CAMPBELL (1777–1844) was a minor Scottish poet who is remembered chiefly for several of his literary ballads.

LEWIS CARROLL (1832–1898), whose real name was Charles Lutwidge Dodgson, was an English mathematician, son of a clergyman. Following his graduation from Oxford in 1854, he lectured in mathematics for the next twenty-seven years. Under the name of Dodgson he wrote his many mathematical treatises. He used the pen name, "Lewis Carroll," for his *Alice's Adventures in Wonderland, Through the Looking-Glass,* and other imaginative volumes that have delighted children and adults alike.

WILLA CATHER (1874–1947) lived on a Nebraska farm during her youth and graduated from the University of Nebraska. She is famous for her novels and short stories which have re-created the spirit of the West and Southwest. *My Antonia* and *Death Comes for the Archbishop* are two of her better-known novels. *April Twilight* is a collection of her poetry.

ELIZABETH J. COATSWORTH (1893————) was born in Buffalo, graduated from Vassar, and now lives in New England. She is a versatile writer of poetry, novels, nonfiction, and of many juvenile stories, one of which, *The Cat Who Went to Heaven,* won the Newberry Medal in 1930.

ROBERT TRISTRAM COFFIN (1892–1955), was born in Maine and graduated from Bowdoin College, where he became professor of English. His published works include poetry, novels, essays, and biography. In 1936 he was awarded a Pulitzer prize in poetry for his volume, *Strange Holiness.*

WILLIAM COWPER (1731–1800) was an English poet who was educated to become a lawyer but retired to the country because of illness and depression. His literary work includes hymns, nature poetry, and other types of verse. Although much of his poetry is religious, Cowper's ability to write light, good-natured humor is evident in "The Diverting History of John Gilpin."

E. E. (EDWARD ESTLIN) CUMMINGS (1894–1962), one of America's greatest lyric poets, was born in Cambridge, the son of a Harvard professor. He graduated from Harvard and served as an ambulance driver in France during World War I. His poetry was sometimes marked by unusual typography and punctuation. This was done to achieve a sense of visual immediacy, as in a painting. His verse includes love poems, humorous character sketches, and satire. In addition to his poetry, Cummings is also known for his war novel, *The Enormous Room,* the play, *Him,* and his many paintings. In 1952, he delivered the Charles Eliot Norton lectures at Harvard. These were later collected into a volume.

JOHN DAVIDSON (1857–1909), the British poet, was born and educated in Scotland. Aside from his poetry, for which he is best known, Davidson was an author of both novels and plays. He is best known for his unusual versification and for the strong individuality his poems reveal.

WALTER DE LA MARE (1873–1956) was born in Kent, England, and educated at St. Paul's School in London. He worked for years in the English branches of Standard Oil. In his musical and imaginative verse he is able to transport the reader into a world of fantasy and make it real and believable. De la Mare is also noted for his short stories and a novel, *Memoirs of a Midget.*

T. S. (THOMAS STEARNS) ELIOT (1888–1965), considered to be one of the most influential poets and critics of our time, was born in St. Louis, graduated from Harvard, and studied at the Sorbonne and at Harvard. In 1927 he became a naturalized British subject. His poems, essays, and plays have received world-wide attention. In 1948, Eliot was awarded the Nobel Prize for Literature. His outstanding works include "The Love Song of J. Alfred Prufrock," *The Waste Land,* and *The Four Quartets*—perhaps the finest long meditative poem in English since Wordsworth's *The Prelude.*

ROBERT FROST (1875–1963), one of the greatest of modern poets, was born in San Francisco but, after the death of his father, settled in New England. He is sometimes referred to as the poet of New England, not only because he spent most of his life there, but because he so often pictures the rural life and people of this region. Although Frost frequently uses the clear language of everyday speech, his poems are, despite their air of conversational ease, most intricately structured and far less simple than they appear. Frost is recognized here and abroad as an extraordinary poet and has won the Pulitzer prize four times. The world witnessed and heard his reading of his own poetry at the inauguration of President Kennedy in 1961.

WILFRID W. GIBSON (1878?–1962) was born in Northumberland, England, and devoted most of his life to writing poetry and plays. His subjects have been the hopes, fears, and activities of common human beings, told in simple, direct language.

WILLIAM S. GILBERT (1836–1911) is the English writer who collaborated with Sullivan in writing the famous light operas. Gilbert was very skilled in devising clever verse forms and in writing humor and light satire.

THOMAS GRAY (1716–1771) was an English poet who is perhaps best known as the author of "Elegy in a Country Churchyard." He also wrote poems of a lighter tone, such as "On the Death of a Favorite Cat." Gray was offered, but refused to accept, the position of poet laureate.

ARTHUR GUITERMAN (1871–1943) was born in Vienna of American parents and brought to the United States as a child. He followed a journalistic career and is known particularly for his humorous verse.

FITZ-GREENE HALLECK (1790–1867), was born in Connecticut, but spent most of his life in the business world in New York City. He has never been considered a "great" poet, but two of his poems, a moving tribute written on the death of his friend, Joseph Rodman Blake, beginning with the line, "Green be the turf above thee," and "Marco Bozzaris," have become part of our literary heritage.

THOMAS HARDY (1840–1928), one of Britain's major novelists and poets, was born in a little village in southern England, a region which he depicted in his novels and poems. He was trained in architecture and won a prize from the Royal Institute of British Architecture. In his early thirties, however, he deserted architecture and devoted himself entirely to his writings. Hardy's more noted works include the novels, *Tess of the D'Urbervilles* and *The Return of the Native*, and his long poem, *The Dynasts*.

RALPH HODGSON (1871–1962), an English poet, was for many years a lecturer in English literature at a university in Japan. He was noted for his retiring nature and intense dislike of publicity. His sympathy for animals is noted in such poems as "The Bull." At the age of eighty-three Hodgson received the Queen's Medal for poetry.

OLIVER WENDELL HOLMES (1809–1894), poet, novelist, and essayist, received a degree in medicine at Harvard and taught in the Medical School there for thirty-five years. His wit and his skill as a conversationalist made him a popular Bostonian during his lifetime. Besides his narrative poetry, his lyric "Old Ironsides" has a place in literature because it was instrumental in saving the historic ship, *The Constitution*, from being scuttled. Holmes' son was Chief Justice of the Supreme Court for thirty years.

A. E. (ALFRED EDWARD) HOUSMAN (1859–1936) was educated at Oxford and taught Latin at University College and in Cambridge. Besides being a great Latin and Greek scholar, he wrote lyric poetry of a classical precision. The scene of many of his poems is the Shropshire section of western England, from which the title of his first volume, *A Shropshire Lad*, is derived.

MARGARET BELL HOUSTON is a contemporary writer of poetry and prose. In 1926 her collection of poems, *Lanterns in the Dusk*, won an award from the Poetry Society of America.

JAMES LANGSTON HUGHES (1902——), an American Negro poet, was born in Missouri, where he attended Columbia College. He taught English in Mexico and traveled widely abroad. Hughes has won many awards for his poetry, which presents the melodic rhythms of Negro folk music. His collections of Negro spirituals have been a contribution to American folk song.

LEIGH HUNT (1784–1859) was an English journalist, essayist, and poet. He was a close friend of Shelley and Keats, and like these more famous poets, devoted himself to the writing of lyric poetry. He is best known, perhaps, as the author of the narrative poem "Abou Ben Adhem."

JAMES WELDON JOHNSON (1871–1938) was born in Florida and educated at Atlanta University and at Columbia. He was a high-school principal, a lawyer, a song writer, and a professor of literature at Fisk University. Johnson has published, aside from his poetry, collections of Negro spirituals and various prose works. One of his best-known books is *God's Trombones*, seven Negro sermons in verse.

JOHN KEATS (1795–1821), the renowned English poet, asked to have inscribed on his tombstone: "Here lies one whose name is writ in water." Although he lived only twenty-six years, he still ranks as one of the world's greatest poets. The poet was the son of a stablekeeper, orphaned at fifteen, frail in health, and finally a victim of tuberculosis. Keats was apprenticed to a surgeon and appointed intern at a London hospital. He later, however, gave up medicine to devote himself completely to poetry. He once expressed his philosophy of writing in these words: "The road lies through application, study, and thought." "Ode to a Nightingale" and "Ode to a Grecian Urn" are, along with the two poems included in this volume, among Keats' most famous works.

CHARLES KINGSLEY (1819–1875) was an English novelist, clergyman, and the author of books on travel, natural history, mythology, and some poetry. His best known novel is *Westward Ho!*, a tale of adventure set in Elizabethan times.

RUDYARD KIPLING (1865–1936), was born in India, son of a renowned British artist. After a relatively brief education in England, he returned to India at the age of seventeen and became an editor with an English-language publication. In the fifty-odd years of his literary life he produced innumerable short tales, longer yarns, animal stories, social commentaries, and poetry. Though his style of writing was sometimes more journalistic than literary, his genius for telling a fascinating story brought him very wide popularity. Among his most famous poetry volumes are *Barrack Room Ballads*, *The Seven Seas*, and *The Five Nations*. Best known among his stories are *Captains Courageous*, *Kim*, and *Puck of Pook's Hill*. His two collections of animal stories, *The Jungle Book* and *The Second Jungle Book*, are among the most widely read of all his works and are, perhaps, his best, from a literary standpoint.

MAXINE W. KUMIN, a contemporary writer, has contributed poems to various magazines—*Harper's*, *The Atlantic Monthly*, *The Saturday Review*; and she has written a number of children's books. Her first collection of poems, *Halfway*, was published in 1961.

VACHEL LINDSAY (1879–1931) was born in Springfield, Illinois, and studied at art schools in Chicago and New York. After his formal education, he spent some time traveling across the country reciting and singing his songs like the old ballad singers, and in campaigning for causes in which he believed. He is distinctly American in his themes, and is famous for his strikingly rhythmical verse.

HENRY WADSWORTH LONGFELLOW (1807–1882), one of America's most widely known and quoted poets, was born in Portland, Maine, and graduated from Bowdoin College, where he later taught modern languages for six years and for eighteen years at Harvard. After his retirement from teaching, he lived at Craigie House, a beautiful mansion in Cambridge, Massachusetts, where he devoted his time to writing. He was a popular and respected man during his lifetime and is honored with a statue in the Poets' Corner of England's Westminster Abbey. His poetry is written in simple language in a variety of verse forms, ranging from simple poems like "The Village Blacksmith" to the long narratives, *Evangeline* and *Hiawatha*.

DAVID LOUGÉE (1928———) is a young American poet whose work has appeared, here and abroad, in most of the leading literary periodicals and anthologies. A book of his poems, *The Passing of Giants*, is scheduled to appear soon.

AMY LOWELL (1874–1925), poet, biographer, and critic, came of a famous New England family and was a cousin of James Russell Lowell, the poet and diplomat. Her early works were written in conventional rhythm and rhyme. Later, however, she became leader of a group of poets known as the Imagists, who believed the primary aim of poetry was to present vivid imagery. Her other main contribution was the breakaway from conventional rhythms and rhyme in poetry, the perfecting of "free verse" forms. Amy Lowell's verse collections include *Sword-Blades and Poppy-Seeds, Pictures of the Floating World, Men, Women and Ghosts,* and *Ballads for Sale.* Her best critical works are *Six French Poets,* and *Tendencies in Modern American Poetry.* Her excellent biography, *John Keats,* may be considered also a volume of literary criticism.

JAMES RUSSELL LOWELL (1819–1891), an American poet, scholar, and literary critic, was educated at Harvard, where he later became professor of modern languages. He was ambassador to Spain and England and the first editor of *The Atlantic Monthly.* His sense of humor is evident in poems like "The Courtin'" and his skill as a serious poet in "The Vision of Sir Launfal," which relates the search for the Holy Grail by one of the knights of King Arthur's Round Table.

EDWIN MARKHAM (1852–1940), an American poet, was the son of pioneer parents. His mother took him to California when he was five years old, and there, after completing his formal education, he became a school teacher and superintendent of schools. His early poems, the most famous of which was "The Man with a Hoe," voiced protest against oppressive social conditions. He is also remembered for his poems about Lincoln.

JOHN MASEFIELD (1878———), Poet Laureate of England since 1930, has written plays and novels as well as poetry. He spent some of his early years wandering restlessly about the world, working as a ship's cabin boy and at various other jobs. The effect of these experiences is reflected in his prose and poems. Masefield is best known as the author of "Sea Fever," two long narrative poems, *The Everlasting Mercy* and *The Widow In the*

Bye Street, which reveal an understanding of, and sympathy with, the sufferings of working-class people.

EDGAR LEE MASTERS (1869–1950) is identified with the Middle West, especially Illinois, where he came to live as a boy and later to attend Knox College. In his *Spoon River Anthology* he presents a series of realistic sketches of life in a small town in the Lincoln country. Through epitaphs in which the dead give facts about themselves, the poet presents the hopes, struggles, successes, and failures of the town's inhabitants.

EDNA ST. VINCENT MILLAY (1892–1950), one of America's most well-known lyric poets, began to write extremely accomplished poetry while she was still in college. It was when she was still an undergraduate at Vassar that she wrote "Renascence," a poem which became widely admired and was the title poem for her first volume of poetry. In 1923 she won the Pulitzer prize for her collection of poems, *The Harp-Weaver*. Miss Millay also wrote the libretto for *The King's Henchman*, an opera which was produced by the Metropolitan Opera Company.

JOAQUIN MILLER (1839–1913), whose real name was Cincinnatus Hiner Miller—Joaquin having been taken as a pseudonym after a famous Mexican bandit—lived a fantastically colorful life. Born in a covered wagon, he ran away from home at an early age, and was to take such various odd jobs as miner and pony-express rider. He was later adopted by an Indian tribe and was finally to marry the chief's daughter. After his wife's death, Miller became a lawyer and a judge. His cowboy-like dress and mannerisms created a sensation when he first visited England in 1871. "Columbus" is Miller's best-known poem.

JAMES MONTGOMERY (1771–1854), was an English poet and journalist, son of a minister. Though born in Scotland, he spent part of his boyhood in Ireland and was educated in England. For more than thirty years he was a newspaper editor. In his poems he showed the influence of Shelley, as his volume, *Pelican Island*, will reveal. His most lasting works, perhaps, are the many hymns that he wrote—hymns that are still sung today in many churches.

WILLIAM MORRIS (1834–1896) was an English poet and prose writer. He studied architecture and painting and was interested in furniture design. He liked to retell old stories—tales of King Arthur, legends of heroes from Greek and Scandinavian literature.

ROBERT NATHAN (1894——), an American poet and novelist, was born in New York and educated privately at home and abroad. He graduated from Harvard and was editor of *The Harvard Monthly*, in which his first prose and poetry appeared. He has devoted his life to a literary career.

HENRY JOHN NEWBOLT (1862–1938), had a varied career as lawyer, editor, novelist, historian, and poet. The son of an English vicar, he studied at Oxford before entering the practice of law. His collections of poems include *Admirals All, The Island Race, Songs of the Sea,* and *Aladore*. He wrote two novels, *The New June* and *The Old Country*. The *Naval History of the Great War* was one of several historical works.

ALFRED NOYES (1880–1958), an English poet, pursued a career of writing following his education at Oxford. His poetry has a singing, vivacious rhythm, which has made him a successful, popular poet in England and America.

WILFRED OWEN (1893–1918), was an English poet who died before his talents had a chance to develop fully. Although he suffered from delicate health throughout his childhood and youth, he enlisted for combat service during World War I. He was invalided home after six months of fighting, but returned to the front as a company commander in August, 1918, three months before the war ended. On November 4, 1918, one week before hostilities ceased, he was killed in action. Inspired by the poems of John Keats, he began to write verse in his early teens and continued to do so during odd moments in service. His favorite theme was war and the pity of war. The first edition of his collected poems appeared in 1920. An expanded edition was published in 1931, containing additional poems that had come to light over a period of the next ten years. Owen's poetry shows remarkable originality, and his influence on contemporary verse has been out of all proportion to the small body of his collected works.

EDGAR ALLAN POE (1809–1849), the famous American poet, was born in Boston. As a young child, after the death of his parents, he went to live in Virginia with a wealthy family, the John Allans. Poe's life was not a happy or successful one; his temperament was moody and unstable. He attended the University of Virginia and West Point, but graduated from neither school. He achieved little financial return for his writings. His wife, Virginia, who was the inspiration behind many of his poems, died while she was very young. Poe worked as an editor and contributor to several literary magazines; he wrote essays as well as poems. Today he is recognized as a major American author. He is considered the originator of the detective story, and his plots of horror and mystery are forerunners of this type of writing. Some of Poe's more famous stories include "The Purloined Letter," "The Murders in the Rue Morgue," and "The Fall of the House of Usher," while his poetry may best be seen in such works as "The Raven," "Annabel Lee," "To Helen," and "Ulalume."

EDWIN ARLINGTON ROBINSON (1869–1935), one of America's major poets, was born in Maine and attended Harvard. He had to leave Harvard after only two years and return home because of his father's illness. President Theodore Roosevelt, an admirer of his work, obtained a position for him in the New York Customs House. He resigned from this work in 1909 and devoted his full time to writing. Robinson won the Pulitzer prize three times and is especially known for his poetic portraits, many of which depict persons whose lives are tragic and unsuccessful. One of his most beautiful poems is the strange and haunting "Eros Turannos."

LEW SARETT (1888–1954) was born in Chicago and educated at Beloit College and at Harvard. He taught at the University of Illinois and at Northwestern. For sixteen years he served as guide and ranger in the Northwest. His interest in the out-of-doors is reflected in his poetry.

Sir Walter Scott (1771–1832) was born in Edinburgh, Scotland, and studied law at Edinburgh University. As a young child he was slightly lamed by a severe illness and was sent to his grandfather's farm to recuperate. There he became fascinated with his grandmother's tales of old Scottish legends, and he said that he read the old ballads "with a delight that can be imagined, but never described." This interest influenced his poetry and his prose. He is especially famous for his Waverley Novels, among which *Ivanhoe* is included, and for his longer narrative poems, such as *The Lady of the Lake*. He achieved fame during his lifetime and retired to Abbotsford, an estate near Edinburgh, which is now a literary shrine.

Robert Service (1874–1958) was born in England and educated in Scotland. He worked in the Yukon region of Canada for eight years and depicts frontier life very realistically in his poems, such as "The Shooting of Dan McGrew" and "The Cremation of Sam McGee." He is sometimes called "the Canadian Kipling."

Karl Shapiro (1913———) was born in Baltimore and attended the University of Virginia. In 1941 he joined the armed services and served overseas in the South Pacific. It was during this time of army duty that he published his first three volumes of poetry. Shapiro received the Pulitzer prize in 1945 for his book *V-Day and Other Poems*. He was editor of the influential literary magazine *Poetry* from 1950 to 1956.

Dora Sigerson Shorter (1866–1918) was born in Dublin, the daughter of a cultured Irish scholar. She married the English editor, Clement Shorter. The English writer, George Meredith, referred to her as "one of the few who can tell a tale in verse . . . the best ballad writer since Scott."

Edward Rowland Sill (1841–1887) a minor American poet and essayist, was a professor of English at the University of California. "Opportunity" and "The Fool's Prayer" are his best-known poems.

Robert Southey (1774–1843) was England's Poet Laureate from 1813 to 1843. He was a close friend of Coleridge and joined him in plans to form an ideal community in America. Because of lack of funds, however, their scheme never materialized. Southey also became closely attached to Wordsworth, to whom Coleridge had introduced him. Byron, who had little respect for most of his contemporaries, made Southey the target of his famous satire, "Vision Of Judgment." Southey is best remembered for a handful of poems and for some of his prose writings, particularly his *Life Of Nelson*. "The Battle Of Blenheim" is one of his better-known works

BAYARD TAYLOR (1825–1878), was born in Pennsylvania. His formal education was relatively brief, but he more than made up for this lack with wide travels throughout the world. For many years he was a journalist, assigned as correspondent for *The New York Tribune*. His travel books, *Views Afoot, A Journey to Central Africa*, and *Northern Travel*, enjoyed great popularity. Among his poetry volumes were *The Poet's Journal, Home Pastorals*, and *Poems of the Orient*. During the last sixteen years of his life he served in various diplomatic posts for the U. S. government.

ALFRED LORD TENNYSON (1809–1892), one of England's greatest Victorian poets, wrote poetry of an extremely varied and accomplished nature. His lyrics are flawless and often very moving. *Idylls of the King* and *In Memoriam* are two of his most famous and finest long poems. Although he was in some ways limited in his responses to life, he was one of the most popular poets England has ever had. Tennyson became Poet Laureate in 1850 and received the title of Lord in 1884. He is buried in Westminster Abbey between two other great writers, Chaucer and Browning.

WILLIAM MAKEPEACE THACKERAY (1811–1863), an English writer born in Calcutta, became famous for his novels which reflect the middle- and upper-class society of England. He was, with Charles Dickens, one of the two dominant novelists of the Victorian Age. His more famous novels include *Vanity Fair, Henry Esmond, The Newcomes*. Although he is best remembered as a novelist, Thackeray also wrote a number of memorable poems and ballads.

ERNEST L. THAYER (1863–1940) was born in Lawrence, Massachusetts, and graduated from Harvard. He worked for years as a journalist on a number of newspapers. "Casey at the Bat" is his best-remembered poem.

DYLAN THOMAS (1914–1953), the great Welsh lyric poet, was born in Swansea, Wales, and published his first volume of poetry, *18 Poems*, at the age of twenty. Thomas' poetry was immediately recognized for its originality, strength of phrasing, and musical drive. Many of Thomas' poems have a complex surface and tightly woven structure, but the difficulties in his work tend to disappear after many readings. The poet's prose is remarkably nimble and witty, as may be seen in both his novel *Portrait of the Artist as a Young Dog* and the play *Under Milk Wood*. Thomas became very well known in this country for the beautiful readings of his work which he gave from coast to coast. It was during one of these American readings that he died suddenly at the tragically early age of thirty-nine.

FRANCIS ORRAY TICKNOR (1822–1874) was a physician in Georgia and a popular poet during the Civil War.

LOUIS UNTERMEYER (1885——) is a contemporary writer, born in New York. He is recognized for his own poetry and as an editor and anthologist who has compiled many collections of British and American poetry.

WALT WHITMAN (1819–1892) was one of America's greatest poets. He was born in New York, and there became engaged in a variety of occupations including teacher, editor, journalist, and writer. During the Civil War, Whitman volunteered as a male nurse at the army hospitals. Though he had little formal education, he was a man of unique genius and exerted a tremendous influence as a poet down to the present time. His verse differed greatly from other poets of the day; he used free verse, often discarding rhyme and regular stanza form, and was fond of a loose but strong rhythmic line. Whitman's most famous single work is *Leaves of Grass*, a long book of poems to which he was continually adding throughout his life. This book has sometimes been described as a glorification of the individual and a song in praise of American democracy.

JOHN GREENLEAF WHITTIER (1807–1892) was born in Haverhill, Massachusetts, the son of a poor farmer. His poetry depicts rural New England life. While he wrote many well-known short poems, such as "Maud Muller" and "The Barefoot Boy," his most famous long poem is *Snow-Bound*. He was an ardent abolitionist and wrote prose and poetry in the cause of the anti-slavery movement.

GEORGE WITHER (1588–1677), an English Puritan poet, wrote poems, hymns, and also pamphlets on controversial religious and political topics.

CHARLES WOLFE (1791–1823), was an Irish priest. He was ordained in 1817, three years after his graduation from Trinity College, Dublin, and spent the few remaining years of his life as curate in two parishes in County Tyrone. Aside from his *The Burial of Sir John Moore*, no poem or other work of his has come down to us.

WILLIAM WORDSWORTH (1770–1850), one of the giants of English poetry and a leader of the Romantic era, graduated from Cambridge and later went to France, where he became sympathetic with the ideals of the French Revolution. Later, however, this enthusiasm cooled. With the poet, Samuel Taylor Coleridge, Wordsworth collaborated on the volume of poems, *Lyrical Ballads*. This became one of the most important events in the history of English poetry. In the famous preface to the 1800 edition, Wordsworth stated that his aim was to write poems "as far as possible in a selection of language really used by men." Coleridge, on the other hand, was to treat of the "supernatural" in as realistic a manner as his collaborator. In this way they intended to do away with the artificial poetic diction of their day. Wordsworth's more famous works include, aside from the lyrics, the long, semi-autobiographical *The Prelude*, the meditative "Ode: Intimations of Immortality from Recollections of Childhood," and such other poems as "Tintern Abbey" and the sonnet "The World Is Too Much With Us." Wordsworth was appointed Poet Laureate in 1843.

WILLIAM BUTLER YEATS (1865–1939), one of the great poets in English of this century, was born in Dublin, the son of a well-known portrait painter. Although he spent a great deal of his life in London, Yeats took an active interest in the literary and political movements of his native country. He was associated with the founding of the famous Abbey Theatre, which he served as director, and to which he contributed many of his verse plays. He was elected a senator of the Irish Free State in 1922. Yeats was continually experimenting with language, and his poetry was continually undergoing changes in both subject matter and technique. It is generally agreed that his later poems constitute his finest achievement. Yeats was awarded the Nobel prize for literature in 1923.

Indexes

■ INDEX OF TITLES

■ INDEX OF AUTHORS

433

■ INDEX OF FIRST LINES